CENTRAL WYOMING COLLEGE

Immigrants in the Ozarks

University of Missouri Studies LXIV

Immigrants in the Ozarks

A Study in Ethnic Geography

Russel L. Gerlach

University of Missouri Press
Columbia & London

Copyright © 1976 by The Curators of the University of Missouri
University of Missouri, Columbia, Missouri 65201
Library of Congress Catalog Card Number 76–4528
Printed and bound in the United States of America

Library of Congress Cataloging in Publication Data

Gerlach, Russel L   1939–
    Immigrants in the Ozarks.

    Bibliography: p.
    1. Minorities—Ozark Mountains.   2. German
Americans—Ozark Mountains.   3. Anthropo-
geography—Ozark Mountains.   4. Ozark
Mountains—Social life and customs.   I. Title.
F472.09G47   301.29'767'1   76–4528
ISBN 0–8262–0201–2

to my wife

Preface

Over the past three centuries, the United States has been the beneficiary of the largest mass movement of peoples in the history of the world. Millions of Europeans as well as smaller numbers of Asians and Africans crossed the oceans to seek their fortunes in America. The United States was irreversibly transformed by the immigrants, just as each immigrant was changed by the experience of leaving his native land and adjusting to life in a new and strange environment.

This study examines the immigrant experience in one small area, the Ozark Highland Region in Missouri. Immigrants are studied in terms of their contribution to the contemporary cultural landscape of the rural Ozarks. It is my hope that the following pages will shed some light on the manner in which the processes of acculturation and assimilation have affected the lives of these immigrants and their descendents in the Ozarks.

The work would not have been possible without the assistance of many people. Although it would be impossible to name all of those who gave so freely of their time and effort, their assistance is, nonetheless, greatly appreciated.

To Leslie Hewes, Professor Emeritus of Geography at the University of Nebraska, Lincoln, I owe a special debt of gratitude. To the extent to which this work represents a scholarly undertaking, Professor Hewes deserves substantial credit. Professor Milton D. Rafferty, my colleague at Southwest Missouri State University, Springfield, contributed greatly, providing both ideas and counsel whenever they were needed. Nancy Schanda, my co-worker at Southwest Missouri State University, Springfield, was always there when I needed her, often performing difficult tasks at a moment's notice. Invaluable assistance in the preparation of maps was afforded by Rev. David Rosen, Joseph Harpine, Mary Fraser, Dennis Hrebec, and Roy Eckert, all former students of mine at Southwest Missouri State University.

Professor Walter Schroeder of the University of Missouri at Columbia freely gave his time during the critical initial phase of this study, as did Professor John Hostetler of Temple University. Vernon Meyr of Perry County extended many courtesies to me, as did the more than one thousand Ozarkians I had the pleasure to interview during the course of my research. Incredibly, never once was I refused an interview.

To the many government agencies that provided assistance, I express my gratitude. In particular, I owe a debt to the many county Agricultural Stabilization and Conservation Service offices and Soil Conservation Service offices, without whose assistance this study could not have been done.

Finally, I acknowledge my indebtedness to my wife, Jean, for her assistance with the organization and typing of the manuscript, but especially for her patience and understanding.

Although many people were involved in the preparation of this study, as the author, I accept full responsibility for the accuracy of its contents.

R.L.G.
Springfield, Missouri
May 1974

Contents

List of Illustrations

List of Tables

1. Introduction

The Ozark Highland in Missouri is a region where many cultures have met and mingled. Far from fitting the commonly held stereotype of a uniform culture reflecting an Appalachian heritage, the Ozark Highland Region contains within its boundaries a wide variety of cultural elements that together have forged a complex cultural landscape. From the Appalachians came the Scottish and English mountain men, whose origins were traced to the first colonists who had settled the tidewater districts of Virginia and the Carolinas in the seventeenth century. From the South came a few slaveholders, who brought with them their plantation economy. From the north and east came even fewer groups of prairie farmers of Midwestern background. These native Americans, particularly those from Appalachia, have dominated the Ozark region numerically and areally for more than a century. Undoubtedly, their contribution to the cultural image of the contemporary Ozarks has been profound. Within this prevailing Old Stock American population matrix, numerous smaller groups that had emigrated directly from Europe have settled. Among the people of ethnic origin who settled in the Ozarks are the French, Germans, Italians, Poles, Belgians, Swiss, Swedes, Yugoslavians, Hungarians, Austrians, Bohemians, and small ethnic religious sects, including the Dunkards, Amish, and Mennonites. These immigrant groups brought the strands of Old World cultures to be woven into the fabric of the rural Ozarks.

It is with the ethnic population of the Ozarks that this study is concerned. It also focuses attention on the landscape imprint of ethnic groups in the rural Ozarks of Missouri. The theory on which this study is based is a simple one. If we can assume, as the eminent American geographer Carl O. Sauer has for so many years, that groups are carriers of culture and that culture through time is the shaping force in the evolution of landscapes, then we can proceed to an analysis of local or regional character and significant variations therein as the result of the impress of contrasting cultures and their human carriers.[1] The differences and similarities in the landscapes of the various ethnic groups and their neighbors can be detected, identified, and analyzed through the application of established techniques of geographic measurement. Through this analysis, I sought to discover whether the rural Ozarks became a mosaic of various ethnic groups that inhabit the region, or whether the individuality of the immigrants, as evidenced in their landscapes, was erased by assimilation.[2]

The study necessarily involves a comprehensive treatment of the settlement in the Ozarks. Central to the study is a need for detailed maps indicating the origins of the region's rural population. Without such knowledge, an examination of ethnic landscapes would perforce be impossible. Therefore, considerable attention and space are given to tracing the settlement history in the Ozarks from the first European and American settlers to the present day. Apart from its usefulness in this study, a concise history of the Ozarks, particularly one emphasizing the geographic dimension, has never been undertaken and is perhaps long overdue.

Rural landscapes are examined with an emphasis on contemporary patterns, but some attention also is paid to the evolution of these patterns. The study focuses on two major, and related, features of the rural landscape: agriculture and settlement, including both form and pattern. A secondary, but essential, focus of the study is an examination of the aspects of cultural identity, including ethnic awareness, language, religion, and other related patterns of social organization that have had an influence on rural landscapes in the region. The study is primarily one of rural groups, and little attention will be devoted to urban centers except in an incidental manner.

Comparison is used liberally in analyzing the rural landscapes. It would be of little use to study ethnic groups alone, for to limit

1. Carl O. Sauer, "The Morphology of Landscape," p. 45.
2. Studies on this same topic in the United States are not too numerous. Some of the better ones that have been made are Terry G. Jordan, *German Seed in Texas Soil*; Walter M. Kollmorgan, "A Reconnaissance of Some Cultural-Agricultural Islands in the South" and "Agricultural-Cultural Islands in the South—Part II"; two articles by Leslie Hewes, "Cultural Fault Line in the Cherokee Country" and "Tontitown: Ozark Vineyard Center"; Russell W. Lynch, "Czech Farmers in Oklahoma," pp. 9–13; and Elaine M. Bjorklund, "Ideology and Culture Exemplified in Southwestern Michigan." Three studies of particular interest to the Ozarks are Joseph R. Castelli, "Grape Growers of Central Missouri"; Arthur B. Cozzens, "Conservation in German Settlements of the Missouri Ozarks"; and Hildegard Binder Johnson, "The Location of German Immigrants in the Middle West."

the investigation would remove the basis for judging whether or not ethnic groups in the Ozarks are different from their neighbors.

By examining ethnic and nonethnic groups side by side, wherever possible, we can assess their cultural influence, as manifested in the rural landscape. And only by comparative analysis can the stated objective of the study be realized. The Ozark Highland Region in Missouri does not present a uniform resource base; conditions vary greatly in places, and any ethnic or nonethnic comparison must be tempered by a knowledge of this fact.

Therefore, comparisons at even the local level are complemented, wherever possible, by evidence indicating significant differences in the quality of the resource base. This is a study of the influence of culture on the rural landscape, and every effort must be made to equate all other variables that might in some way influence the landscapes of either or both groups. Because cultural geography is not a laboratory science, extraneous variables cannot be controlled, but they can be accounted for.

If comparison is the device of this study; then, its major method is field investigation. The information has been drawn from several major sources, including systematic road traverses, field mapping, direct field observation, and interviews. These sources are supplemented by a liberal usage of census materials and other government documents, church records, archival research, and a variety of plats and maps. Because of the unavailability of data on the landscapes of ethnic groups in the Ozarks of Missouri, the emphasis in this study is on direct field observation.

The primary sources for information on the lineages of the rural population in the Ozarks are the manuscript census schedules of population from 1860 to 1880.[3] On the manuscript schedules of population, the name of each person is listed along with his or her birthplace. Field interviews and a variety of secondary sources provide information on changes in the makeup of the rural population of the region since the turn of the century.

Information on land use was obtained through field mapping of more than one-hundred thousand acres in six widely separated Ozark areas. Areas were selected to contrast ethnic and nonethnic agriculture on land of comparable quality in each of the locales. Information on settlement patterns was obtained along fifteen hundred miles of systematic road traverses and on more than five

3. The manuscript population schedules for Missouri covering the period from 1860 to 1880 are available on microfilm at the Springfield, Missouri, Public Library.

thousand farmsteads. The traverse areas have been selected in such a way in which comparably sized ethnic and nonethnic populations are included, while at the same time extremes in land quality between the two groups have been avoided as much as possible. Several aerial reconnaissances were carried out to ascertain information on general settlement patterns for the entire study area.

Material on ethnic identity is the most subjective of all the data used in the study. Most of this material was obtained through interviews with more than five hundred residents throughout the study area, including farmers, clergymen, community leaders, and government officials. In some cases, such as religion and political attitudes, quantitative data are available.

Definition of Terms

One of the first problems in any study involving ethnic groups in the United States is that of defining the term *ethnic group*. The word *ethnic* derives from the Greek *ethnos* meaning "people" or "nation." The term clearly implies that members of such a group share a sense of unity. *Ethnic* is ordinarily used to refer loosely to groups who identify or are identified on the basis of common racial, religious, or national origins.[4] Further, an ethnic group suggests some degree of cohesion among its members, at least in a historic sense. Although not implicit in the term ethnic group, a degree of geographic concentration is inferred to the extent that cohesion assumes contact and contact is partly a function of the spatial dimension.

For the purposes of this study, the following working definition is used in determining what constituted an ethnic group. The term ethnic is used in its more limited sense to refer to people of more or less direct foreign origin who identified or were identified by their national origins at the time of their settlement in the Ozarks, that is, the Germans, Italians, or Poles. The Anabaptist groups (Amish and Mennonites) are considered borderline, because they identify and are identified primarily by their distinctive religious beliefs. However, because the overwhelming majority of the Amish and Mennonites are of German, Swiss, and Dutch background, they are included as ethnic on that basis. An individual settlement qualified as an ethnic group if it met one of three conditions: (1)

4. E. K. Francis, "The Nature of the Ethnic Group."

the group settled as a colony in a given location in the Ozarks; (2) the group comprised in its core at least 75 per cent of the total rural population; and (3) the group was recognized by itself and others as being ethnically distinctive. Most ethnic groups in the Ozarks fit the latter two qualifications and many fit all three. In choosing the settlements, I have set no limitations on size or minimum percentage of the total rural population in a locale, because such a limitation would have eliminated some of the Amish and Mennonite groups. Most of these groups are less than twenty-five families in size, and several are quite dispersed; yet, they are recognized by their neighbors as being ethnically distinctive. On the other hand, most counties contain small numbers of various European groups, who drifted in at various times with no association among them. Under the definition used here, these groups would not constitute ethnic groups.

To avoid confusion, another term is used to refer to the non-ethnic or native American population of the Ozarks. This term is *Old Stock American*. Although the Old Stock Americans came from ethnic stock and many traced their origins to central Europe as well as to the British Isles, by the time they had reached the Ozarks they had become, in most cases, true Americans in a cultural sense.

The Ozark Highland Region

The study was done in the Missouri portion of the Ozark Highland Region, which is locally known as "the Ozarks." The entire Highland Region lies in five states — Missouri, Arkansas, Oklahoma, Kansas, and Illinois. Of the more than fifty thousand square miles that comprise the Ozarks, approximately thirty-five thousand are in southern Missouri. There is little agreement on the boundaries of the Ozarks; one definition excludes much of southwestern Missouri because of its different physical characteristics.[5] The boundaries employed are those most geographers have traditionally used. By limiting the study to Missouri, the southern boundary and portions of the eastern and western boundaries are fixed by state boundaries. The southeastern boundary, where the Ozarks meet the Interior Lowlands, is evidenced by a pronounced escarpment — for example, near Poplar Bluff. The northern boundary is less distinct. Here, the Ozarks and the Dissected Till Plain of northern Missouri meet. The boundary lies generally

5. Tom Beveridge, "Look at the Ozarks," pp. 6–8.

north of the Missouri River, reaching its most northerly position near Glasgow. Moving east, the boundary gradually tips to the south to a point approximately thirty miles east of St. Louis, where the boundary breaks sharply to the southeast crossing into Illinois in southern Jefferson County. Thus, metropolitan St. Louis is excluded from the Ozarks, as is Columbia. Jefferson City, however, is included in the region. The western boundary, where the Ozarks meet the Osage Plain, has been the most troublesome. A recent study examining this boundary acknowledged the difficulty in precisely separating the Ozarks from the Osage Plain but concluded that Sauer's choice of a boundary nearly sixty years ago remains the most logical.[6] This is the boundary that I have used. By so placing the western boundary, both Springfield and Joplin are included in the Ozarks (Figure 1–1).

The Ozark Highland Region lies several hundred miles southeast of the center of the United States. It is the most centrally located highland in the country, and together with the adjacent Ouachita Mountains constitutes the only large area of elevated land between the Appalachian and the Rocky mountains.

Elevation in the Highland Region is generally higher than that of surrounding regions, and relief is greater. The most appropriate term describing the topography of the Ozarks is *hilly*, although the term *plateau* is descriptive of the topography over much of the western Ozarks. By contrast, the Ozarks are bounded on all sides by plains. The Ozarks consist of rocks that are predominantly Ordovician or older, which contain a high percentage of dolomite (magnesium limestone) and chert (which resembles flint). Because the area is not glaciated and is underlain in most parts by cherty dolomites, it contains numerous caves, springs, clear streams, and relatively thin acid soils on the uplands. Geologic, topographic, and climatic conditions have resulted in a distinctive floral and faunal assemblage. Although most of the Ozark Highland Region was forested — primarily with oak — numerous natural prairies of varying sizes were interspersed with the woodland areas.

The Highland Region is a poor resource base. It is true that the richest lead deposits in the United States are located in the Ozarks, and significant barite and coal deposits are also scattered throughout the region. However, these resources have affected few of those who have settled in the Ozarks. For most, the future lay in agri-

6. Michael W. Jinks, "Some Aspects of Regional Delimitation: The Western Ozarks — A Case Study"; Carl O. Sauer, *The Geography of the Ozark Highland of Missouri*, p. 3.

Figure 1–1. Ozark Highland Region. The region contains fifty thousand square miles and is located in Missouri, Arkansas, Oklahoma, Kansas, and Illinois.

culture, and the resources for this activity were meager. The combination of soil and topography in the Ozarks, with a few exceptions, lacks the qualities necessary to support a prosperous agricultural economy. The Ozark Highland is a region poor in material resources.

2. Settlement of the Ozarks

Although ethnic groups constitute an important element in the population of the Ozarks and are the focus of this study, numerically they represent a minority of the region's population. Except for the early period of French settlement, the Ozarks have been dominated numerically by an Old Stock American population and remain so today. Therefore, it is essential that both the Old Stock American and ethnic populations be considered in this study, in terms of both the evolution of the Ozark's population and the makeup of the region's present population.

Settlement Under the French and Spanish, 1673–1803

The first European to enter the territory now known as Missouri, possibly as early as 1541, was a Spaniard. However, the exploitation and settlement of the Mississippi Valley, including the Ozark Highland Region in Missouri, were not begun until the late seventeenth century, when the French, probing south from their lower St. Lawrence settlements in Canada, renewed the search for wealth in interior North America. Shortly after René de la Salle had claimed the Mississippi Valley for France in 1682, French explorers, hunters, and fur traders were operating on both sides of the Mississippi from the Gulf of Mexico to Canada.[1] As early as 1687, the salt springs near Ste. Genevieve were known to the French, and prior to 1700 they had learned of the lead deposits on the Missouri side. In 1704, the French were reported to be settling on the Missouri side of the Mississippi River. By 1720, the French had acquired substantial and favorable information concerning the potential wealth of the middle Mississippi Valley.[2]

1. For an account of early French activities in the Mississippi Valley see John Finley, *The French in the Heart of America*, and J. H. Schlarman, *From Quebec to New Orleans.*
2. Carl O. Sauer, *The Geography of the Ozark Highland of Missouri*, pp. 74–75; Louis Houck, *A History of Missouri*, vol. 1, p. 243.

The earliest permanent French settlements in the Mississippi Valley were established in the Illinois country. Shortly after the expeditions of both Jacques Marquette and La Salle, a number of riparian settlements, or *cotes*, were founded along the eastern bank of the Mississippi River opposite the Ozarks (Figure 2–1). The first riparian settlement was Cahokia (1699); followed by Kaskaskia (1700); Fort Chartres (1720); St. Phillips (1723); and Prairie du Rocher (1733). The importance of the Illinois settlements

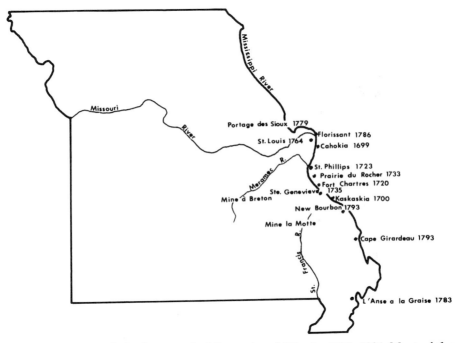

Figure 2–1.   French Settlements in Missouri and Illinois, 1699–1804. Most of the early French settlements were on the Illinois side of the Mississippi River. Later, settlements were established on the Missouri side; at first near the river and then farther inland in the mining country. (Note: Present boundaries of Missouri are shown for perspective.)

lies in the fact that the earliest permanent pioneers in the Ozarks, with a few exceptions, were from these Canadian French settlements, especially from those settlements along the eastern bank of the Mississippi, which was known as the American Bottom. The movement into Missouri, then, was a continuation of the movement by Canadian French into the Illinois country. It was not until the 1760s that French settlers began entering the American Bottom by way of the lower Mississippi via New Orleans.[3]

Despite the absence of permanent settlements on the Missouri side of the Mississippi, the French still were active in the exploitation of salt, furs, and lead. By 1720, Philippe François Renault, with a large contingent of Frenchmen and slaves, was developing the lead deposits along the Meramec River. In 1723, one of Renault's agents, Antoine de la Mothe Cadillac, discovered a rich deposit of lead south of the Meramec along the St. Francis River, and thereafter numerous other mines were opened, some of which produced well into the twentieth century. The diggings of Renault and other Frenchmen are scattered throughout the St. Francis region.

Most of the early Frenchmen, whether fur traders or miners, maintained their permanent habitations on the Illinois side of the Mississippi. It was not until 1735 that a permanent settlement was established on the Missouri side, serving as a shipping point for the mines. The settlement was established four miles south of the present Ste. Genevieve. Significantly, this settlement, which was subsequently transferred to the present site of Ste. Genevieve, remained the only permanent settlement in Missouri for the next three decades. Apparently, Ste. Genevieve served the needs of the limited French population on the Missouri side, which by 1745 was estimated to be only three hundred. Because the mining country was rough and uninviting to the early French, they preferred to retain their residence in either Ste. Genevieve or across the river in Illinois. It was not until the 1790s that a permanent settlement was established in the interior mining country. The farming population stayed on the Illinois side, and those who crossed over into Missouri "did not take up land, clear farms, and settle permanently." Thus, by 1760 the French population on the Missouri side consisted of one permanent settlement and a floating population of hunters, fur traders, and miners.[4]

In 1762, France ceded its Louisiana Territory west of the Mississippi River to Spain. Three months later in 1763, France relinquished its hold on Canada and all of the areas to the east of the Mississippi; these territories were yielded to England. The French in the Mis-

3. John R. Henderson, "The Cultural Landscape of French Settlements in the American Bottom," pp. 24–33; E. M. Violette, "Early Settlements in Missouri," p. 39; Herman R. Friis, *A Series of Population Maps of the Colonies and the United States, 1625–1790*, plate following p. 16.
4. J. Viles, "Population and Extent of Settlement in Missouri Before 1804," pp. 201–3; Violette, "Settlements in Missouri," p. 41.

sissippi Valley, including the American Bottom, were aware of the British cession, but for several years remained nescient of the Spanish cession. Many Frenchmen soon left the territories that had been ceded to Protestant England in favor of areas still thought to be under French Catholic control. Some of them returned to France; and some of them went down river toward New Orleans; while others crossed the river into Missouri, which was still believed to be under French control. In 1766, the inhabitants of Kaskaskia and Fort Chartres were reported as having gone largely to the western bank of the river.[5]

Although Missouri was under Spanish control, the territory remained French in population and character. Billion said of the period of Spanish control in Missouri:

> The intercourse of the people with each other and their governors, their commerce, trade, habits, customs, manners, amusements, marriages, funerals, services in church, parish registers—everything was in French. The governors and officials all spoke French. . . . The few Spaniards that settled in the country soon became Frenchmen, and all married French wives; no Frenchman became a Spaniard.[6]

The areas greatly increasing in French population under Spain were the bottomlands within a few miles of the Mississippi and the lead-mining districts (Figure 2–2). In addition to the population increase in Ste. Genevieve, several new settlements were established, mostly by Frenchmen. The settlements included St. Louis (1764); Portage des Sioux (1779); L'Anse a la Graise (1783); Florissant (1786); New Bourbon (1793); and Cape Girardeau (1793) (Figure 2–1). Major lead deposits also were discovered at Mine à Breton (Potosi) and Mine a Gerbore (Flat River), with a resulting increase in French population. Apparently, only a few of the two thousand inhabitants in Missouri in 1786 were not descended from French stock.[7]

The Spanish regime officially forbade the predominantly Protestant Americans to settle in Missouri until 1795. The Spanish previously sought immigrants from Catholic countries, including, in addition to Spain, France, Germany, and Italy. With few exceptions, however, only the Frenchmen came. New Bourbon was settled by a group of French Royalists, who were refugees from

5. Duane Meyer, *The Heritage of Missouri—A History*, p. 44; Sauer, *Ozark Highland*, p. 79.

6. *Annals of St. Louis*, pp. 67–77, quoted in Violette, "Settlements in Missouri," p. 44.

7. Lucien Carr, *Missouri: A Bone of Contention*, pp. 56–57.

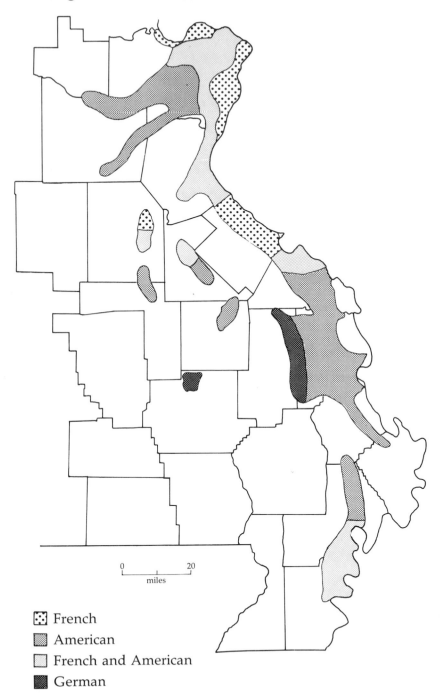

French

American

French and American

German

Figure 2–2. Extent and Character of Settlement in Missouri, 1803. Settlement was concentrated near the two great transportation routes, the Mississippi and Missouri rivers. Those settlements in the interior were centered in the mining districts.

the French Revolution.[8] The early records of St. Joachim's Catholic Church in Old Mines indicate that the majority of that settlement's population came to Missouri from France during the period of Spanish control.[9]

In 1803, the villages of Ste. Genevieve and New Bourbon were still almost exclusively French, as was the vicinity of St. Louis. Excluding the Old Mines claim, by 1803 the French were forced to share the mining districts with Americans who had come into Missouri in the 1790s. By then, Canadian French hunters and fur traders south of New Madrid (L'Anse a la Graise) were mixed with Americans. In northern Perry County, the French dominated in the creek bottoms, while Americans were dominant in the upland areas. North of Ste. Genevieve in Jefferson County, French and Americans were settled along a number of creeks well up to their sources. In the areas around St. Louis, Americans were rapidly gaining on the French. By 1803, the French still constituted approximately 44 per cent of Missouri's population, with this figure steadily declining.[10]

It is not known when the first American arrived in Missouri. However, it was not until the last decade of the eighteenth century that Americans began coming in large numbers. Initially, Americans were reluctant to enter a territory under a foreign flag, and the Spanish were equally unwilling to allow the Protestant Americans to settle in their territory. Yet, it would seem that the overriding factor that kept the Americans east of the river was distance. It was during the eve of the American Revolution that they settled permanently west of the Alleghanies (Figure 2–3). Between the Alleghanies and the Mississippi lay a vast stretch of unsettled land. In 1785, Kentucky had a population of 12,000, whereas by 1790 the figure had increased to 73,677.[11] The westward movement of the settlement into the frontier, as it followed the Ohio River, moved slowly toward Missouri. By 1790, the advance element of settlement was approaching the Mississippi Valley and by 1800 it was there.

8. Louis Houck, *The Spanish Regime in Missouri*, vol. 1, pp. 153–55; Sauer, *Ozark Highland*, p. 80.

9. St. Joachim's Church parish records of births, baptisms, marriages, and deaths, dated from 1787. The records are incomplete but do indicate that a substantial portion of the original population was composed of miners who came directly from France in the 1780s and 1790s.

10. Hattie M. Anderson, "Missouri, 1804–1828: Peopling a Frontier State," p. 150.

11. Violette, "Settlements in Missouri," p. 45.

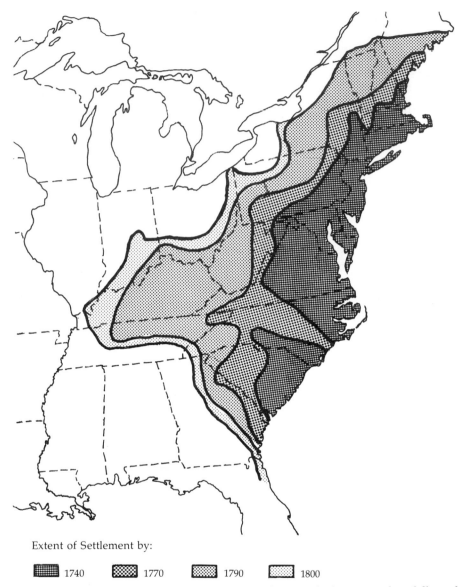

Extent of Settlement by:

▓▓ 1740   ▒▒ 1770   ░░ 1790   ⬚⬚ 1800

Figure 2–3.   Moving Frontier. After crossing the Appalachians, settlers followed the Ohio River and its tributaries, the Cumberland and Tennessee, on their trip west. By 1800, the frontier had reached the confluence of the Ohio and Mississippi rivers—at the doorstep of Missouri. Sources: Friis, *A Series of Population Maps of the Colonies and the United States, 1625–1790*, and Paullin, *Atlas of the Historical Geography of the United States.*

Several factors are instrumental in determining the direction the frontier moved, as it approached the Mississippi. The Northwest Ordinance of 1787 prohibited slavery in those territories north of the Ohio; thus, many slaveholding settlers were deflected toward Missouri. Missouri was largely forested in contrast to the prairies north of the Ohio, which, at that time, were considered unsuitable for agriculture. Missouri, on the whole, had a good reputation for its agricultural potential and its mineral wealth. Finally, a more romantic factor was involved to some degree:

> To understand the early settlement of our western country, one must keep in mind the desire of the early pioneer to get a little farther beyond the existing frontier line. The love of independence and of freedom from restraint and the relish for hazardous enterprise, led many people to forsake the old community and settle in a new and remote country.

Many accounts, if not most, of the settlers' westward movement into the frontier mention this factor. The attraction of new land to the frontiersman, with all the unknown hazards and challenges, is a part of American folklore. Yet, it may be that, in many instances, the frontiersman was pushed from his home rather than lured by the frontier. For example, some early settlers in Kentucky and Tennessee did not make the effort to secure land titles, and the following incomers who did file claims on this same land forced some of the earlier pioneers out into the frontier. Apparently, Daniel Boone, who failed to secure a title to his land in Kentucky, was forced to move on west, eventually settling in Missouri.[12]

The final inducement to the American pioneer came from the Spanish government. In 1797, the Spaniards opened Missouri to the Americans, who were already located on the eastern bank of the Mississippi. They offered the pioneer free land, exemption from taxes, and, in some cases, free animals, seed, and tools. These land grants, which are irregular in shape and positioning, represent one of the few visible reminders of the Spanish era in Missouri. The grants that were made in the early years of Spanish control were for mining, and most of the recipients were French. The later grants that were predominantly for agricultural purposes attracted mostly Americans. These grants, which were made to American settlers shortly before the United States gained control of Missouri, covered virtually all of the chert-free limestone

---

12. For a more detailed treatment of this subject see Friis, *A Series of Population Maps*, and William O. Lynch, "The Westward Flow of Southern Colonists Before 1861."

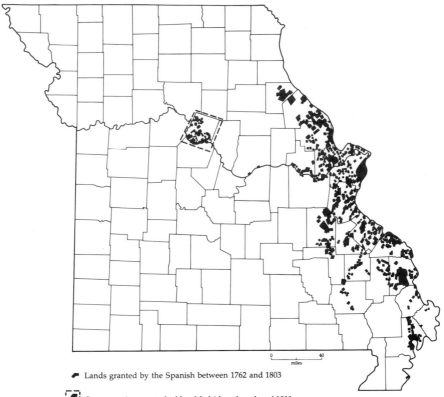

 Lands granted by the Spanish between 1762 and 1803

Compensation grants for New Madrid earthquake of 1811

Figure 2–4. Spanish Land Grants in Missouri. The Spanish granted land to settlers, including many Americans, between 1762 and 1802. The Spanish grants covered both mining and agricultural areas in the eastern Ozarks. The grants in the interior Ozarks were made by the American government after 1811 to compensate those whose land had been destroyed in the New Madrid earthquake. Sources: Saalberg, "The New Madrid Land Claims in Howard County, Missouri," and U.S.G.S. Topographic Quadrangles.

basins in the eastern Ozarks. The U.S. government later agreed to honor most of these grants, which are even more evident on maps than in the field (Figure 2–4).[13]

The original American migration into Missouri went via the Ohio Valley, with most settlers claiming first Kentucky and Tennessee as their former homes. Soon other states easily connected to the Ohio system were represented, namely, New York, Pennsylvania, Maryland, Virginia, and the Carolinas. General Morgan's

13. Meyer, *Heritage of Missouri*, pp. 102–3; Russel L. Gerlach, "Spanish Land Grants in Missouri," p. 11; Curtis F. Marbut, *Soils of the Ozark Region*, p. 251; Ada Paris Klein, "Ownership of Land Under France, Spain, and the United States," p. 282.

colony from Kentucky, which located near New Madrid in 1788, was probably the first distinctly American settlement in Spanish territory. The majority of the Americans entering Missouri under the Spanish came as individuals or in small groups and represented the advance element in the westward-moving settlement of the frontier.[14]

The first American settlement was in southeastern Missouri in the areas adjacent to the mouth of the Ohio River. But by 1800, American settlements were spotted up and down the Mississippi, from New Madrid to the north of St. Louis, with substantial penetration inland in several areas. By 1803, Americans made up 56 per cent of Missouri's population and were dominant in several locations. North of New Madrid on a slightly elevated ridge known as Big Prairie, Americans receiving Spanish grants had settled north to the present location of Sikeston. The soils and drainage on the ridge were favorable, whereas the lowlands to the east were frequently overflowing. Generally, the Americans showed a preference for upland areas in contrast to the French, who seemed to prefer riparian locations. Although the town of Cape Girardeau was founded by the French, by 1803 the district was overwhelmingly American. Again the Americans moved back from the river and settled on upland soils in the Eastern Whitewater Drainage Basin, where some of the most fertile soils in the entire Eastern Ozark Border occur. Farther north in present-day Perry County, a group of Kentuckians located at the "barrens," an almost treeless tract similar to those found in Kentucky. A few miles to the east in the creek bottoms, adjacent to the Mississippi, the population was almost exclusively French.[15]

In the north, the French remained supreme in the vicinity of St. Louis, while Americans dominated the outposts. The movement of Kentuckians up the Missouri River was well underway by 1803, including Daniel Boone's settlement at Femme Osage Creek, which was organized in 1797. Americans had also established settlements southwest of St. Louis in the Meramec River valley.[16]

14. Violette, "Settlements in Missouri," p. 45; Viles, "Missouri Before 1804," p. 191.

15. Anderson, "Missouri, 1804–1828," p. 150; Houck, *History of Missouri*, vol. 2, pp. 381–87. For a discussion of the "barrens" of Kentucky see Carl O. Sauer, *Geography of the Pennyroyal*, p. x; Viles, "Missouri Before 1804," p. 201.

16. Sauer, *Ozark Highland*, p. 109; Cardinal L. Goodwin, "Early Exploration and Settlement of Missouri and Arkansas," p. 396.

As the French, many Americans were attracted to Missouri by the lead mines. In 1798, Moses Austin was granted land at Mine à Breton and soon an American settlement including farmers was well established. Americans were responsible for the discovery and development of several important lead deposits in the St. Francis region during this period. Several small agricultural settlements had been established by Americans in the mining districts by 1800. The most important of these were the Bellevue and Caledonia valleys and near the present location of Farmington.[17]

Besides the French, the only ethnic settlements during this period were in the Whitewater Creek bottoms of Cape Girardeau and Bollinger counties, where a group of German-Swiss from North Carolina settled in 1798. Several small groups, apparently Germans from the Whitewater settlements, continued west and, by 1800, were located in several small settlements in present-day Wayne County.[18]

By 1803, several differences among the various ethnic groups in Missouri were evident. First, the French showed a definite propensity for village settlement, whereas the Americans and Germans were much more inclined to settle on detached farms. At Ste. Genevieve, the French utilized a combination of gardens and orchards in the village—a large agricultural field subdivided into long, narrow strips of cropland—with common pasture and woodland outside the village. As a result, almost the entire French population in Missouri was included in the villages. By contrast, when the U.S. government took over Louisiana in 1804, no town or village in the largely American district of Cape Girardeau existed to serve as the center of government. Although the district was well populated, all of the population was scattered on farms.[19]

Significant agricultural differences among the various groups are also apparent. It has already been noted that the French employed the European farm village, whereas the other groups settled largely on dispersed farms. The French were apparently less inclined toward agriculture than their American and German neighbors, who were considered to be superior farmers. Violette notes that

17. Sauer, *Ozark Highland*, p. 106; Houck, *History of Missouri*, vol. 1, pp. 372–75; Viles, "Missouri Before 1804," p. 202.

18. Floyd C. Shoemaker, "Cape Girardeau: Most American of Missouri's Original Five Counties," p. 51; Goodwin, "Missouri and Arkansas," p. 394.

19. Henderson, "American Bottom," p. 23; Marbut, *Soils of the Ozark Region*, p. 251; Shoemaker, "Cape Girardeau," p. 54; Walter A. Schroeder, *The Eastern Ozarks*, p. 19; Sauer, *Ozark Highland*, p. 85.

the three classes of Frenchmen who came to Missouri were miners, soldiers, and hunters and fur traders. Obviously, very few farmers came, and many who did farm out of necessity were ill prepared to do so. A possible explanation for many Frenchmen going into agriculture, beyond the fact that their agricultural needs had to be met, is that the French government granted free land only to those who engaged in farming.[20]

Within the large agricultural field, the French divided the land into long, narrow strips (Figure 2–5). No advantage was gained

Figure 2–5.   French Long Lots at Ste. Genevieve. The French in Missouri employed the European village system of agriculture. Common tracts of land were used for wood and pasture. A third large tract was divided into long, narrow strips of cropland. Each farmer was given one or more strips of cropland as well as access to the wood and pasture tracts. Source: Land ownership plat, Ste. Genevieve County, Missouri, 1970.

20. Violette, "Settlements in Missouri," p. 90; Henderson, "American Bottom," p. 17.

by using the long lot system in Missouri, particularly in upland areas where attenuated strips did not enhance accessibility. It is possible that the long lot system was brought to Missouri from the lower St. Lawrence and implemented merely from habit. The long, narrow subdivisions of agricultural land, characteristic of the subdivisions of European village communities, are found only at New Madrid and Ste. Genevieve, indicating that the French did not contribute a great deal to the permanent agricultural development of the Ozarks. Even in areas of mining claims such as Old Mines this system of land division was utilized occasionally (Figure 2–6).[21]

The habitations of the French, Americans, and Germans differed in several respects. Among the differences are the design of dwellings, building materials, and quality. Distinguishing features of French dwellings during this period included the technique of placing the logs side by side in a vertical rather than the more common horizontal position. With this method, referred to as *poteaux en terre*, the logs were driven several feet into the ground, resulting in eventual rotting of the lower sections. This may well account for the few examples of this type of architecture to be found today. The Bolduc house in Ste. Genevieve represents a well-preserved example of the *poteaux en terre* technique (Figure 2–7). French houses were noted for their large porches, or galleries, which were built on two, three, or four sides of the house (Figure 2–8). The use of large porches in French domestic architecture was a technique brought over from the West Indies.[22]

These styles are descriptive of Ste. Genevieve, where they have been preserved, and for other French villages where the upper class had lived. The average Frenchman, however, probably did not fare so well. Anderson observes that the majority of Frenchmen lived in small plastered huts, which presented a vivid contrast to the Americans' log cabins and the Germans' stone structures. An official report to Spain in 1798 concerning the incoming Americans stated, "Their homes are already better than those of the Creoles and Canadians who were settled in villages thirty years ago." The image of the ever-moving American and his "temporary" log cabin, which often survived more than a century of use, and the German with his very permanent stone structures

21. Sauer, *Ozark Highland*, pp. 85–86; Marbut, *Soils of the Ozark Region*, p. 251.
22. Rexford Newcomb, *Architecture of the Old Northwest Territory*, p. 21; Sauer, *Ozark Highland*, p. 92.

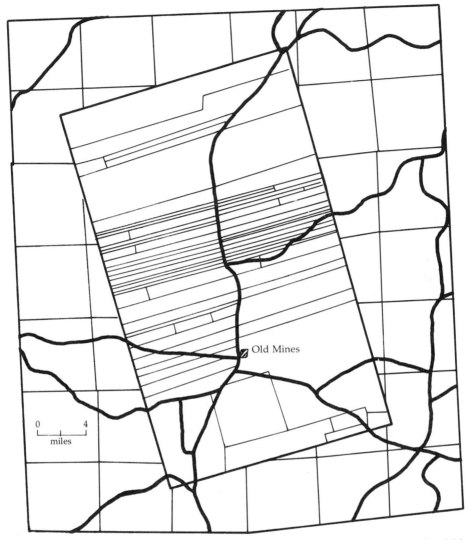

Figure 2–6. Old Mines Mining Claim, Washington County, Missouri. The Old Mines mining claim represents a rare combination of a Spanish land grant and French long lots on the same tract of land. The rectangular survey employed by the U.S. government can be seen in the same area. Source: Land ownership plat, Washington County, Missouri, 1970.

are themes interwoven throughout much of Missouri's early history and will be discussed later.[23]

It was also during this period that the supremacy of the Catholic church in Missouri was first challenged. Many American settlers

23. Anderson, "Missouri, 1804–1828," p. 158; Houck, *Spanish Regime*, vol. 2, p. 256.

Figure 2–7. Bolduc house in Ste. Genevieve, Missouri, featuring vertical log construction.

Figure 2–8. Early French house in Ste. Genevieve with large porches.

in Missouri, it is true, remained indifferent to religion. However, in the areas where Catholic influence was least, the American was able to express his religious beliefs at an early date. The English Protestant religions first entered Cape Girardeau, a district dominated solely by Americans, sometime before 1800. The two frontier sects, the Methodists and Baptists, crossed the Mississippi here. Since both religions were extremely evangelistic, they found a fertile field in Missouri, where many settlers were members of no church or only nominally adherents of Catholicism. After the ground had been broken by the Methodists and Baptists, other denominations made their appearance, including Scottish-Irish Presbyterians who came by way of Pennsylvania, "separate" Baptists of New England origin, and German Lutherans from North Carolina.[24]

American Settlement, 1804–1830

In 1802, control of Louisiana was returned by Spain to France, and negotiations were quickly begun by the United States to secure the title to this vast territory from France. On 30 April 1803, the United States agreed to pay France some $15 million, or four cents an acre, for the 828,000 square miles of Louisiana. On 9 March 1804, Capt. Amos Stoddard of the U.S. Army arrived in St. Louis to take possession of the entire territory in the name of the United States.

The immediate effect of the Louisiana Purchase on Missouri was a rapid increase in immigration from the eastern bank of the Mississippi. By 1810, Missouri's population had reached 19,783, almost twice the figure for 1804. By 1814, the figure had increased to 25,845. After the lull caused by the War of 1812, emigration again picked up, and the figure for 1820 was 66,586. Included in this number were many veterans of the War of 1812, who had been granted land west of the Mississippi as a bounty for their wartime service to the United States. Immigration continued unchecked for the next decade, and by 1830 Missouri, now a state, had a population of 140,455. The overwhelming majority of the settlers migrating to Missouri from 1804 to 1830 was from areas to the east of the Mississippi and was American.[25]

24. Shoemaker, "Cape Girardeau," p. 54; Wilbur Zelinsky, "An Approach to the Religious Geography of the United States: Patterns of Church Membership in 1952," p. 158; Anderson, "Missouri, 1804–1828," p. 174.

25. *Fifteenth Census of the United States, 1930: Population,* vol. 1, p. 11; Houck, *History of Missouri,* vol. 3, p. 140.

American settlers at first located within the limits of the original settlement areas, either locating in those settlements already established or in the unoccupied territory within the frontier lines. Within a decade of the Louisiana Purchase, a noticeable change had occurred in the character and extent of settlement in Missouri. The population had more than doubled, and it was estimated that four-fifths of the people then in Missouri were Americans. Moreover, the American settlers had, by the close of the first decade of American control, begun to make their way into the interior, some going as far as two hundred miles from the settled areas.[26]

The first significant movement into the interior was via the Missouri River. The Missouri represented, by far, the greatest natural route leading into the interior. The mining areas to the south were rough and hilly and were ill suited for agricultural purposes. Farther south, the swampy regions of Bollinger and Stoddard counties proved to be significant obstacles to movement and settlement for the years ahead. Thus, the area just to the west of the original strip of settlements was difficult to pass through and ill adapted to the purposes of the majority of the American settlers. The newcomers sought lands suitable for farming, which they could best find in abundance along the Missouri River. As a result of this deflection of the current of American migration into Missouri, the central interior of the state was fairly well populated before the second tier of counties west of the Mississippi.

At the same time, settlers were moving north from St. Louis and establishing settlements along the Mississippi, where they found few natural obstacles to hamper inland settlement as compared to those mentioned in southeastern Missouri. The settlement of northern Missouri is beyond the scope of the study; however, in the early stages many of the causes and patterns of settlement in northern Missouri are similar to those in the Ozarks.

Prior to the movement of American settlers up the Missouri River—a movement that started in earnest in 1810—there were only a few scattered settlements west of St. Charles. One of the few settlements was at Cote Sans Dessein near the mouth of the Osage River, where some Frenchmen had established a hunting village in 1807 after Louisiana had passed to American control. Houck reports that the French also settled on the south side of

26. Violette, "Settlements in Missouri," p. 48.

the river at Bonnots Mill in 1805. Sauer describes the French in the Missouri Valley at this time as follows:

> It was quite natural that a few half-wild French traders should locate on the great route to one of the most important fur districts of the New World. . . . Their villages were a collection of poor huts and their habits of life very primitive. As a result of their associations with the Indians, intermarriages were frequent.

Thus, the French in the Missouri Valley presented a quite different picture than those in the Ste. Genevieve district.[27]

In all practicality, it can be said that the entire Missouri Valley west of St. Charles was unsettled at this time. Among the first Americans to ascend the Missouri were the Boones, who passed beyond the French and settled in present-day Howard County. The settlement became known as Boone's Lick because of the presence of salt in the vicinity and soon achieved the reputation in the eastern and southern states as the most desirable land in Missouri. By 1820, settlers largely from Kentucky at first were coming in droves. In October of 1819, it was estimated that ten to fifteen thousand settlers crossed the Mississippi at St. Louis, and most of the settlers headed for Boone's Lick. In a decade, the Missouri River area between St. Louis and Boone's Lick was dotted with settlements, and by 1830 settlement had reached the western boundary of Missouri.[28]

By this time, flank movements of population on both sides of the river had begun. While frontiersmen were building homes along the Missouri, others were moving up the major tributaries of that stream and were occupying valleys and uplands. Settlers had moved south and had established themselves along the Gasconade River by the time Long made his expedition in 1819. Farther south and west, the area included within the boundaries of present-day Maries County was occupied about this time.[29]

By 1820, some settlement was occurring in southwestern Missouri. In 1819, Schoolcraft smelted lead in the vicinity of Springfield. Sometime prior to 1819, a settlement at the present site of Forsyth in the White River Hills had been occupied for some time. The year 1830 is given for the founding of Springfield. To the east,

27. Houck, *History of Missouri*, vol. 3, p. 159; Sauer, *Ozark Highland*, pp. 90–91.
28. Anderson, "Missouri, 1804–1828," p. 169; Violette, "Settlements in Missouri," p. 51.
29. Houck, *History of Missouri*, vol. 3, p. 154.

settlements were beginning along the Current River in present-day Carter County by the early 1820s.[30]

The most apparent change in the population of Missouri between 1803 and 1830 was the Americanization of most of the state (Figure 2–9). By 1830, the population of Missouri was more than 90 per cent American. Although most Americans moving west from the eastern seaboard were still stopping to the east of Missouri, those who had gone west from the Atlantic at an earlier date accounted for most of the emigrants in Missouri. The main artery along which population was funneled to Missouri was the Ohio River and its tributaries the Cumberland and Tennessee; thus, emigrants in

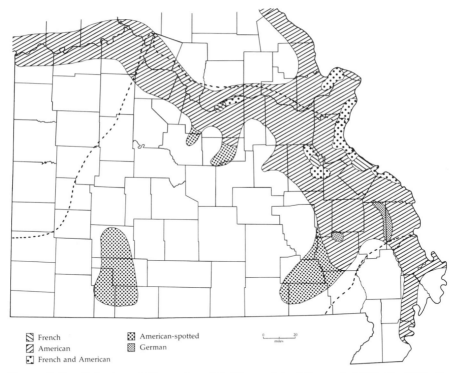

Figure 2–9. Extent and Character of Settlement in Missouri, 1830. By 1830, the settlement frontier had passed through Missouri, avoiding the rougher Ozark Highland Region and following the Missouri Valley. Settlements were beginning to reach toward the rougher interior areas.

30. Henry Rowe Schoolcraft, *Schoolcraft in the Ozarks*, p. 112; Houck, *History of Missouri*, vol. 3, p. 159; Milton D. Rafferty, "Persistence Versus Change in Land Use and Landscape in the Springfield, Missouri, Vicinity of the Ozarks," p. 40; Goodwin, "Missouri and Arkansas," p. 402.

Missouri were moving pretty much along parallels of latitude at this time. This accounts for the larger Kentucky migration into Missouri at this time and a similar movement of Tennesseans to Arkansas.[31]

The effect the Americanization of Missouri had on the French was quite pronounced. By 1811, American manners and the language were beginning to predominate among the French, and by 1830 the strongholds of French culture were severely constricted so that only Ste. Genevieve, Old Mines, and Bonnots Mill remained. St. Louis, in particular, had lost its French flavor. Anderson observes about the French in Missouri in 1830:

> Probably it is not too much to say that by the end of the third decade of American rule, most of the French looked on hopelessly while they were being absorbed and overwhelmed by the more numerous, wrangling, covetous, liberty-loving, equality-demanding Americans.[32]

One factor that may well have contributed to the decline of French culture in Missouri was the absence of schools in most of their settlements. Brackenridge notes that nearly every American settlement had a school, which was in sharp contrast to the "majority of the unenterprising French Creoles, many of whom did not know a letter of the alphabet."[33] As late as 1850, neither Ste. Genevieve nor Washington counties, both still French strongholds, had a library; whereas, the neighboring American counties all had libraries at that time.

Because of the American settler, by 1830 Missouri's culture was no longer dominated by the Roman Catholic church but more correctly reflected the religious diversity of its inhabitants. By that date at least two-thirds of Missouri's population were either Protestant or nonreligious. While there were no Baptist churches in Missouri in 1803, there were 230 in 1836. Methodists ranked with Baptists as the dominant Protestant denomination in Missouri, and by 1830 most Protestant denominations were represented to some degree.[34]

Although the growth of Missouri's population from 1803 to 1830 was overwhelmingly American, foreign immigrants from central

31. Floyd C. Shoemaker, "Missouri's Tennessee Heritage," p. 130.
32. Anderson, "Missouri, 1804–1828," pp. 156–57.
33. Henry M. Brackenridge, *Recollections of Persons and Places in the West*, p. 117, quoted in Anderson, "Missouri, 1804–1828," p. 162.
34. R. W. Heintze, "Religious Organization in Missouri Before 1839," p. 94; R. W. Heintze, "The Religious Situation in Missouri up to 1839," p. 71.

Europe began arriving in small numbers. In 1818, in anticipation of the large number of foreign immigrants expected, an emigrant aid society was organized in St. Louis, especially for the Germans and Irish. In 1820, Missouri already numbered the Welsh, Scottish, and Irish among her settlers. Although data for this period are somewhat sketchy, naturalization records for Perry County indicate that Germans were present in that county prior to 1820.[35]

In addition to the Germans in southeastern Missouri, a few had passed beyond St. Louis and ascended the Missouri River. Most notable was Gottfried Duden, an educated Rhinelander, who immigrated into Missouri in 1824, and farmed near the present location of Dutzow in Warren County. Duden published a report in 1829 entitled *Reise nach dem westlichen Staaten*. In his report, Duden described the northern Ozarks as geographically similar to southern Germany but without the social drawbacks; a region where one could practice hillside horticulture and, yet, be free of the convention-ridden society of nineteenth-century Germany. Duden's report was widely read in Germany, and in subsequent years thousands of his countrymen came directly into Missouri as a result of this glowing and somewhat exaggerated description of the Ozarks. In addition to Duden's writings, at least a dozen other German-language travel books dealing with Missouri were in circulation by 1830.[36]

Anderson's observation that "by 1828 Missouri was a true melting pot" may have been somewhat premature; but the seeds for future growth were present. The Americans, of course, were still coming in large numbers. And the European has sent word back to his old homeland that Missouri was not only available to them for settlement but was the best possible place for their settlements in all of the United States.[37]

35. Anderson, "Missouri, 1804–1828," p. 167; County court records, 1821, vol. 1, p. 2.

36. Lewis W. Spitz, "The Germans in Missouri: A Preliminary Study," pp. 34–35. Duden's report has been translated to English by William G. Bek and published in the *Missouri Historical Review*, October 1917–April 1919. This was followed by another series of articles entitled, "The Followers of Duden," which appeared in the *Missouri Historical Review*, October 1919–January 1925. Both series deal with Duden's many written accounts of his years in the Missouri Ozarks and the impact his writings had on subsequent German immigration to Missouri. Spitz, "A Preliminary Study"; pp. 30–42; Carl E. Schneider, *The German Church on the American Frontier*, p. 14.

37. Anderson, "Missouri, 1804–1828," p. 174; Richard O'Conner, *The German-Americans: An Informal History*, pp. 68–70.

Passing of the Frontier, 1830–1860

The Ozark region was settled from 1830 to 1860, pushing the frontier into the plains of Kansas. According to the census figures for 1860, every county in the Ozarks had surpassed a population density of two people per square mile.[38] Although the majority of Missouri's population growth during this period was American, this was the time when large numbers of foreign settlers, primarily Germans, entered the Ozarks.

The settlement frontier did not proceed through the Ozarks on a north-south axis; rather, a more circuitous route was taken. With the Missouri Valley filling up rapidly, settlement proceeded south along the Western Ozark Border toward the Springfield Plain, thus avoiding the rugged Ozark interior (Figure 2–10). A corresponding movement west from the Mississippi border lagged behind for several decades. The White River Hills were settled at about the same time as the Springfield Plain and to a degree were settled from the south as well as from the east by frontiersmen who bypassed the Ozark interior to get to the more preferred hunting grounds of southwestern Missouri. Gradually, settlement spread inward toward the Ozark center from the Northern, Eastern, and Western Ozark Border regions and appeared more as an "unobtrusive infiltration" than the passing of the frontier. The dominance of Americans during this period in the frontier is evidenced by various religious groups in the Ozarks in 1850. With a few exceptions, American churches were the only ones present in the frontier areas.[39]

Three states dominate as source areas of the Ozark's Old Stock American population during this period. These states are Tennessee, Kentucky, and Virginia. The Kentuckians, many of whom were slaveholders, continued their movement up the Missouri and filled in the areas around Boone's Lick, which by the 1830s had come to mean almost any place between the mouth of the Osage River and Kansas City. From the Missouri, Kentuckians moved

38. *Eighth Census of the United States: 1860, Preliminary Report*, pp. 268–71.
39. Houck, *History of Missouri*, vol. 3, p. 159; Sauer, *Ozark Highland*, pp. 148–50; E. Joan Wilson Miller, "The Ozark Culture Region as Revealed by Traditional Materials," p. 55; *The Seventh Census of the United States: 1850*, pp. 684–91. Of the 178 churches present in the frontier areas, defined as those Ozark counties not bordering on either the Missouri or the Mississippi rivers, excluding the mining counties of the eastern Ozarks, 96.7 per cent were of the various American denominations as defined by Zelinsky, "Religious Geography," p. 146.

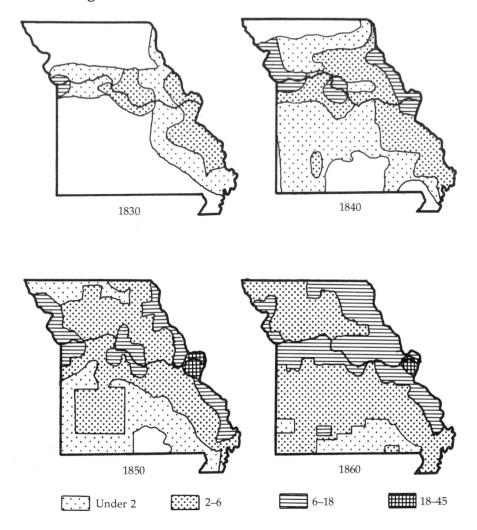

Population Density Per Square Mile, 1830–1860

Figure 2–10. Passing of the Frontier. Sources: Emerson, *Geography of Missouri*, Sauer, *Ozark Highland*.

north and south along the larger streams, particularly along the Osage to the south (Figure 2–11). The Virginians also reached their greatest numerical strength along the Missouri. Virginia was situated at the terminus of the only route then available across the southern Appalachians. Many of those filtering through Cumberland Gap found Kentucky already somewhat crowded by 1830 and, as a result, moved directly to Missouri. Having passed through

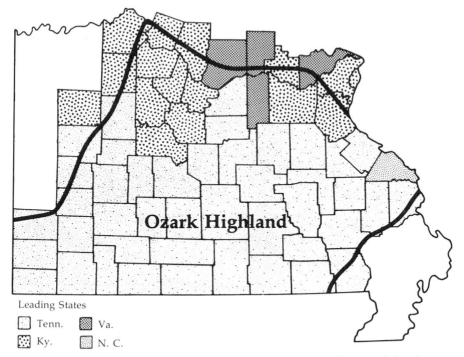

Figure 2–11. Nativity of the Old Stock American Population of the Ozarks, 1860. The pattern of Old Stock American settlement in the Ozarks was characterized by a dominance of Tennessee stock over much of the rougher and less productive Ozarks, while Kentucky and Virginia stock dominated the more productive Ozark borders. Source: Manuscript schedules of population, 1860.

Kentucky, they were aware of Boone's Lick, which was then the focus of settlement in Missouri.

The remainder of the Ozarks was dominated by settlers from Tennessee. Shoemaker states that:

> During the early decades of the nineteenth century the Tennessee settlers spread themselves all over the State of Missouri but later made their homes mainly in our Ozark highlands. Here they occupied almost solidly an area . . . of 31,000 square miles. . . . And, they still hold it.[40]

Sauer adds, "It is no rare thing to find some remote valley [in the Ozark center] in which every inhabitant is descended from Tennessee stock."[41]

North Carolinians lead only in Perry County. Unlike Virginians, who traveled through a crowded state on their way to Missouri,

40. Shoemaker, "Missouri's Tennessee Heritage," p. 130.
41. Sauer, *Ozark Highland*, p. 159.

North Carolinians moving west entered a less crowded Tennessee. However, because the settlement frontier moved more rapidly through Kentucky than Tennessee, many North Carolinians apparently stayed in Tennessee, since abundant land was still available there. Many of the Tennesseans who migrated into Missouri at a later date were probably descendents of these North Carolinians.

Although most of Missouri's American settlers during this period were from these states, there were significant differences among them. The Kentuckians were either slaveholders or sympathetic to slavery, suggesting that they had come originally from the middle and southern Atlantic seaboard, possibly by way of the South (Figure 2–12). This is also true of many Tennesseans in the eastern Ozarks, who were referred to as "plantation" Tennesseans. Sauer

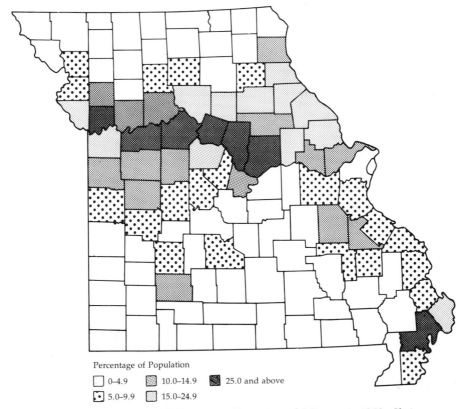

Percentage of Population

☐ 0–4.9   ▨ 10.0–14.9   ▨ 25.0 and above
⊡ 5.0–9.9   ▨ 15.0–24.9

Figure 2–12. Percentage of Slaves in Counties of Missouri, 1860. Slaves were concentrated in Missouri in the more productive areas such as the Missouri Valley and in areas populated by Kentuckians and Virginians. Source: Laughlin, *Missouri Politics During the Civil War.*

agrees, adding, "Some of the Missouri and Mississippi River portions of the state of Missouri still retain in large part dominant southern traits, and are referred to occasionally by their political antagonists as Bourbon districts." Several of the counties along the Missouri are included in the region referred to as "Little Dixie," an area that has maintained political and cultural ties with the South since the early days of settlement. The river counties contained the overwhelming majority of the slaves in the state and are said to reflect to this day their inherited Southern culture through their overwhelming support of the Democratic party.[42]

The settlers of the central and western Ozarks were largely from eastern Tennessee, and their culture was more characteristic of the North than the South. They owned few slaves partly because slavery was not in their cultural background, but also because many of the eastern Tennesseans were hill people from the poorest classes and, thus, financially unable to own slaves. The probability that many eastern Tennesseans were of northern origin and moved down the Great Valley in reaching Tennessee is supported by the presence of Quakers in Jasper County during this period. In addition, Pennsylvanians by birth were well represented among the Tennesseans in the central and western Ozarks but were largely absent in the northern and eastern Ozarks. In contrast to the Southerners in the river districts, the highland Tennesseans became Republicans and have remained so to this day.[43]

German Settlement to 1860

Due to adverse social, political, and economic conditions in various parts of nineteenth-century central Europe, the largest outpouring of immigrants ever from German lands occurred. German immigrants moved out in various directions. Some immigrants moved eastward into the Slavic lands of eastern Europe and Russia; others selected homes in temperate areas of Latin America; and the British Empire attracted significant numbers,

42. Shoemaker, "Missouri's Tennessee Heritage," p. 132; Sauer, *Ozark Highland*, p. 102; Robert M. Crisler, "Missouri's 'Little Dixie'," p. 131.
43. Carl O. Sauer, "Geography and the Gerrymander," p. 410; Shoemaker, "Missouri's Tennessee Heritage," p. 132; Marbut, "Soils of the Ozark Region," p. 253; Sauer, *Ozark Highland*, p. 159; Friis, *A Series of Population Maps*, plate following p. 16; R. A. Campbell, *Campbell's New Atlas of Missouri*, p. 34; Russel L. Gerlach, "Geography and Politics in Missouri: A Study in Electoral Patterns," p. 28; Harbert L. Clendenen, "Settlement Morphology of the Southern Courtois Missouri Hills, 1820–1860."

particularly Australia and Canada. The vast majority, however, chose the United States, where Missouri was a major focus of German settlement in the nineteenth century.[44]

During the years following the publication of Duden's report in 1829, Germans began coming in larger numbers to Missouri. The early German settlements in Missouri were spotty and composed mostly of Germans from Ohio, Kentucky, Tennessee, Virginia, Maryland, and North Carolina. Later, German immigration into Missouri was much better organized, with many settlers coming directly from Germany through New Orleans. The majority of Germans who settled in the Middle West, however, continued to enter the United States via New York and settled primarily in Wisconsin and Minnesota rather than more southerly areas such as Missouri. From the beginning, St. Louis served as the distribution center on the Mississippi River for those immigrants going up the Mississippi and, as a result, exerted a significant influence on the location of German communities in the middle Mississippi Valley.[45] The timing of German immigration into Missouri, and the Midwest in general, was a result of both the westward movement of the frontier and the greater number of Germans who immigrated into the United States after 1830.[46]

The Northern Ozark Border

The following statement appeared in *Niles' Register* on 8 November 1834:

> A large number of German emigrants who arrived in the last and present years, have settled in the 'forks of the Missouri and Mississippi' Rivers—preferring the rich bottom lands. The population of Missouri is rapidly advancing and many of the old settlers are proceeding towards the 'Far West' to make room for the newcomers.[47]

Three years later, *Niles' Register* gave the following account of German immigration to the United States:

> In the late second annual report of the Immigrants' Friends Society, at Cincinnati, Ohio, it is stated by their traveling agent, the Rev. Mr.

44. For a discussion of these factors see Terry G. Jordan, *German Seed in Texas Soil*, p. 32.

45. Theodore Huebener, *The Germans in America*, pp. 88–89; John Fraser Hart, "The Middle West," p. 260; Hildegard Binder Johnson, "The Location of German Immigrants in the Middle West," p. 12.

46. The large-scale immigration of Germans into the United States began around 1820 but reached Missouri somewhat later. For more information see Wilbur Zelinsky, *Cultural Geography of the United States*, pp. 23–28.

47. *Niles' Register*, 8 November 1834, p. 273.

Lemonowsky, that there are in that part of Pennsylvania belonging to the valley 15,000 (Germans), of which number the majority are in and about Pittsburgh. In Virginia, the majority in and about Wheeling, 10,000. In the state of Ohio, 40,000, of which 10,000 are in Cincinnati. In Indiana, 20,000. Kentucky 20,000, of which 5,000 to 6,000 are in Louisville; Missouri, 30,000, of which 6 to 7,000 are in St. Louis; Tennessee, 5,000; Louisiana, 15,000; Alabama, 2,000; Mississippi, 5,000; making in all an aggregate of 117,000 German immigrants, who are not citizens of our country. Besides these about 450,000 are preparing in various parts of Germany to immigrate to this country.[48]

The first report notes the location of German settlements in Missouri. The second report indicates the magnitude of German immigration into Missouri, which was second at that time only to Ohio. The latter report also gives an indication of the volume of German immigration into the United States that was anticipated in the following years.

Duden's location in Warren (then Montgomery) County had attracted many farmers and laborers from Hannover and Westphalia. Many people of higher social class followed, including counts, barons, scholars, preachers, gentlemen farmers, officers, merchants, and students, all possessing some means but little inclination to work. The educated German settlers, known as the "Latin Farmers," because many were educated in the German gymnasia and received thorough instruction in Greek and Latin, came to Missouri seeking a utopian life based on Duden's exaggerated descriptions of Missouri. Many of these settlers failed; some returned to Germany; many settled in St. Louis; and some committed suicide. However, the farmers, who accompanied the scholarly Germans, did quite well and prospered in most cases.[49]

In addition to the general causes of immigration already mentioned, the desire to establish a *"Germania in America"* drew many thousands of Germans to Missouri in the mid-nineteenth century. The first of the two groups to attempt the founding of a German state in Missouri was the so-called *Giezener Gesellschaft.* In regard to this society, the following item appeared in *Niles' Register:*

> The *Stuttgard Universal Gazette* of September 2d announces that a plan is in progress in the southwest of Germany, to make up a state and

48. Ibid., 18 December 1837, p. 357.
49. Albert B. Faust, *The German Element in the United States,* vol. 1, p. 441. Such idealistic schemes were tried in other parts of the United States by other ethnic groups. A good example of one such experiment involving the English was Rugby, Tenn. For details see Walter M. Kollmorgan, "A Reconnaissance of Some Cultural-Agricultural Islands in the South," pp. 417–18.

ship it over to the United States, to become a twenty-fifth member of the confederacy. The following notice of the project appears in that publication: 'According to accounts from the southwest of Germany, a society of liberal men are organizing a grand plan for emigrating to North America. The emigration has hitherto been precarious, because the means were not concentrated. But now it is different, as the object is to form a *New Germany* beyond the ocean, which is to receive all those whose hopes and claims to liberty and right are disappointed in Old Germany. In order to be admitted into the confederation of the United States of America, the law requires the number of free inhabitants, above 25 years of age, to be 60,000, and this number is to be assembled before any further measures can be taken. Many of the Germans established in North America will join their countrymen, and the plan is so popular in Germany, that scarcely any doubts are entertained of its being successful.[50]

The Gieszen Emigration Society was founded in the year following the story in *Niles' Register*, and a large-scale immigration into the Mississippi Valley was planned "to make a model state in the great republic." Wisconsin and Texas were also foci of efforts to create a German state in the United States. With Missouri as their destination, five hundred members from all over Germany sailed for the United States. The immigrants arrived in 1834 and most located on the northern bank of the Missouri River near Duden's farm in present-day Warren County. During the next several years, other organized German settlements were established in this same general area, including the Berlin Society that founded the town of Washington in Franklin County and the Solingen Society that established a settlement on Tavern Creek, also in Franklin County.[51]

The second, and by far larger, effort to create a German state in Missouri followed by only three years after the attempt made by the Gieszen Society. In Philadelphia, which was the cradle of German colonization in America, a society called the German Settlement Society of Philadelphia was established in the 1820s. Its purpose was to establish a German colony somewhere in the "Far West." Its promoters were prompted by several motives. They believed that in partial isolation German settlers could enjoy both the advantages of America and the pleasures of the fatherland. They felt a "Far West" location would allow them to settle as a unit and, thus, to preserve their heritage more fully. The costs of such a

---

50. *Niles' Register*, 3 November 1832, p. 148.
51. Faust, *The German Element*, vol. 1, p. 443; Spitz, "A Preliminary Study," p. 47; Melvin B. Roblee, *Historical Review of Franklin County, Missouri*, p. 52; Schneider, *The German Church*, p. 19.

venture in the West would be moderate compared to Pennsylvania. Finally, they believed that, being somewhat familiar with American laws, customs, and conditions, they could accomplish what others had failed to do.[52]

The society selected a site in Gasconade County where they purchased more than 12,000 acres in 1838. In the first year, 230 immigrants from all over Germany arrived at the new settlement in Gasconade County, and many moved directly to the newly established town and focal point of the colony, Hermann.[53]

The German settlers continued coming up the Missouri and established, in the process, overwhelming German majorities in the river counties for one hundred miles west from St. Louis. By the late 1830s "a veritable German highway had been formed from St. Louis to Manchester, Tavern Creek, and Missouritown, and particularly . . . to Marthasville and the Femme Osage Valley." The newly arrived Germans bought out the established Americans as they went, including Daniel Boone at Femme Osage. The region became so German that many of the Americans in the vicinity of Washington learned to speak fluent German, and in northern Gasconade County the same was said to be true of the small Negro population in the vicinity of Hermann. Yet, the "New Germany" plan failed. It appears that those who were most enthusiastic about the idea failed as pioneers, while those who simply wanted a good life, caring little about preserving everything German, went to work and prospered.[54]

At the same time efforts were being made to establish a German state in Missouri, thousands of Germans seeking religious freedom were settling in the northern Ozarks. In 1833, a colony of Catholics from Muenster established a settlement on Maries Creek, four miles above the Osage River in Osage County. The next year a group of Catholic Rhinelanders arrived in the same area and founded the settlement of Westphalia. In 1837, there were about

52. William G. Bek, *The German Settlement Society of Philadelphia and Its Colony, Hermann, Missouri*, pp. 1–2.

53. Hermann and its environs have been the subject of several studies. In addition to Bek, *German Settlement Society*, they include Arthur William Apprill, "The Culture of a German Community in Missouri"; A. B. Cozzens, "Conservation in German Settlements of the Missouri Ozarks"; Martha Langendoerfer, "Geography of the Hermann (Missouri) Region"; and Samuel T. Bratten and Martha Langendoerfer, "The Hermann, Missouri, Region."

54. Schneider, *The German Church*, p. 19; Faust, *The German Element*, vol. 1, p. 446. The German who purchased Boone's farm was an early arrival since Boone was in Howard County by 1810. Spitz, "A Preliminary Study," p. 47; Bek, *German Settlement Society*, p. 128; O'Conner, *The German-Americans*, pp. 81–82.

fifty Catholic families in the settlement. In the years that followed, seventeen German Catholic communities were established from the original settlement at Westphalia, and by 1840 there were more than six hundred families in these new settlements. The settlements had spread to Maries, Miller, and Cole counties, and included a German-Belgian colony at Taos near Jefferson City.[55]

Since abundant land was available in this area, the German Catholics had much latitude in selecting locations for their settlements. Most settlements were probably located on the basis of site factors and, to some extent, intuition; however, one settlement owes its location to a rather unique set of circumstances. Ten miles south of Westphalia a Protestant landowner, who had purchased several thousand acres for speculative purposes, conceived that the best means of attracting the incoming German settlers would be to erect a Catholic church. The landowner donated the land and the money for the church with the result that the settlement of Koeltztown, almost exclusively German Catholic, grew rapidly. Other Catholic settlements were established downriver at Washington and Augusta in the 1830s.[56]

A filling-in process followed the initial phase of German settlement whereby Americans sold their land to the incoming Germans and moved on. From the modest beginnings of the Philadelphia Society in Gasconade County, German settlement continued until virtually all of the northern two-thirds of the county was German. In Westphalia, Americans were present at the time of the initial German settlement, but by 1840 all of the landowners within three miles of Westphalia were both German and Catholic. The Richfountain School District, which numbered more than two hundred families, had but one non-German, non-Catholic landowner within its boundaries.[57] In discussing the tendency of Germans to acquire additional and higher quality land after the initial settlement, Schneider observes:

> After acquiring some means [in the city], the [German] peasant usually moved to the country and readily adjusted himself to more con-

55. Emmet H. Rothan, *The German Catholic Immigrant in the United States (1830–1860)*, p. 50; Joseph H. Schmidt, "Recollections of the First Catholic Mission Work in Central Missouri," p. 84; W. A. Willibrand, "A Forgotten Pioneer of Westphalia, Missouri," p. 7.

56. Gilbert J. Garraghan, "The Mission of Central Missouri," pp. 178–79; Rothan, *German Catholic Immigrant*, pp. 51–52.

57. *Souvenir of the Centennial Celebration of St. Joseph's Parish, Westphalia, Missouri, August 6, 1935*, pp. 5–12; Rev. John Rothensteiner, *History of the Archdiocese of St. Louis*, vol. 1, p. 690.

genial conditions. On occasion he hired out to his neighbor, while the women and children cleared the underbrush from his farm. Much of the best bottom land finally fell into the hands of these frugal people, who procured it from the restless Yankees. . . . Flourishing farms began to appear; the German-American farmer came into being.[58]

Marbut notes that wherever the region was occupied by Germans, "the original population was bought out and the German population took the place of the original."[59]

Germans continued to move north on the Missouri River in search of homes. In the late 1830s, settlement was begun in Pettis County. Originally, the settlement consisted of only nine families, but after 1840 the settlement grew rapidly, eventually totaling more than six hundred Germans. The settlements extended beyond the western Ozark boundary into Lafayette County, and south into Benton County, where large numbers of Lutherans settled at Cole Camp and Lincoln.[60]

Other central Europeans settled among the Germans and, in most cases, blended in rather easily. South and southwest of Owensville in Gasconade County was an area settled largely by Bohemian Catholics. The settlement extended east into Franklin County in the vicinity of Japan. In addition there were some agricultural Swiss settlements, the largest of which were in Moniteau and Gasconade counties. The Belgian colony at Taos, which originally attracted approximately fifty immigrants from Ghent, was the only Belgian settlement in the Northern Ozark Border.[61]

South of Washington in Franklin County, a sizeable group of Polish farmers settled. They later established the communities of Krakow and Clover Bottoms. Although these settlements were not large, the first Polish newspaper in the United States, the *Polish Eagle*, began publication in Krakow in 1870.[62] German immigrants subsequently moved into the Polish settlements, and soon these settlements were predominantly German. Although smaller numbers of other European nationalities are included in the

---

58. Schneider, *The German Church*, pp. 25–26.
59. Marbut, *Soils of the Ozark Region*, p. 251.
60. Spitz, "A Preliminary Study," pp. 76–77.
61. Prior to 1914, Bohemia was a province of Austria. It is probable that more Bohemians settled in the Ozarks but claimed nationalities other than Bohemian, most likely Austrian or German. Rothensteiner, *Archdiocese of St. Louis*, vol. 2, p. 418; John Paul von Grueningen, *The Swiss in the United States*, p. 28; Rothensteiner, *Archdiocese of St. Louis*, vol. 2, p. 373.
62. Rothensteiner, *Archdiocese of St. Louis*, vol. 2, p. 413; Roblee, *Historical Review*, p. 26; the paper was later moved to Chicago.

manuscript census returns for 1860, those listed above represent the major nuclei of European settlement in the northern Ozarks to 1860.

The Eastern Ozark Border

German settlement of the Eastern Ozark Border followed that of the Northern Ozark Border by only a few years. However, there was little effort directed toward the goal of a "*Germania* in America" among the Germans south of St. Louis. The two main factors responsible for the Germans locating south of St. Louis are inexpensive land and the desire to attain religious solidarity through compact group settlement, which was only possible in more remote areas. After the establishment of Colonel Bollinger's colony on the Whitewater in 1798, a gradual trickle of Germans came into the eastern Ozarks. Records in Perry County indicate that Germans were applying for naturalization as early as 1821, and by 1830 the number of Germans entering the county was sizeable. By 1828, a Catholic chapel had been built by Germans at Apple Creek, and it was reported that the French priest had learned to speak German and English in order to serve his parishioners, who represented all three nationalities.[63]

The majority of the Germans entering the Eastern Ozark Border after 1830 was Catholic, who came in colonies or grouped themselves along religious lines after arriving. The first German Catholic colony to establish a settlement along the Mississippi River arrived in 1834 and selected a site near Cape Girardeau. In 1836, a Catholic colony of both Germans and Swiss settled west of Cape Girardeau at Dutchtown. Several other German Catholic colonies located farther south just beyond the Ozark boundary at Kelso, Illmo, New Hamburg, and Diehlstadt.[64]

In Ste. Genevieve County, German Catholic colonies were established at New Offenburg and Zell in 1840. Later, settlements were founded nearby at Weingarten and Coffman, and Germans moved into formerly French settlements such as River Aux Vases and even Ste. Genevieve itself. Of the Germans in Ste. Genevieve, Franzwa noted:

> The old town like any number of others in the Middle West was innundated with industrious Germans in the immigration wave of

63. County court records, 1821, vol. 1, p. 2; *Centennial Remembrance of St. Joseph's Parish at Apple Creek, Missouri, 1828–1928*, p. 3; Rothensteiner, *Archdiocese of St. Louis*, vol. 2, p. 68.
64. Sauer, *Ozark Highland*, p. 167.

1825–45. By the middle of the nineteenth century there were far more Germans there than French.[65]

The German settlements in Ste. Genevieve County expanded rapidly until the county possessed a German-speaking majority. German Catholics were attracted to Ste. Genevieve County apparently by the French Catholic residents nearby. The in-movement of German Catholics continued south into Perry County, where large numbers of settlers from Baden located in the 1840s and 1850s.[66]

One of the most intriguing religious groups from Germany to settle in the Ozarks was the Saxon Lutheran, or "Old Lutheran," who established a colony in eastern Perry County in 1839. The Saxon Lutherans, who feared continued repression if they remained in Germany, represented a conservative minority in the Saxon state church. By immigrating to the United States, they hoped to establish a semiautonomous theocratic community. They first went to St. Louis in search of a suitable location for their colony. The desire of the leaders of the Saxons for isolation is apparent from their choice of a site for their settlement. They were offered a parcel of 15,000 acres on the banks of the Meramec near St. Louis; this land was inexpensive and appropriate for agriculture. However, they selected a track of approximately 4,500 acres of very hilly land 110 miles south of St. Louis in eastern Perry County. The Perry County site was almost completely unsettled and "so utterly remote from civilization that seldom any travelers trespassed upon it." The leaders, at least, considered the agricultural quality of the land secondary to a remote location. Their selection of a site allowed them to keep "nonbelievers" out, but as Sauer observes, "their choice of rough hill land was most unfortunate and was due to their inefficiency in matters of practical judgment."[67]

The Saxon settlement in Perry County was very carefully planned in every detail. Five boroughs were designated; each was to have its own church. Of the five original boroughs, only Altenburg, Wittenberg, and Frohna materialized. Later immigrants who were

65. Gregory M. Franzwa, *The Story of Old Ste. Genevieve*, p. 92.

66. Sauer, *Ozark Highland*, p. 167; Rev. S. P. Hueber, ed., *The Centennial History of Perry County, Missouri, 1821–1921*, p. 22.

67. The Perry County Saxons have been the subject of several studies, including Walter O. Forster, *Zion on the Mississippi*; P. E. Kretzmann, "Saxon Immigration to Missouri, 1838–1839"; E. F. Stegen, "The Settlement of the Saxon Lutherans in Perry County, Missouri"; Sauer, *Ozark Highland*, p. 167.

adherents of the Saxon Lutheran religion settled in the vicinity of the original settlements. They established parishes at Paitzdorf (later changed to Uniontown to demonstrate the support of the Saxons for the Union cause in the Civil War) and Farrar, which are both in Perry County, and New Wells in Cape Girardeau County. Thereafter, congregations were established at Perryville, Friedenburg, Longtown, and Crosstown in Perry County, and Pocahontas in Cape Girardeau County. These later settlements were based partly on new arrivals in the 1860s and partly on expansion from the older settlements. These settlements represent the beginning of the Missouri Synod of the Lutheran Church. Trinity Lutheran, the mother church of the Missouri Synod, is located in Altenburg. Concordia Seminary, the major training institute for Missouri Synod ministers, originated in Altenburg and was later moved to its present location in St. Louis.

As in the Northern Ozark Border, Germans continued to move into the settlements along the Mississippi throughout the remainder of the nineteenth century. They showed a preference to settle among their own kind; first, along ethnic lines, and, second, along religious and other intranational lines. The German settlements along both the Northern and Eastern Ozark Border regions reflect the strength of regional loyalties that had long existed within Germany, and whole communities of Rhinelanders, Hannoverians, Badish, and other groups are not uncommon in the Ozarks.

New parishes were founded by both German Protestants and German Catholics from southern Jefferson County to the Ozark boundary in the south and as far west as Iron and Madison counties. Although the majority continued to come directly from Germany, many were now coming to Missouri from other states, according to Spitz, because of the climate of Missouri, which was preferable to the cold winters of Wisconsin and the hot summers of Texas. One group of Germans and Dutch came from Ohio in 1856 and established a colony near Leopold in Bollinger County.[68]

Other smaller groups of Europeans entered during the same period. In 1837, a French colony settled in southwestern Perry County. It is doubtful that this colony came from France; rather, it is more likely that the colony came from Illinois or Canada. Sometime in the 1860s, a colony of Belgian Catholics located in the lowlands along the Mississippi in northern Perry County, where the

68. Spitz, "A Preliminary Study," p. 77; Rothensteiner, *Archdiocese of St. Louis*, vol. 2, p. 239.

town of Belgique was founded. In northern Cape Girardeau County, a group of Austrian Lutherans settled in the 1860s and soon became closely identified with the Saxon Lutherans in Perry County.[69]

One final ethnic settlement located near the Eastern Ozark Border during this period. A group of approximately forty Irish families settled in the very rugged and hilly country of Shannon County in the late 1850s. Their choice of a home in the Ozarks is a result of some interesting circumstances. They left Ireland because of the potato famine of the 1840s and found work building railroads in the midwestern United States. They became nearly destitute in St. Louis by the mid-1850s. A Catholic priest from St. Louis purchased land on their behalf in Shannon County and assisted them in establishing an agricultural settlement. Their choice of land for an agricultural settlement was most unfortunate but was only one of the difficulties they faced in their new Ozark home. During the Civil War, both sides sent recruiters into the area to conscript the settlers for military service. Those who remained during the war were caught in the middle of the vigilante actions, which plagued parts of the interior eastern Ozarks. As a result, by the conclusion of the Civil War, this settlement, which never was named, had virtually ceased to exist. However, the area where the Irish settled in Shannon County is still commonly referred to as the "Irish Wilderness."[70]

European Settlement and the Railroads

The Europeans continued to settle in the Ozarks in the years following the Civil War, but immigration was more sporadic than before and involved smaller numbers. However, the immigration represented a much greater variety in terms of ethnic background. This period of European settlement was closely associated with railroad construction in the Ozarks in the years immediately preceding and following the Civil War (Figure 2–13).

Many Europeans who were influenced very little by the railroads, particularly the Germans, continued to locate in the older and more established settlements. In fact, immigrants coming from Germany continued to filter into the Northern and Eastern Ozark Border regions well into the twentieth century, and even today a few still are coming. Some expansion also occurred from

69. Hueber, *History of Perry County*, p. 22.
70. Ruth F. Van Doren, "Myth—History of the Irish Wilderness," p. 6.

Dates of Railroad Completion

╫ To 1864
╫ 1864–1870
— Post–1870

Figure 2–13. Dates of Railroad Construction in the Ozarks. In general, railroads came late to the Ozarks, and the density of rail coverage was never sufficient to remove the barriers that had contributed to the region's isolation. Sources: Gates, "The Railroads of Missouri, 1850–1870"; Mann, "Frisco First: A Source Materials of the St. Louis and San Francisco Railroad, 1845–1947"; and Miner, *The St. Louis-San Francisco Transcontinental Railroad.*

the original German settlements in the late nineteenth century, probably because of the land shortages in the older settlements. In Miller County, a German colony from the eastern counties settled around Marys Home and St. Elizabeth during this period. In the 1890s, some Germans and Bohemians moved farther southwest and settled near the western Ozark boundary in Cedar County near Jerico Springs.[71] Some of the other Europeans were brought in as colonies by the railroads; while, on the other hand, some were

71. H. G. Lewis and F. V. Emerson, *Soil Survey of Miller County, Missouri,* p. 7; E. B. Watson and H. F. Williams, *Soil Survey of Cedar County, Missouri,* p. 8.

A	Austrian	G	German	S	Swedish
B	Bohemian	H	Hungarian	Sw	Swiss
D	Danish	I	Italian	Y	Yugoslavian
F	French	P	Polish		

Figure 2–14. Ethnic Railroad Settlements and Major Rail Lines. More than twenty ethnic settlements were established on or near railroad grant land in the Ozarks. Although most of the railroad settlements were small, they represented a variety of foreign source areas.

located by land companies that specialized in European immigrants; and some were influenced indirectly through the advertising by railroads and land companies.[72] For a few groups the Ozarks represented a second location since leaving Europe; their first location for various reasons being unsuitable.

The railroad settlements are widely distributed throughout the Ozarks. However, three broad clusters of settlements can be noted when viewing all of the settlements (Figure 2–14). First, the main

72. A search through the archives of the St. Louis-San Francisco Railroad Company in St. Louis turned up no records dealing with the railroad's colonization activities. Apparently, these records were destroyed when the headquarters of the Frisco were transferred from Springfield to St. Louis.

line of the Frisco to the southwest from St. Louis was a major focus of colonization. Second, the Springfield Plain north to and beyond the border between the Ozarks and the Osage Plain was a major area of railroad settlement. Finally, several settlements were situated along the Ozark escarpment in the southeastern part of the state. Railroad settlement was begun at the conclusion of the Civil War and reached its greatest intensity during the late 1870s and early 1880s. A few settlements were located as late as the first decade of the twentieth century. All of the rural settlements associated with the railroads are summarized in Table 2–1.[73]

The first cluster of settlements was along the main line of the St. Louis-San Francisco Railroad between St. Clair and Rolla. The railroad was completed to Rolla in 1861, but little settlement occurred until the end of the Civil War. In 1866, a colony of several hundred Danish and Swedish immigrants was brought from Europe by the American Emigrant Aid and Homestead Company, with most settling in Rolla township in Phelps County. Although the Frisco was instrumental in establishing several ethnic settlements in the Ozarks and elsewhere, it had no formal and organized program of colonization comparable to those of the Burlington and Union Pacific railroads. In the early 1870s, several additional agricultural colonies were established in this vicinity with the help of the Frisco. These settlements included Frenchmen, at Dillon (near Rolla); Austrians, a few miles south of Rolla; Germans, a few miles east of Rolla; Swiss, to the southwest of Rolla; and Swedes, in Franklin County near St. Clair. Later, two additional European settlements appeared along the main line. A Swedish colony located in Pulaski County in 1876. They established the town of Swedeborg on land purchased from the railroad. Beginning in 1876, an Austrian group migrated to the Ozarks from Hungary, which then was part of the Austrian Empire. They settled near Steelville in Crawford County.[74]

Farther southwest, along the main line of the Frisco, several

73. The information in Table 2–1 and in the text regarding the various railroad settlements was obtained through a series of field interviews unless otherwise noted.

74. H. Craig Miner, *The St. Louis-San Francisco Transcontinental Railroad,* map following p. 84; Charlotte Erickson, *American Industry and the European Immigrant, 1860–1885,* pp. 79–80; Castelli, "Grape Growers of Central Missouri," p. 115; "Ozark Vineyards: Fresh From the Hills," *Chicago Tribune;* Von Grueningen, *The Swiss,* pp. 28–30; Mabel Manes Mottaz, *Lest We Forget: A History of Pulaski County, Missouri, and Fort Leonard Wood,"* p. 22; John Zahorsky, Jr. *The Austrian Immigration of Crawford County,* pp. 1–5.

Table 2-1

Summary of Railroad Settlements

Year	Nationality	Location	Moved from	No. of Families
Main Line Settlements				
1866	Danish, Swedish	near Rolla	Europe	approximately 150
1970s	Austrian	near Rolla	Europe	12
	French	Dillon	–	small
1876	Swedish	near St. Clair	Europe	small
1878	Austrian	near Steelville	Europe	40
1880s	Swedish	Swedeborg	Europe	approximately 50
	Swiss	near Rolla	Europe	approximately 35
1900	Italian	Rosati	Arkansas	60
Southwest Settlements				
1871	German	Rader	Tennessee	15
1873	Swedish	Verona	Europe	approximately 100
1874	German	Freistatt	Minnesota	50 (by 1883)
	(also at Stone's Prairie, Sarcoxie Prairie, and Meinert in the 1870s)			
1875	French	Monett	Uruguay, Europe	30 (by 1880)
1880s	Bohemian	near Bolivar	Europe	small
	German	Billings	Eastern U.S.	35
	(also at Monett, Verona, Pierce City, and Springfield)			
	Moravian	Lebanon	Eastern U.S.	small
	Swiss	Greene County	Europe	small
1880	Polish	Pulaskifield	Europe	approximately 45
1881	German	Lockwood	Illinois	40 (by 1883)
	Swiss	south of Lockwood	Illinois	10
Southeast Settlements				
1870s	German	White Rock	Wisconsin	small
1880s	German	near Thayer	Europe	approximately 20
1890s	Hungarian	near Poplar Bluff	Europe	approximately 25
1905	German	Glennonville	Europe via St. Louis	100
1910	Yugoslavian	Naylor	East	small
1915	German-Polish	Doniphan	East	small

European colonies settled in the 1870s and 1880s. The first settlement occurred in 1871, when a group of German Lutherans from Tennessee founded the community of Rader in southwestern Laclede County. They had heard that the railroad was selling good land at a low price.[75] However, the brunt of the colonization in southwestern Missouri occurred farther down the line in Greene, Christian, Lawrence, and Barry counties.

The southwestern settlements, particularly those involving Germans, were encouraged by the city of Springfield. In 1867, an editorial in the Springfield *Missouri Weekly Patriot* commented, "We regard them [Germans] as the most thrifty and desirable citizens, and should be glad to welcome them to our midst. No other class of population would do more to develop our country." With the encouragement of Springfield, the railroads were reported to be sending executives directly to Germany to attract settlers to southwestern Missouri. The Springfield residents were motivated to seek German immigrants, as well as native American immigrants, to southwestern Missouri, believing that prosperity required growth and growth required large numbers of highly productive settlers.[76]

In 1874, a small group of Germans, who then lived in Minnesota and found the climate too severe, accepted an offer from the Frisco to buy land west of Springfield in Lawrence County for six dollars an acre. They selected a prairie site eight miles north of the railroad in Lawrence County. In the next two decades, the settlement grew rapidly, with Germans coming from New York, Ohio, Wisconsin, Illinois, in addition to Minnesota. All of the settlers had one thing in common: they were German Lutherans who wanted to establish a "real" Lutheran community composed primarily of farmers. By 1883, the settlement had grown from the original nine families to approximately fifty, and a town called Freistatt had been established in the center of the settlement. Because of the success of the Freistatt settlement, several other German Lutheran settlements were established nearby. The settlements that resulted were near Sarcoxie Prairie, at Meinert in Newton County, and at Stone's Prairie in Barry County.[77]

75. *Centennial of Immanuel Lutheran Church, Rader, Missouri*, p. 1.
76. *Missouri Weekly Patriot*; Charles K. Piehl, "The Race of Improvement: Springfield Society, 1865–1881," p. 485.
77. *Great Churches in America: Trinity Lutheran, Freistatt, Missouri, The Christian Century*, p. 753; *Diamond Jubilee, 1874–1949: Trinity Lutheran Church, Freistatt, Missouri.*

In 1881, the Kansas City, Fort Smith, and Gulf Railroad was completed through Dade County. In that same year, four Germans from Illinois arrived and purchased land. Four more contingents of Germans arrived in the next two years and established a sizeable German Lutheran community around Lockwood. At the southern end of this settlement, a small group of Swiss Methodists established a settlement in the 1880s.[78]

A group of German Catholics settled near Billings in Greene and Christian counties in the 1870s, and some German Catholics also settled near the Lutherans in the area of Sarcoxie Prairie. Many of the German Catholics chose the urban centers, including the railroad towns of Monett and Pierce City, as well as Springfield.[79]

A colony of Protestant French Waldensians, or Savoyards, established a settlement south of Monett on railroad land following the Civil War.[80] The Waldensians had long suffered religious persecution in their native home in the Cottian Alps on the French-Italian border.[81] Many Waldensians who sought asylum immigrated to Switzerland and Germany, and one group went to Uruguay in the 1850s. Concerned with violence and repeated revolutions in Uruguay, the colony was enticed to relocate in Missouri by the advertisements of the Atlantic and Pacific Railroad, the parent company of the St. Louis-San Francisco Railroad Company. They selected a forested location near Monett instead of the fertile prairie, later known as the Freistatt Prairie, because having lived in Uruguay where wood was scarce, they felt a wooded location offered greater advantages to settlement. Originally, nine families from Uruguay established the colony in 1875; later, more than twenty families emigrated from Europe to the Monett settlement.[82]

In 1873, a colony from Sweden settled in the vicinity of Verona in Lawrence County on a grant land sold to them by the railroad. The colony was fairly large, consisting of about one hundred families. Unlike most of the ethnic colonies in Missouri, however,

78. A. J. Young, *History of Dade County and Her People*, pp. 151–54.

79. *Christian County: Its First 100 Years*, pp. 84–88; Rothensteiner, *Archdiocese of St. Louis*, vol. 2, p. 285; Miriam Keast Brown, *The Story of Pierce City, Missouri, 1870–1970*, p. 57.

80. A. T. Sweet and E. W. Knobel, *Soil Survey of Barry County, Missouri*, p. 1934.

81. The name Waldensian comes from the founder, Peter Waldo, of this religious sect. Waldo led one of the Anabaptist splinter groups that broke from Luther at the time of the Reformation. For more information see George B. Watts, *The Waldenses in the New World*, and Cornelius J. Dyck, *An Introduction to Mennonite History*.

82. Watts, *The Waldenses*, p. 3.

the Verona Swedish settlements were composed of a variety of religious groups, Methodists, Lutherans, and Baptists. In 1880, a colony of Polish settlers arrived in Barry County and purchased land from the railroad south of Pierce City near Bricefield, which was later renamed Pulaskifield in honor of the Polish general Pulaski. In the early 1880s, a small Moravian settlement was established near Lebanon in Laclede County. According to the 1850 census, other Moravian colonies had located in the Ozarks at an earlier date. In 1850, two colonies were listed for Dade County and one colony for Ripley County, although no evidence can be found of these earlier settlements. Sometime later in the 1880s, a number of Bohemians from Illinois located north of Springfield near Bolivar. The connection of this settlement with the railroad, if any, is not clear.[83]

The final phase of railroad settlement occurred at the beginning of the twentieth century. One of the most interesting ethnic settlements in the Ozarks is the Italian colony at Rosati in Phelps County. In 1895, a philanthropist named Corbin brought approximately two hundred poor families from Italy to Sunnyside, Arkansas, located in the Delta country. Corbin hoped to establish on his land a thriving agricultural community by growing cotton. Soon after their arrival at Sunnyside, many of the colonists became dissatisfied with conditions there: housing was poor; promised services such as education never materialized; the climate was not what they were led to believe it would be; and nearly one hundred members of the colony died of malaria shortly after their arrival at Sunnyside. Therefore, the majority of the colonists left the Sunnyside settlement. Some returned to Italy, and some moved on to South America. One contingent accompanied by the group's spiritual leader, Father Bandini, moved to northwestern Arkansas where they founded the community of Tontitown. In 1900, approximately sixty families were brought by the Frisco to an unsettled area east of St. James in Phelps County, where the railroad owned land. This settlement, later named Rosati, has become the only significant area of grape production in the state of Missouri.[84]

83. A. W. Haswell, *The Ozark Region: Its History and Its People*, pp. 16–18; Brown, *The Story of Pierce City*, p. 55; *Seventh Census of the United States: 1850*, pp. 687–88.

84. Joseph Velikonja, "The Italian Contribution to the Geographic Character of Tontitown, Arkansas, and Rosati, Missouri," pp. 7–8; Leslie Hewes, "Tontitown: Ozark Vineyard Center," pp. 125–43; Castelli, "Grape Growers," pp. 114–15; Arch C. Gerlach, *The National Atlas of the United States*. Note the single dot in south-central Missouri on the map of grape production, p. 175—this is Rosati.

In the southeastern Ozarks, several settlements were established along the St. Louis, Iron Mountain, and Southern Railroad, which was completed in 1880. Around 1900, a small Hungarian group established an agricultural colony near Poplar Bluff. In 1910, a small group of Yugoslavians from New York bought railroad land near Naylor, Missouri. One small group of Germans located in southern Oregon County in the 1880s along the right of way of the newly constructed Frisco line from Thayer to Springfield. Sometime prior to 1915, a colony of German Poles settled in Ripley County east of Doniphan in the "flatwoods." However, efforts by the railroads to establish ethnic settlements in this part of the Ozarks were not always successful:

> Attempts by land companies at colonization have in the main proved a failure. The colonists, mostly Poles and Austrians from northern cities, had little or no capital to pay expenses while they were clearing and otherwise fitting their land for cultivation. As a result, many of them became discouraged and left. The absence of local markets and the type of farming also added to the lack of success of these settlers.[85]

One final ethnic settlement deserves mention, even though it is located slightly beyond the southeastern Ozark boundary, and its origins are not tied to the coming of the railroads in any way. At the turn of the twentieth century, the Catholic church in St. Louis became quite concerned about the large number of indigent German Catholics who were then residing in St. Louis. Since most of these German Catholics had been farmers in the Old World, the church decided to establish an agricultural colony somewhere in Missouri for them. At that time, land was being drained and cleared in the bottomlands along the Ozark escarpment in Butler County in southeastern Missouri, and large blocks of land suitable for group settlement were available for sale. The St. Louis diocese purchased fourteen thousand acres in 1905 and settled approximately one hundred German families from St. Louis in the following two years. The community of Glennonville, named for Cardinal Glennon of St. Louis, was founded. The settlement proved quite successful, and in 1910 a daughter colony was established at Wilhelmina in Dunklin County.[86] The presence of large numbers

85. Clair V. Mann, ed. "Frisco First: A Source Materials History of the St. Louis-San Francisco Railroad, 1845–1945," pocket map; Leslie Konnyu, "Hungarians in Missouri," p. 261, and *Hungarians in the United States: An Immigration Study*, p. 50; F. Z. Hutton and H. H. Krusekopf, *Soil Survey of Ripley County, Missouri*, p. 8.
86. Sister Teresa, *The Eye, Arm, Spine of the Wilderness*.

of German Catholics in southeastern Missouri probably influenced the church in its decision to locate the Glennonville community in that part of the state.

In addition to the ethnic groups already mentioned, there were some that located in urban centers—Springfield, Joplin, and Jefferson City—and some that located in smaller towns, particularly the mining communities. For example, in the town of Desloge in St. Francois County, small Greek and Russian colonies were established in the early part of this century. They had come from St. Louis to work in and around the mining industry. Since these groups, in a functional sense, are rural nonfarm, which is to say they were urban but lived in towns not classified as urban places, they do not qualify as rural ethnic groups and therefore have not been included in this study.[87]

Amish and Mennonite Settlement

The extent of settlement by religious sects in the Ozarks during the nineteenth century is somewhat obscure. The 1850 census lists a Mennonite congregation in Warren County, in addition to three Moravian congregations and one under the title of minor "sect." In the 1890 census, seven congregations of Dunkards and two congregations of Quakers are listed for the Ozarks. By 1890, the Mennonite congregation in Warren County was no longer listed, but five Mennonite congregations and one of the Amish were represented in the Ozarks. Three congregations, including the Amish, were in Hickory County; two were in Jasper County, and one was in Moniteau County. Of these early congregations, only the General Conference Mennonites in Moniteau County and a splinter group that was affiliated with the (Old) Mennonite Church have remained active to date. Little is recorded of these early settlements that are now extinct, and virtually no imprint remains on the landscape.[88]

Between 1890 and 1964, two small Mennonite settlements located in the Ozarks; one in Benton County, and the other in Shannon County.[89] However, broadly speaking, the Ozark region was never

87. According to the U.S. Bureau of the Census, a community must have a minimum population of 2,500 inhabitants to be classified as an urban center. The population of all nonfarming communities with less than 2,500 is rural.

88. *Seventh Census of the United States: 1850*, pp. 687–90; *Eleventh Census of the United States, 1890: Report on Statistics of Churches*, p. 360.

89. Mary I. Detwiler, *History of the Berea Mennonite Church*.

a focus of the Amish and Mennonites until recently. As long as land of higher quality and greater accessibility was readily available at moderate prices in other parts of the United States and Canada, this situation persisted.

By the mid-1960s, two changes affecting the suitability of the Ozarks for Amish-Mennonite settlement were apparent. First, population growth in the older areas of Amish-Mennonite settlement had caused crowding to the extent that some people were being forced into nonfarm employment. Second, land in the older core areas of settlement had been selling at a premium price, thus making land expansion a prohibitively expensive undertaking for many groups. With the Amish, whose population growth is approximately 2 per cent annually, it has become increasingly difficult to maintain farming as a living for all without some out-migration from the older core areas.[90]

Since 1964, the Ozark region of Missouri has been a major focus of Amish and Mennonite settlement. In fact, the movement of the Amish and Mennonites to the Ozarks as well as northern Missouri during the past decade has been the largest interstate migration involving these groups during this period. The flow of the Amish and Mennonites to Missouri from the older core areas over the past decade is depicted in Figure 2–15. The reasons most often cited by the Amish and Mennonites for selecting the Ozarks as a home at this time cover a wide range. First, and most important, was the price of land; all groups mentioned this factor. One Amish farmer, for example, stated that he had sold his Corn Belt land for $1,200 an acre and, in turn, purchased four times as much land in the Ozarks at $250 an acre. Several commented that the potential for future expansion of landholdings in the Ozarks also appeared to be good as compared to the areas from which they had migrated. A related consideration, particularly for those using horse-drawn machinery, was that in a region, where the economy depends predominantly on livestock, such as in the Ozarks, they would be at less of a competitive disadvantage as a result of their traditional ways than in a region with a crop-oriented economy, as the Corn Belt. Even among those using powered farm machinery, the difference required in capital outlay for agriculture beyond land investment favored the Ozarks by a wide margin.

Several groups mentioned the general conservatism of the Ozarks as a positive factor. The stereotyped isolation of the Ozarks, prob-

90. James E. Landing, "Amish Population Changes, 1947–1964," p. 4.

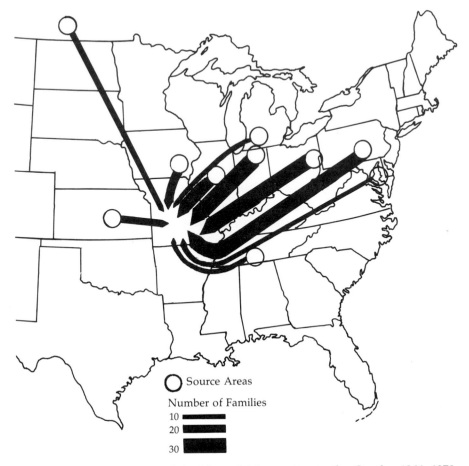

Figure 2–15.   Movements of Amish and Mennonites to the Ozarks, 1964–1972. The Amish and Mennonites who have settled in the Ozarks have migrated from a variety of source areas. The area of the agricultural interior stands out, but other areas ranging from Canada to Kansas to Maryland are represented.

ably more fiction than fact, attracted some. Laws regarding both the education and public schools in the Ozarks are considered, in general, to be more favorable toward the needs of both the Amish and Mennonites.[91]

Since 1964, twelve separate groups of Amish and Mennonites have established settlements in the Ozarks of Missouri (Figure 2–16 and Table 2–2 summarize these settlements). The total of six-

91. For a discussion of the Amish-Mennonite education controversy see John A. Hostetler and Gertrude Enders Huntington, *Children in Amish Society: Socialization and Community Education*.

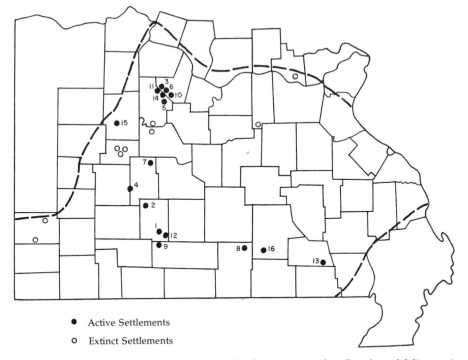

Figure 2–16. Amish and Mennonite Settlements in the Ozarks of Missouri, 1972. The majority of Amish and Mennonite settlements are of relatively recent origin. Although the Amish and Mennonites are concentrated in two small areas, much of the Ozarks has been affected by these groups. (Note: The numbers refer to Table 2–2.)

teen settlements in the Ozarks represent nine different affiliations, with a total population of 230 families.[92] Although the distribution of Amish and Mennonites in the Ozarks is somewhat dominated by two clusters (Morgan-Moniteau and Webster counties), a broad area in the Ozarks has felt the impact of their settlement. This clustering may well have been the result of enterprising real estate agents in those two areas. One realtor in Webster County follows the Amish and Mennonite movements closely, and he contacts those groups he thinks would be interested in settling in the Ozarks. It is doubtful that land prices or other similar conditions favor these two areas. Although other Amish and Mennonite groups were settled in the Ozarks, only three settlements main-

92. For a discussion of the differences among the various Amish and Mennonite groups see Harold S. Bender, *Mennonite Encyclopedia*; John A. Hostetler, *Amish Society*; Charles Henry Smith, *The Story of the Mennonites*; and Dyck, *Mennonite History*.

Table 2–2

Amish and Mennonite Settlements in the Ozarks of Missouri, 1972

No. on Map	Location	No. of Families	Year Originated	State of Origin
Old Order Amish				
1*	Seymour	22	1968	Ind.
2*	Elkland	10	1970	Can.
3*	Fortuna	13	1967	Ohio, Ind., Mich.
Amish-Mennonites (Beachy)				
4	Buffalo	28	1964	Ill.
Church of God in Christ (Holdeman) Mennonites				
5	Versailles	11	1969	Kans.
Black Bumper (Old Order) Mennonites				
6	Latham	5	1970	Pa.
Stauffer Mennonites				
7*	Leadmine	10	1970	Md.
Old Order (Wisler) Mennonites				
8*	Mt. View	9	1970	Tenn., Ohio
9*	Dogwood	8	1969	Ohio
10*	Latham	21	1970	Pa.
General Conference Mennonites				
11	Versailles	28	1867	Ohio
Conservative Mennonite Church				
12	Seymour	25	1967	Ohio, Ind., Iowa
13	Grandin	16	1969	Ohio, Iowa
(Old) Mennonite Church				
14	Versailles	13	1871	Ohio
15	Warsaw	8	1949	Iowa, Mo.
16	Birch Tree	5	1895	Ill.

* Indicates groups still using horse-and-buggy transportation.

tain that their selection of a location in the Ozarks was not influenced by the presence of these settlements. The most common responses to the question, "Why did you choose this specific location?" are: (1) we saw it advertised in a real estate catalog; and (2) we were passing through and liked what we saw. On this basis, much of the Ozarks would be open to future Amish and Mennonite settlement.

Summary

The main cultural groups that together have forged the cultural landscapes of the Ozarks are outlined in the preceding pages (Figure 2–17). All told, ethnic groups account for somewhat more than 10 per cent of the region's total population. This represents an ethnic population of approximately 150,000, of which more than 80 per cent are of German descent. It is not my contention that the population patterns described in the preceding pages still persist in all, or even in most cases. There are significant in- and out-

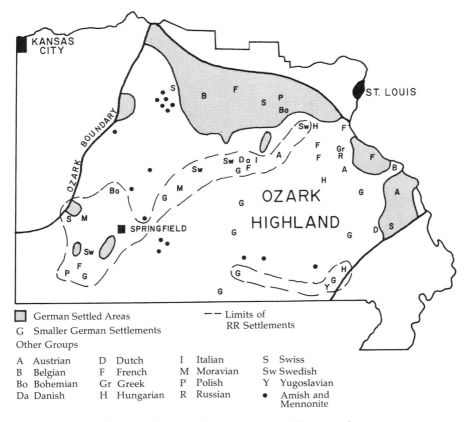

Figure 2–17. Ethnic Settlements in the Ozarks. Ethnic settlements are concentrated in the border areas of the Ozarks where some of the most productive agricultural land is found. Most of the ethnic settlements in the interior Ozarks were small and were associated with the coming of the railroads.

migrations of people that have affected the Ozark region of Missouri in the twentieth century. However, the Ozark region is less affected by an out-migration than the other rural areas in the state. This fact coupled with the small immigration into the Ozark region in the twentieth century, and this flow has been and is still directed primarily to urban centers and the lake districts, suggests that the rural population of the region is rather stable. Marbut commented on population growth in the Ozarks earlier in this century, noting that, "it is the result of natural growth of the active population. The influx from the outside has been small."[93] The following chapters will analyze how the various population elements of the Ozarks have forged their cultural landscapes and also to what extent their cultural imprint has persisted. Emphasis will be on the contribution of the ethnic population of the Ozarks, but the cultural landscapes of the ethnic population will be analyzed and interpreted within a broader regional context.

93. Marbut, *Soils of the Ozark Region*, p. 250.

3. The Germans
Settlement

Expansion and Growth of Settlements

The German settlements in the Ozarks increased rapidly around the original nuclei of settlement. Although some expansion pushed outward, for the most part growth took the form of a filling-in of areas within the bounds of the original settlements. The population densities in both the Northern and Eastern Ozark Border regions were quite low when the major German settlements were established. In 1840, after the initial phase of German settlement, the population density along the Eastern Ozark Border averaged between two and six people per square mile. Along the eastern half of the Northern Ozark Border, the population density was between two and six people per square mile, while in the western half it was less than two people. By 1850, the density along the Eastern Ozark Border was between six and eighteen people per square mile, but along the Northern Ozark Border the population remained less than six people per square mile. Thus, abundant land was available for newly arrived Germans along both borders during the decade following initial German settlement.[1]

Germans preferred to settle among their own kind. Zelinsky refers to this as a "chain migration," and in his words:

> Once a viable ethnic nucleus takes hold in a given location, chain migration may be triggered. If communication lines are kept open between the new settlements and relatives and neighbors back home, positive information may induce the latter to pack up and follow. In this way, a great many . . . rural ethnic neighborhoods have been expanded.[2]

This process operated throughout the Ozarks in areas of German settlement. No case can be found where German settlements de-

---

1. Frederick V. Emerson, *Geography of Missouri*, p. 43.
2. Wilbur Zelinsky, *The Cultural Geography of the United States*, p. 29.

creased in size, or contracted in area, after the original settlement.

The literature is replete with references to the German practice of buying out non-German neighbors, as a means both of expanding landholdings and of obtaining land of higher quality. This process was facilitated both by a willingness among Germans, in many cases, to pay higher than market value for their neighbors' land and, frequently, by a desire among non-Germans to move away from the areas dominated by the clannish Germans. In so doing, the Germans, whose original settlements were often on land of lower quality, were able to obtain the more fertile lands — bottoms and uplands — along the Eastern and Northern Ozark Border regions. The magnitude of the displacement of non-Germans by Germans in Gasconade and Perry counties is portrayed on Figures 3–1 and 3–2.[3]

Once established on the land, Germans in the Ozarks have shown remarkable stability as landowners. Sauer observes:

> Stability remains the most distinguishing characteristic of the German stock. Where Germans have located in most cases they have remained. The selling of real estate is not a thriving business in their communities. Property is handed down from father to son, and in many cases the descendents of the original entrymen still retain the land.[4]

Interviews with local officials throughout the German areas in the Ozarks indicated that locational stability remains a distinguishing characteristic of German stock. Numerous farms in Gasconade, Perry, and Osage counties are owned presently by the descendents of the original entrymen. In the core of the Saxon area of eastern Perry County, 60 per cent of the surnames of the original Saxon immigrants — 164 out of 272 original surnames — are represented in the rolls of the present population. Furthermore, only 13 per cent of the surnames representing all landowners in the core of the fifty square mile Saxon area are not found on the original rolls.[5]

3. Albert B. Faust, *The German Element in the United States*, vol. 1, pp. 445–46; Richard O'Conner, *The German-Americans: An Informal History*, p. 81; Carl O. Sauer, *The Geography of the Ozark Highland of Missouri*, p. 171; Lewis W. Spitz, "The Germans in Missouri: A Preliminary Study," p. 75; Curtis F. Marbut, *Soils of the Ozark Region*, p. 251; Carl E. Schneider, *The German Church on the American Frontier*, pp. 25–26. Due to the different dates for the earlier period of landownership on Figures 3–1 and 3–2, the two maps are not directly comparable as measures of the magnitude of change in the ethnicity of landowners. The different dates on the two maps are the result of limitations imposed by the need to use different data sources. The date for the more recent period of landownership, however, is the same for both maps.

4. Sauer, *Ozark Highland*, p. 173.

5. Walter O. Forster, *Zion on the Mississippi*, pp. 540–58.

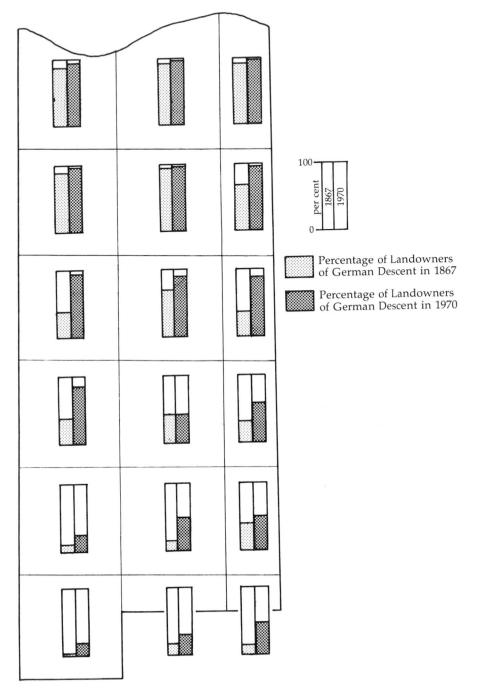

Figure 3–1. Increase of German Landowners in Gasconade County Between 1867 and 1970. Sources: Land register for 1867, Gasconade County, Missouri, and Land ownership plat, Gasconade County, Missouri, 1970.

Percentage of Landowners
of German Descent in 1860

Percentage of Landowners
of German Descent in 1970

Figure 3–2. Increase of German Landowners in Perry County Between 1860 and 1970. Sources: Abstract of original land entries, Perry County, Missouri, 1894, and Land ownership plat, Perry County, Missouri, 1970.

To determine if locational stability varied along ethnic lines, three sample townships, one German and two non-German, were selected for detailed analysis. Roark Township is located in northeastern Gasconade County and includes all of the land originally purchased by the German colony centered at Hermann. Since 1867, more than 90 per cent of the landowners in this township have been of German descent. Bourbois Township is located in extreme southwestern Gasconade County. Since the earliest white settlement, Bourbois Township has been dominated by an Old Stock American population. Bellevue Township is located in southeastern Washington County. This township contains the northern part of the Bellevue-Caledonia Valley. One of the earliest, and most prosperous, American agricultural settlements in the entire eastern Ozarks was established in the limestone basins comprising this valley. The present population of Bellevue Township is nearly 100 per cent of Old Stock American descent.[6]

6. Louis A. Houck, *A History of Missouri*, vol. 1, pp. 372–75.

For each of the three sample townships, a list of the surnames of all farmers was prepared for 1870. This list was then compared with a list of the surnames of all rural landowners in 1970 for each township.[7] Each surname is recorded in one of the following three categories: (1) still represented by a landowner in the township; (2) not represented in the township, but still represented by a landowner in the same county; or (3) no longer represented by a landowner in the same county. The results are presented in Table 3–1.[8]

Table 3–1

Locational Stability in Selected German and Non-German Townships in the Ozarks, 1870–1970

Townships	Total of different surnames of all farmers in township in 1870	Surname of 1870 present in same township in 1970		Surname of 1870 not present in same township but present in same county in 1970		Surname of 1870 not present in county or township in 1970	
	Number	No.	%	No.	%	No.	%
Roark (German)	182	107	58.8	29	15.9	46	25.3
Bourbois (non-German)	127	36	28.4	22	17.3	69	54.3
Bellevue (non-German)	221	60	27.2	33	14.9	128	57.9
Total	530	203	38.3	84	15.9	243	45.8

Sources: Manuscript schedules of population for 1870 and plat books for Gasconade and Washington counties, 1970.

The findings in the sample townships support the contention that locational stability is more pronounced in the German settlements than in Old Stock American areas. The literature, as well, tends to support the conclusion that the Old Stock American population in the Ozarks has traditionally demonstrated mobility,

7. The surnames were obtained from the manuscript schedules of population for 1870 and from 1970 plat books for Washington County.
8. Using only surnames does not provide an exact measure of locational stability. One family that left a township may have been replaced by a family with the same surname but of no blood relationship. This is highly probable with such names as Smith and Schmidt. However, all three townships should be affected similarly by this. Thus, the results, although less than exact, should not be biased by this factor in favor of one group.

as opposed to locational stability. Sauer describes one instance of the migratory character of the Old Stock American:

> The ancestor of one of the pioneers of Howell County came from Ireland and settled in South Carolina. His descendents removed to Alabama, thence to Tennessee, Illinois, and Arkansas successively drifting with the stream courses. The final removal was from Arkansas to Missouri.

Jordan found that many hill people, who had migrated from the Appalachians to the Missouri Ozarks continued their migratory movement, settling in the hills of central Texas, the Cascades and Coast ranges of Washington, Oregon, and the northern Rockies.[9]

Interviews with recorders of deeds in eight Ozark counties, four of which are largely German or have a sizeable German minority, and four of which are almost exclusively Old Stock American, were conducted concerning land transfers in recent years.[10] From these interviews, the following generalizations concerning present patterns of locational stability and land transfer can be made:

1. The rate of land transfers is small in all four German counties and somewhat greater in the four non-German counties.[11]

2. In the counties with a German and non-German population (Perry, Gasconade, Lawrence, and Osage), the rate of land transfer is greater for the non-German in the county than it is for the German.

3. The rate of land transfer has increased dramatically in three of the four non-German counties in the past decade, but the rate has remained constant in the four German counties.

4. In the German counties, land passes primarily from German to German, and there is a definite tendency for land to be retained within the ethnic group and, to some extent, the family.

5. In the German counties, where land transfers involved Germans and non-Germans, the Germans are more often the buyers than the sellers.

9. Leslie Hewes, "Tontitown: Ozark Vineyard Center," p. 117; Marbut, *Soils of the Ozark Region*, p. 251; Sauer, *Ozark Highland*, p. 103; Terry G. Jordan, "The Texan Appalachia," p. 410.

10. The four German counties are Gasconade, Perry, Osage, and Lawrence; the four non-German counties are Dallas, Stone, Shannon, and Oregon. The interviews were conducted from June through September of 1972.

11. Statistics obtained from the recorders of deeds confirm this conclusion. For example, the four non-German counties average nearly 900 land transfers per year between 1969 and 1972, compared with a figure of just over 600 for the four German counties. However, so many variables are involved in the buying and selling of real estate, that such figures are only a crude indicator of locational stability. Location, access to urban areas, and quality of land must be considered in interpreting such data.

6. In all eight counties, it was pointed out that "good" agricultural land is rarely sold.

To a limited extent, it appears that Germans in the Ozarks are still buying out their non-German neighbors. Furthermore, interviews with German farmers in the Ozarks confirmed that the practice of keeping the land in the hands of Germans is often done consciously.

The results of more than a century of filling-in are most evident in Perry and Gasconade counties. The core of the Saxon area in Perry County, consisting of more than fifty square miles, contains no non-German landowners. A small pocket of non-Germans near Farrar, at the eastern edge of the Saxon core, consists of a group of North Carolinians who settled there in 1817, and they appear as determined to retain their land as are their neighbors, the Saxon Lutherans. In the Catholic settlements of south central Perry County, Germans control more than 90 per cent of the land. However, the attitude that land must pass on to other Germans is much less pronounced than among the Saxons.[12]

The northern two-thirds of Gasconade County are more than 90 per cent German owned, and in the northern third of the county, Germans own nearly 100 per cent of the land. In the southern third of the county, German landowners constitute a minority but continue to increase.

Similar patterns of landownership exist in several other parts of the Ozarks. Most notably, Franklin, Lawrence, Osage, Ste. Genevieve, and Warren counties contain German settlements in which ownership exceeds 90 per cent in the core, with this percentage holding stable or on the increase.

Settlement Patterns

The way man disperses himself on the land, and the buildings he constructs to shelter himself, his produce, and his animals represent important individual cultural expressions that are manifested in the landscape of a region. Awareness of differences in settlement patterns and types within a region can add important details to our knowledge of the nature of culture and its areal expression. Particularly, the study of the type, form, appearance, variety, materials of construction, condition of upkeep, climatic and economic adequacy, functional efficiency, and environmental harmony of

12. Willis Knox, *A History of the Brazeau Presbyterian Church, Brazeau, Missouri, 1819–1970*, p. 4.

man's settlement features has much to offer in a regional study. Because settlement patterns are distinguished through the areal distribution of the various features, and are thus mappable, they deserve attention by cultural geographers. In regions such as the Ozarks, where written records of the historical-cultural geography are in short supply, data on the geography of settlement can provide needed insight into the geography of the present and the past.[13]

Settlement Distribution

On the whole, the organization of villages in the Ozarks was haphazard in the early days of settlement. Since water was of extreme importance, many of the early pioneers preferred to settle in areas with springs. They lived a self-sufficient life, which included both some hunting and some farming.[14] The early village in the Ozarks most commonly owed its origins to the location of a general store at a crossroad. Settlers would tend to congregate around the general store, with a few urban functions developing in the village as time passed. Many villages in the Ozarks today still retain this basic pattern, as evidenced by the casual arrangement of streets and irregularly shaped lots.

Later, improvements in transportation elongated the village along highways and other improved roads. The people who settled along the edges of these villages came largely from surrounding rural areas, where they had abandoned their old farmsteads but not necessarily their farms. By moving to the village, one could continue to maintain his farm on a part-time basis and find employment in the village or nearby urban centers. The farmer who had not moved into the village had located his dwelling along all-weather roads in rural areas. This is evidenced by the distribution of abandoned dwellings, which increase in frequency with increasing distance from all-weather roads.

Although some of these same tendencies can be seen in the German settled areas of the Ozarks, there are also marked differences in the distributional patterns of settlement in these areas. The German village, from the beginning, had shown a tendency to

13. Jean Brunhes, *Human Geography*, pp. 585–87; Carl O. Sauer, "The Morphology of Landscape," pp. 27–30; J. E. Spencer, "House Types in Southern Utah," p. 444; K. H. Stone, "The Development of a Focus for the Geography of Settlement," p. 347.

14. Milton D. Rafferty, "Persistence Versus Change in Land Use and Landscape in the Springfield, Missouri, Vicinity of the Ozarks," pp. 225–26; Marbut, *Soils of the Ozark Region*, pp. 251–60; and Sauer, *Ozark Highland*, pp. 112–29.

elongate, regardless of topographic or other physical conditions. In some cases, the village was established as a farm village with each farmer having a town lot and an attenuated strip of farmland stretching back from the village, or a totally detached farm some distance from the village. This was the case with the Saxon settlements in eastern Perry County and with several of the Catholic settlements in Osage County. These villages were all established by the Germans. Since many of them were intended beforehand to serve as farm villages, they were carefully planned and laid out. The church was normally placed near the center of the village, with public lands nearby. The outskirts of the village were used exclusively for residential purposes. A typical example is Altenburg in Perry County. The elongation of Altenburg occurred early. The village originally was platted to include one full section of land, with the church in the center. Additions were made to the village in 1856 and 1860; in both cases, the additions were long, narrow strips of land oriented with the narrow dimension facing the road, thus producing a string pattern. The elongation continued with more strips added periodically, until the village reached its present dimensions, sometime before 1915. This village today is two miles in length and two lots in width.[15]

A number of these German villages in the Ozarks are shown in Figure 3–3. In some cases, such as Freistatt in Lawrence County, parallel streets were added, but the recency of these additions is apparent from the differences in architectural styles. The only explanation for this form being used in German towns that were not farm villages is that Germans settled by colonies and were thus able to implant directly certain Old World cultural forms. Nelson observes:

> It is important to note that village settlement is usually the result of the occupation of an area of land by a group; and a group that is essentially homogeneous, ethnically, religiously, or otherwise.[16]

Whether or not the string-shaped village served the same function in the Ozarks as it did in Germany is secondary. The point is that the string-shaped village, or *Strassendorfer*, was a form of settlement that the Germans were acquainted with, and one that could be established in the Ozarks with little difficulty.[17]

15. "Plat of the Colony of Altenburg, August 5, 1840," *Plat Book, Towns, and Villages*, p. 7; *Surveyor's Plats*, no. 1, p. 334; *Illustrated Atlas of Perry County, Missouri*, pp. 36–37.

16. Lowry Nelson, *The Mormon Village*, p. 10.

17. Robert E. Dickinson, "Rural Settlement in the German Lands," pp. 260–63.

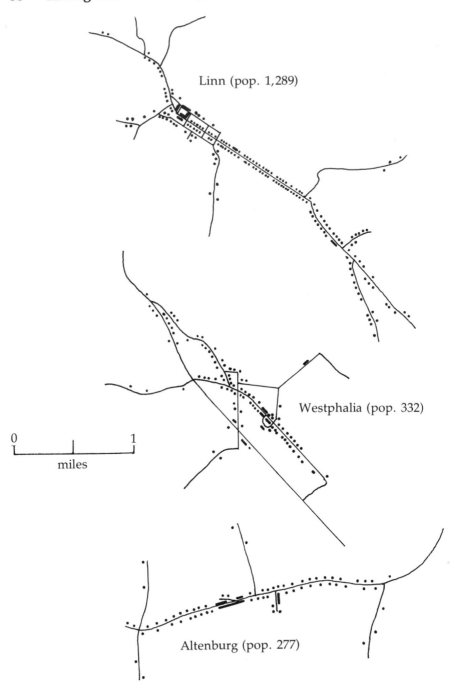

Figure 3–3. German String-Shaped Villages in the Ozarks. Approximately twelve agricultural string-shaped villages were established by groups of Germans who settled in the Ozarks.

Figure 3–4. Houses without front yards, positioned directly by the street in Westphalia.

A distinctly Old World feature of several German string-shaped villages in the Ozarks is the absence of front yards. This is particularly noticeable in Westphalia, where nearly all of the houses in the village are positioned in such a way that only a narrow sidewalk separates the entrance of the dwelling from the street (Figure 3–4).

The German villages in the Ozarks have been subjected to minimal alteration. Most are located at some distance from major highways and do not have a continued string-like growth. Some have filled in, in the sense that there are now more houses in the village than there were previously, but this has happened in most cases within the original limits of the village. Few have shown significant lateral growth. Marbut describes the German village in the Ozarks earlier in this century as "solidly built and neatly kept. . . ."[18] Although many have suffered some population loss, the German village in the Ozarks today appears to be quite healthy. Most still offer a full complement of goods and services. This can be partly accounted for by the smaller out-migration from the rural German areas when compared to the Ozarks as a whole. A second factor

18. Curtis F. Marbut, *Soil Reconnaissance of the Ozark Region of Missouri and Arkansas*, p. 26.

involved to some degree is the importance of the village church and parochial school to the German in the Ozarks. As long as these institutions remain viable, the German village will hold its own.

The pattern of dispersed farmsteads in the German rural areas in the Ozarks is evidenced by a more regular distribution of the farmsteads than in the non-German areas. The concentration of farmsteads along public roads and the presence of abandoned dwellings away from all-weather roads are much less noticeable in the German areas. An examination of two townships, one German and one non-German, was made to test this contention. The German township is located in northern Gasconade County, and the non-German township is located in the southern part. Topographic conditions in the two townships are similar. Farmsteads are divided into two categories: (1) those within one hundred yards of a public road; and (2) those more than one hundred yards from the nearest public road. A visual examination of the distribution of farmsteads indicated that the spacing in the German township is less closely tied to public roads than is the case in the non-German township (Figure 3–5). In the non-German township, 77.1 per cent of all farmsteads are located within one hundred yards of public roads, compared to a figure of 52.6 per cent for the German township. The tendency of farmsteads to be located near public roads is seen in areas of both level and hilly topography in the Ozarks. Apparently, this phenomenon cannot be explained simply by differences in surface configuration or land quality from area to area.[19]

Structural Occupance Features

Structural occupance features, including the structures man builds, the styles, numbers, sizes, conditions, and patterns of arrangement to form farmsteads, are highly visible and are variable features of the rural landscape in the Ozarks. This fact is confirmed whenever one drives through the Ozarks in almost any direction. The causes of these differences are, surely, multiple and varied. Rafferty found variations in settlement characteristics to be related to areal differences in physical, economic, and cultural conditions, as well as accessibility.[20]

To determine if differences in structural occupance features existed between German and Old Stock American areas in the

19. Milton D. Rafferty, "Population and Settlement Changes in Two Ozark Localities," pp. 46–56.
20. Rafferty, "Persistence Versus Change," pp. 314–20.

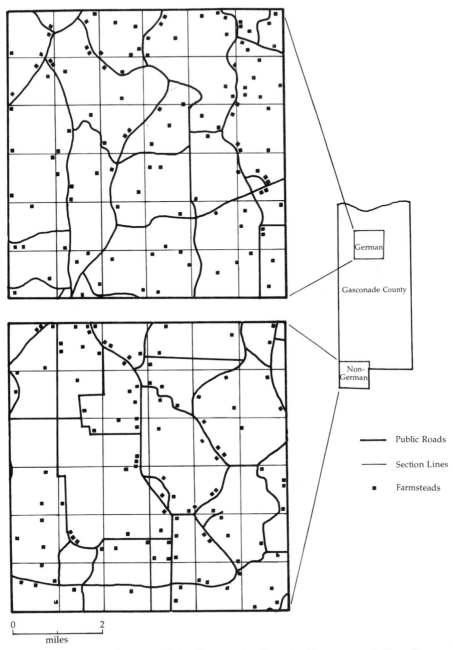

German

Gasconade County

Non-German

——— Public Roads

——— Section Lines

■ Farmsteads

0   2

miles

Figure 3–5. Distribution of Settlement in Sample German and Non-German Townships in Gasconade County, 1970. German farmsteads are located away from roads more often than those of their neighbors, suggesting that Germans have remained on the old, or original, farmsteads, whereas their neighbors have abandoned the old places for ones that offer easy access to the city. Source: General highway map of Gasconade County, Missouri.

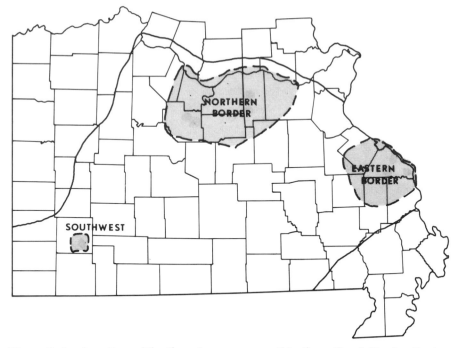

Figure 3–6. Location of the three traverse areas (Northern Ozark Border, Eastern Ozark Border, and Southwest).

Ozarks, data were collected in three widely separated areas, included were fifteen hundred miles of systematic road traverses encompassing approximately forty-five hundred farmsteads (Figure 3–6).[21] Selected features were then mapped and compared with overlays showing the distribution of Germans and Old Stock Americans.

The three traverse areas encompass approximately fifty-six hundred square miles. Included in the three traverse areas are portions of six different physiographic provinces of the Ozarks. The quality of land varies significantly from one traverse area to another (Table 3–2). Therefore, German-owned farms of various land quality could be compared. However, within each traverse

21. In the two larger traverse areas (Northern and Eastern Ozark Border regions), the selection of specific traverse lines is based on two considerations: (1) that the traverses be oriented in such a way as to result in a rough grid, and (2) that sufficient traverses be included to provide adequate coverage for the entire traverse area. These two conditions were stipulated to insure that the data when collected would be representative of the areas. Beyond these considerations, the traverses were randomly selected. In the third traverse area (Lawrence County), all public roads in the 100 square miles of the traverse area were utilized as traverse lines.

Table 3-2
Land Capability for Traverse Area According to Nativity of Residents

Traverse Area	Soils definitely suited to continued crop use	Soils of moderate fertility, occasional areas of which should be retired from crop use	Soils used for crops much of which should be retired from crop use	Soils definitely submarginal for crops
	Percentage of All Land in Traverse Area			
Lawrence County				
German Portion	42	7	51	0
Non-German Portion	35	9	56	0
Eastern Ozark Border				
German	1	42	54	3
Non-German	2	29	60	9
Northern Ozark Border				
German	1	3	87	9
Non-German	0	1	75	24

Source: Based on planimetric measurements of soil classification map in Hammar, *Factors Affecting Farm Land Values in Missouri*, p. 9.

area, an effort was made to avoid extremes in land quality between the areas of German and Old Stock American settlement. This was not entirely possible. The Germans did acquire much of the best land in the Ozarks, and they avoided most of the less productive land in the region. Therefore, any large traverse areas selected in the Ozarks that included German and non-German settlements would favor the areas of German settlement relative to land capability. As Table 3–2 indicates, land capability is generally higher in the German portions. However, the magnitude of the differences in land quality between the German and non-German areas is not overwhelming. The majority of the land in each traverse area is of similar quality for both groups.

House Types and Other Features

Houses are classified according to style, size, and condition. Sixteen different types are included in the classification. The sixteen types are then reduced to five broader categories that are based on similarities of several house types. These similarities are sufficient to warrant several house types to be included into one category. I have designed a classification system to categorize houses according to very general specifications in style and size.

Contemporary Houses. These houses were built largely in the period after World War II. They present a myriad different styles that were influenced by national home magazines, among other things, and, therefore, no attempt is made to distinguish between different styles of contemporary houses. For purposes of data collection, they are divided into two categories based on age: (1) houses built between 1945 and 1960; and (2) those built since 1960.

One, and One-and-a-Half Story Bungalows. These houses are generally several decades in age and range from small to relatively large in size. Most are constructed of finished lumber and reflect professional workmanship (Figure 3–7). However, a few bungalows constructed of native stone are also encountered in the three traverse areas. The majority are oriented with the narrow dimension as the front of the house. Also included in this category are small box-shaped houses and pyramid style houses.

Two-Story Linear Houses. This type was popular from the mid-nineteenth century until the time of World War I. There are many variations of this type, but most have in common a two-story, I section, which the dimensions are two rooms by three rooms. The longer dimension normally serves as the front of the house (Figure

Figure 3–7.   One-and-a-half story bungalow.

3–8). In most cases, a second section of either one or two stories was added to the house. The house types that resulted include (1) the L-shaped house; (2) the T-shaped house; and (3) the linear with a shed located in the rear of the house. These houses are built from a variety of materials, including logs, bricks, and native stones, but most are constructed of sawed lumber of varying quality, depending on the affluence of the builder and the time the house was built (Figure 3–9). Also included in this category is a type called the "saltbox." In appearance this type is similar to the linear with a shed, except there is no break in the roofline.[22]

Small, Low-Quality Houses. These houses were built up to the time of World War II, and a few are still being built today. However,

22. Information on the chronology of construction for all of the house types was obtained from interviews with realtors in the study areas. The dates mentioned herein are approximations based on these interviews. Although the reference to an I section here is meant to be descriptive of the shape of this style house, the original designation of this style as an I house was in reference to its association with the states of Indiana, Illinois, and Iowa. Fred B. Kniffen, "Louisiana House Types," p. 187; Dorothy J. Caldwell, *Missouri Historic Sites Catalog*, p. 55.

Figure 3–8.   Two-story L-shaped house.

Figure 3–9.   Linear house constructed of finished brick in Gasconade County.

the majority is of pre-World War I origin. Several distinct types are included in this category, namely, the shed-room house, the Ozark type house, and the one-room shack (Figure 3–10). Most are constructed of rough and sawed lumber, or occasionally logs, and are either unpainted or covered with tar paper, or composition roll-type siding. Many are in poor condition and are surrounded by clutter.

Mobile Homes. The mobile home, which has gained popularity in recent years as a dwelling unit in rural areas, is a separate category. They range from the modern, three-bedroom unit to the older and smaller units, which were probably intended as travel trailers.

Some types, such as the Corn Belt style house, are not covered, since their occurrence along the traverses is so few as to be insignificant.

Regional differences of importance along ethnic lines are found in the distribution of several house types (Table 3–3). The linear, or I style, is the most common type in all three traverse areas. This is especially true for the German portions of the three traverse areas. By contrast, the linear is a minority in all three non-German portions of the traverse areas. In the core of the Saxon area of eastern Perry County and in the vicinity of Hermann, the linear

Figure 3–10. Shed-room type.

Table 3–3

Summary of House Types and Related Settlement Characteristics for Northern Ozark Border, Eastern Ozark Border, and Lawrence County Traverse Areas, 1972

	Traverse Areas															
	Freistatt				Northern Ozark Border				Eastern Ozark Border				All			
	German		non-German		German		non-German		German		non-German		German		non-German	
House Type	No.	%	No.	%	No.	%	No.	%	No.	%	No.	%	No.	%	No.	%
Contemp.	15	9	44	17	365	25	305	25	72	14	231	24	452	21	580	24
Frame	35	20	132	50	242	16	351	29	140	28	360	37	417	20	843	35
Linear	117	68	57	22	735	50	160	13	265	53	150	16	1,117	52	367	15
Small	1	1	16	6	58	4	330	28	10	2	190	20	69	3	536	22
Trailer	3	2	12	5	66	5	57	5	16	3	29	3	85	4	98	4
Total	171		261		1,466		1,203		503		960		2,140		2,424	
Roofing Material																
Comp.	160	94	223	85	1,150	78	742	62	378	75	714	75	1,688	79	1,679	70
Metal	11	6	37	15	310	22	430	36	121	24	223	23	442	21	690	28
Other	0	–	1	0	6	–	31	2	4	1	23	2	10	–	55	2
Presence of Light. Rods	145	85	64	25	1,129	77	314	26	440	87	178	19	1,714	80	556	23

Note: The total number of farms in all three sample areas is 4,564. However, not all of the farms are considered under each settlement characteristic, because in some cases these characteristics were not applicable. Source: Compiled from field data sheets.

Table 3-3—Continued

	Freistatt				Northern Ozark Border				Eastern Ozark Border				All			
	German		non-German		German		non-German		German		non-German		German		non-German	
Const. Material	No.	%	No.	%	No.	%	No.	%	No.	%	No.	%	No.	%	No.	%
Finished																
Lumber	154	90	209	80	1,247	85	932	78	456	91	775	81	1,857	87	1,916	79
Brick	12	7	7	3	193	13	29	2	39	8	49	5	244	11	85	3
Comp.	5	3	39	15	24	2	189	16	7	1	124	13	36	2	352	15
Rough																
Lumber	–	–	6	2	2	–	51	4	1	–	7	1	3	–	64	3
Other	–	–	–	–	–	–	2	–	–	–	5	0	0	–	7	–
Total	171		261		1,466		1,203		503		960		2,140		2,424	
Barn Size																
Small	19	8	32	19	314	16	239	32	80	13	169	21	413	15	440	26
Medium	177	77	121	71	1,361	71	444	61	451	70	611	75	1,989	71	1,176	68
Large	34	15	18	10	256	13	49	7	111	17	34	4	401	14	101	6
No. of Barns																
0	20	12	113	43	251	17	557	46	70	14	301	31	341	16	971	40
1	87	51	127	49	669	46	548	47	265	53	528	55	1,021	48	1,203	50
2	49	28	19	7	376	26	74	6	127	25	107	11	552	26	200	8
3	15	9	2	1	170	11	12	1	41	8	24	3	226	10	38	2

Traverse Areas

Table 3-3 – Continued

	Traverse Areas															
	Freistatt				Northern Ozark Border				Eastern Ozark Border				All			
	German		non-German		German		non-German		German		non-German		German		non-German	
No. of Outbldg.	No.	%	No.	%	No.	%	No.	%	No.	%	No.	%	No.	%	No.	%
2 or less	37	22	136	53	320	22	670	56	84	16	430	45	441	21	1,236	51
3–5	67	39	101	39	629	43	451	37	189	38	439	45	885	41	991	41
6–8	56	33	17	7	378	26	60	5	189	38	74	8	623	29	151	6
9 or more	11	6	2	1	139	9	21	2	41	8	17	2	191	9	40	2
Overall Condition																
Good	131	77	113	43	982	67	409	34	406	81	451	47	1,519	71	973	40
Medium	38	22	124	48	440	30	590	49	90	18	384	40	568	27	1,098	45
Poor	2	1	24	9	44	3	204	17	7	1	125	13	53	2	353	15
Total No. of Barns	230		171		1,931		732		642		814		2,803		1,717	
No. of Barns per Farm	1.36		.67		1.31		.61		1.28		.85		1.31		.71	

style, and its variants, accounts for more than 80 per cent of all rural dwellings. On the periphery of the German areas, the linear accounts for less than half of the dwellings. All told, 52 per cent of rural dwellings in the German portions of the traverses are of the linear style, compared to a figure of 15 per cent for the non-German portions of the three traverse areas.

The second most common house type in all three of the traverse areas is the one story or one-and-a-half story bungalow. Approximately one-fifth of the houses in the German areas represents this type, as compared with a figure of one-third for the non-German areas. In the German areas, this type is found primarily on the periphery and, to some extent, along better roads. In the non-German areas, the bungalow type is widely distributed but tends to be most prevalent on level land and along better roads.

The third most common type for all three traverse areas is the contemporary house. This type comprises more than 20 per cent in both the German and non-German areas. The contemporary house is especially concentrated near urban centers, as in Jefferson City, Cape Girardeau, Perryville, and Ste. Genevieve. It is interesting that relatively few contemporary houses are found on the periphery of the German town of Hermann, while non-German Owensville, in the southern part of the same county, is ringed with contemporary houses. Second, contemporary houses are closely associated with better roads, especially state and federal highways. The fewest contemporary houses are found in the more rugged sections of the non-German areas and in the core of the Saxon area in Perry County, Hermann, and Freistatt.

The small, low-quality house is the least common type in all three traverse areas, with the exception of mobile homes. Small, low-quality houses account for 3 per cent of the dwellings in the German areas and 22 per cent in the non-German areas. The number of low-quality houses in the German areas is small, and those that are found tend to be on the periphery and on back roads. These houses are widely distributed in the non-German areas, but they appear to be most concentrated in the more rugged sections of the traverse areas and in areas that appear to be nonagricultural. Thus, this type is found mostly on back roads of both the German and non-German areas.

Mobile homes are relatively few in number, comprising 4 per cent of the total number of dwellings in the German and non-German areas. Other than a noticeable concentration along all-weather roads, many mobile homes are also located next to abandoned houses, which suggests that the mobile home is an inexpensive replacement for deteriorating farmhouses.

The distributional patterns of house types in the three traverse areas are reflective of both the culture of the groups involved and the quality of the resource base in the different areas. Closely related to these considerations is the quality of the agricultural economy, which varies widely in each of the three traverse areas.

The most striking contrast between the German and non-German traverse areas is the dominance of the linear style house in the German areas and the dominance of the small, low-quality house in the non-German areas. According to Kniffen, the linear style has traditionally been an indicator of agricultural prosperity in the United States. The linear is not a German house type per se; in fact, no rural dwellings of uniquely German style are found in any of the traverse areas. With the exception of Hermann, Westphalia, and a few other villages in the Northern Ozark Border, the Germans almost completely adopted American architectural styles. The linear type house is, nonetheless, the style preferred by rural Germans in the Ozarks. Rafferty observes this same preference for this style near Springfield, Missouri, where the German settlement near Billings is the only sizeable area where linear style houses are dominant. Since the majority of the Germans in the Ozarks came directly from Germany, it is improbable that they picked up their preference for the linear anywhere in the United States outside the Ozarks. An exception to this would be the Germans in Freistatt, who went to the Ozarks from the area of the upper Corn Belt.[23]

The apparent prosperity of the German areas in the Ozarks supports the contention that the linear style house is associated with economic well-being. Numerous references to the agricultural affluence of the German settlements in the Ozarks appear in the literature. By contrast, small, low-quality houses are more commonly associated with a lower standard of living. Expenditures for public aid programs in the late 1950s demonstrate the disparity in the level of economic well-being between the German and Old Stock American populations in the Ozarks. The German areas are reported to have a much lower need for aid programs than any

23. Fred B. Kniffen, "Folk Housing: Key to Diffusion," p. 555; Rafferty, "Persistence Versus Change," p. 273.

other rural area in the state. Gregory notes, "Payment from governmental welfare and quasi-welfare programs constitutes about as great a source of revenue in some of the counties as any single industry including the return from agriculture."[24]

The majority of houses in the German areas is found to be of pre-twentieth-century origin. Many, although it is impossible to determine exactly how many, are the original dwelling units built by the first German settlers. Although most of the houses have been remodelled, occasionally the original construction materials of some houses are still visible. The predominance of older traditional houses in the German areas suggests that the houses were originally well built, and by people who, from the beginning, settled with the intention of permanent residence in the Ozarks. This may well stem from the tradition of locational stability in German rural areas, which encouraged substantial long-range investments in the farm toward the goal of improving the farm for future generations. On the concern of the German farmer in the Ozarks for future generations, Gregory notes, "The expected pattern among German families, in many instances, has been for the sons to take over the farm land and continue in the occupation of their parents. . . ." On the periphery of the German areas, especially those areas facing the interior Ozarks, Germans moved in at a later date, and the lesser dominance of the linear style house and the greater presence of bungalows and other houses of more recent origin probably indicate a general shift in architectural preferences at this later date, affecting Germans and non-Germans alike.[25]

By contrast, the predominance of both small, low-quality houses and bungalows in the non-German areas is indicative of a somewhat different attitude toward the land. Virtually the entire Old Stock American population in the Ozarks had moved at least once before they moved into the Ozarks. They were less concerned with the future in the Ozarks, including the building of dwellings, due to their uncertainty as to how long they would be in a given loca-

24. James E. Collier, *Geography of the Northern Ozark Border Region*, p. 52; A. B. Cozzens, "Conservation in German Settlements of the Missouri Ozarks," pp. 286–98; Conrad H. Hammar, "Institutional Aspects of Ozark Decline," p. 845; Marbut, *Soils of the Ozark Region*, p. 26; Sauer, *Ozark Highland*, pp. 164–74; Walter A. Schroeder, *The Eastern Ozarks*, p. 20; Rafferty, "Persistence Versus Change," pp. 274–75; Jordan, "The Texan Appalachia," p. 421; and Cecil L. Gregory, *Rural Social Areas in Missouri*, p. 26.

25. Terry G. Jordan, *German Seed in Texas Soil*, pp. 37–38; Gregory, *Rural Social Areas in Missouri*, p. 24.

tion. Many of those who remained in the Ozarks as permanent settlers did so more by accident than conscious intent:

> The first settlers were not farmers seeking agricultural land but timber workers who were left stranded with the exhaustion of the forests. Some of them left the area. . . . Others stayed on to establish a permanent settlement in the area with part-time employment in the greatly reduced lumber operations combined with a subsistence type of agriculture.[26]

This account suggests that many who did stay were simply biding their time and waiting for better opportunities. For large numbers, the opportunities never came, with the result that they did become permanent settlers in the Ozarks.

The dwelling units they built were intended to satisfy immediate needs, and as conditions changed, new dwellings were periodically constructed until, in many cases, a permanent dwelling resulted. The first dwellings built were crude structures, serving merely as a place to escape the elements. The small, low-quality houses so common today represent an intermediate stage in the evolution of the early temporary shelter to the finished house. The prevalence of the bungalow style of post-World War I origin indicates the general time span when many people finally realized their desire for a permanent structure to serve as a home.

In total, fewer than half of the houses in the German areas were built in this century, while more than 80 per cent of the houses in the non-German areas have been built since 1900, and the majority since World War I. It appears that the Germans made a large initial investment in their dwellings that have served them quite well into the future, while the Old Stock Americans made a modest initial investment and have upgraded their dwelling units into the more permanent structures of today.

The location of contemporary houses along major highways and near urban centers is consistent with Rafferty's findings in the Springfield area. This pattern holds true for both German and non-German areas. The majority of contemporary houses is occupied by either nonfarmers or part-time farmers, judging from the small size of farmsteads and absence of machinery. Both nonfarmers and part-time farmers are dependent on urban employment and, therefore, have located along routes more quickly and easily accessible to urban centers. This fact is further confirmed by the small number of contemporary houses in the Freistatt area, which

---

26. Gregory, *Rural Social Areas in Missouri*, p. 32.

has no major highway passing through the traverse area. By contrast, Jefferson City, the largest urban center in all three traverse areas, pulls commuters from a large surrounding area. The highest percentage of contemporary houses in all three traverse areas is found within a fifteen-mile radius of Jefferson City.[27]

The urban worker who lives in a rural area has had a significant impact on rural land values in Missouri. Forty years ago, the factors affecting the value of rural land in Missouri were largely related to the capability of the land to produce agriculturally. Today, this is no longer the case. The most important factors affecting the value of land in the rural Ozarks bear little relationship to traditional measures of land capability. The important factors today are access to urban areas, the presence of all-weather roads, the availability of lake sites, and the area's social climate. In Gasconade County, for example, the poorest land in the county, from an agricultural point of view, often brings a higher price than the best agricultural land if it possesses any of the qualities above.

Broadly speaking, the pattern of land and building values in the traverse counties is somewhat chaotic (Table 3–4).[28] The value of land and buildings is influenced by factors in addition to land capability. For example, Perry County has the highest land capability rating, yet it ranks third in value of land and buildings. The same is true at the opposite extreme. Madison County has the lowest land capability rating, yet it ranks fourth from the bottom in land values. Location appears to be a most significant variable in determining land values. Three of the four counties with the highest values are urban or urban oriented. Cole and Cape Girardeau counties both contain sizeable urban centers. Eastern Franklin County forms part of the St. Louis commuter belt. All three of these counties have a lower land capability rating than Perry County, but two of the counties have a significantly higher value of land and buildings per acre. The counties with the lowest value per acre are the most isolated. Madison, Maries, and Miller counties are at some distance from the Missouri-Mississippi river system, the main railroad lines, and the interstate highway system. Osage

27. Rafferty, "Persistence Versus Change," p. 266; Conrad H. Hammar, *Factors Affecting Farm Land Values in Missouri*, pp. 61–62.

28. The majority of the land area in the Old Stock American-dominated counties in Table 3–4 is not included in the traverse areas. The major portions of most of the Old Stock American counties are located in the more rugged geographic divisions of the Ozarks. They are included in Table 3–4 for two reasons: (1) the data were available only by county unit, and (2) their inclusion demonstrates the tenuous relationship between land capability and land values.

Table 3–4

Value of Rural Land and Buildings per Acre for Selected Ozark Counties, 1969

	Value of land and buildings for 1969 (per acre)	Average land capability (1.0 good to 4.0 poor)
Northern Ozark Border		
German-dominated counties		
Cole	$160	3.20
Franklin	$248	3.25
Gasconade	$139	3.05
Osage	$104	3.15
Old Stock American-dominated counties		
Crawford	$146	3.70
Maries	$ 87	3.40
Miller	$112	3.70
Moniteau	$174	2.65
Phelps	$136	3.55
Eastern Ozark Border		
German-dominated counties		
Cape Girardeau	$233	2.50
Perry	$208	2.45
Ste. Genevieve	$162	2.90
Old Stock American-dominated counties		
Bollinger	$136	3.00
Madison	$115	3.75
St. Francis	$175	3.10

Sources: U.S. Department of Commerce, Bureau of the Census, *Census of Agriculture, 1969: Area Reports, Missouri,* vol. 1, part 17, sec. 1, 268–69, and Hammar, *Factors Affecting Farm Land Values in Missouri,* p. 9.

County appears well situated at first glance. However, the nearest bridges across the Missouri are upstream at Jefferson City and downstream at Hermann. Phelps and Crawford counties, on the other hand, have easy access to both the main line of the Frisco Railroad and the interstate highway system leading from Springfield to St. Louis. Excluding the variable of relative location, or access, land values undoubtedly would more closely reflect land capability.

To determine if significant differences in the values of houses exist within the same county, data were obtained at the minor civil division level on the value of all rural houses that are occupied by the owners for three counties, one for each traverse area. The minor civil divisions for each county are divided into those over 50 per cent German and those over 50 per cent Old Stock American. In most cases, the boundaries separating Germans and Old Stock Americans coincide approximately with minor civil division boundaries. The differences in the value of houses for the three counties are summarized in Table 3–5. Houses valued at less than $5,000 in 1970 occur more frequently in the Old Stock American portions of the three counties. This is consistent with the findings presented previously on the distribution of house types. Small, low-quality houses, which presumably would have the lowest dollar value, are found with greatest frequency in the non-German areas. Except for Gasconade County, a high percentage of the houses in the German areas are moderately valued between $5,000 and $10,000. Since the majority of these houses are quite old, this seems logical. It appears that the bungalow style prevalent in the Old Stock American areas is valued in the same general range. The houses valued at more than $10,000 include, in addition to contemporary houses, the best of the linear and bungalow styles. The magnitude of the differences in the value of houses in the German and Old Stock American portions of the three counties indicates that the Germans have invested more heavily in their dwelling

Table 3–5

Value of Owner-Occupied Rural Dwellings by Minor Civil Division for Selected Ozark Counties, 1970

	Less than $5,000		$5,000–$10,000		More than $10,000	
	No.	Percentage	No.	Percentage	No.	Percentage
Lawrence County						
German Portion	4	(4.8)	60	(71.4)	20	(23.8)
Old Stock American Portion	162	(47.5)	111	(32.6)	68	(19.9)
Perry County						
German Portion	74	(18.6)	144	(36.3)	179	(45.1)
Old Stock American Portion	83	(38.1)	82	(35.5)	61	(26.4)
Gasconade County						
German Portion	15	(2.2)	135	(19.7)	537	(78.1)
Old Stock American Portion	109	(10.2)	386	(36.0)	576	(53.8)

Source: *Census of Housing: 1970*, Tapes of small area returns, provided by the Public Affairs and Information Service, University of Missouri — Columbia.

units than have their neighbors. These data also indicate that the Germans are more successful in maintaining the value of their houses than are their neighbors.[29]

An examination of assessment records for the Lawrence County traverse area was made to further check on the reliability of the data obtained through direct field observation. The Lawrence County sample includes approximately 50 per cent of all land in the entire traverse area and is based on an examination of alternate sections of land. The built-up areas around the towns of Monett and Pierce City are excluded, as in the collection of field data for the same area. Land and buildings are assessed as a unit for each separately owned parcel of land. There is no way to determine what portion of the assessed value represents buildings only. However, the assessor stated that all land in the traverse area is considered to be of equal value for purposes of assessment, and any differences in assessed values would represent structural improvements, such as houses, barns, fences, and general upkeep. The assessed value of land and buildings for the entire sample is quite low, averaging $29.45 per acre (Table 3–6). However, it was estimated that land

Table 3–6

Assessed Value of Land and Buildings in Lawrence County, Missouri, by Nativity of Owner, 1973

Nativity of Owner	No. of Parcels of Land	Total Acreage	Assessed Value of Land and Buildings per Acre[1]
Non-German	160	13,813	$26.51
German	154	14,223	$32.32
Total	314	28,036	$29.45 (avg.)

[1] Assessed value is approximately 10 per cent of current market value. Source: Assessment records, Lawrence County, Missouri, 1973.

and buildings in the sample area are currently assessed at approximately 10 per cent of real market value. The assessed value of land and buildings averages 18.0 per cent higher for German-owned land than for non-German-owned land. The difference in assessed value is nearly $6.00 per acre between Germans and non-

29. The counties are Perry, Lawrence, and Gasconade. The computer printouts for Gasconade County did not provide data on rural minor civil divisions. Only those three minor civil divisions containing towns over 1,000 population were available. Therefore, the data for Gasconade County include the German town of Hermann and the Old Stock American towns of Bland and Owensville.

Germans, which in terms of real market value would be $60.00 more per acre for German-owned land. For an average farm, which is approximately 160 acres for Lawrence County, the difference in value at current market prices is $9,296. This supports the previous findings of both the direct field observation and census sources that improvements, such as houses and barns, are more substantial in the German portions of the traverse areas.

Construction Materials. Materials used in house construction for the three traverse areas are summarized in Table 3–3. The majority of houses in all three traverse areas is of frame construction. However, certain regional differences and differences between Germans and non-Germans are found. Composition siding, roll-type siding, and rough lumber, which are associated with small, low-quality houses and a lower standard of living, are almost totally absent from the three German areas but are somewhat more prevalent in the three non-German areas. This is consistent with the house type associations previously discussed.

The use of brick, stone, and rock as construction materials shows some differences from area to area and between Germans and non-Germans. Yet, in all three areas, houses constructed of these materials account for only a small minority of the total. With the exception of the German area in the Northern Ozark Border, the majority of brick houses are of contemporary styling. In the German settlements of the Northern Ozark Border, more than half of the brick houses are old traditional dwellings of the linear style previously discussed. Sauer states that the Germans in the Northern Ozark Border have a tendency to use finished brick and limestone as their building materials.[30] Rural brick and limestone (locally referred to as freestone) houses are most concentrated in the immediate vicinity of Hermann. Their small number is somewhat overshadowed by their impressive appearance (Figure 3–9).

A few red brick linears are found in the German settlements of the Eastern Ozark Border, particularly in the Saxon areas of eastern Perry County. Very few limestone linears are found outside the Hermann vicinity of Gasconade County. The red brick linear and other traditional styles constructed of brick are found to be quite common in a number of German villages and towns, including Hermann, Westphalia, Washington, Ste. Genevieve, and Uniontown. Hermann, in particular, is dominated by traditional style houses built from red brick (Figure 3–11). No examples of the

---

30. Sauer, *Ozark Highland,* p. 173.

Figure 3–11.   Traditional styles of architecture in Hermann, Missouri.

traditional German technique of half-timbering are found along any of the traverses.[31] However, a few examples of this type of construction are seen in the Northern Ozark Border area (Figure 3–12). The German style of architecture featuring the double fake chimneys is quite common in several villages and is seen occasionally in rural areas.

Roofing Materials. The material used for roofing presents an interesting contrast between the German and non-German areas (Table 3–3). Except for the Freistatt traverse area, sheet-metal roofs are common in both the German and non-German areas. Metal roofs are normally a sign of poor economic conditions, which is obvious in the non-German areas of the Northern and Eastern Ozark Border regions, where metal roofs are found primarily on small, low-quality houses. Yet, in the German areas, metal roofs, usually painted, are also found on a large percentage of high quality traditional houses. A somewhat facetious answer given more than once to queries concerning the metal roofs is, "We Germans like

31. Terry G. Jordan, "German Houses in Texas," pp. 24–26.

Figure 3–12. Half-timbered construction in Gasconade County.

to know when it is raining." However, further investigation turned up three plausible explanations.

The German's reputation for frugality, the modest cost, and long life of metal roofs can be a possible explanation. It is also feasible that metal roofs were initially installed and maintained to the present as a means of fire protection, since, as recently as 1950, two-thirds to three-fourths of German farm families in the Northern and Eastern Ozark Border regions reported using wood for cooking and heating.[32]

The third, and possibly the most realistic explanation, concerns the use of cisterns in German areas of the Northern and Eastern Ozark Border regions. Germans in these two areas represent the second wave of settlers; the first wave was American. By the time of the German's arrival, most of the lowland areas were settled, particularly the choice spring sites. The German found himself on the uplands and without a source of fresh water. Since deep wells were not widely used in the Ozarks, he was forced to rely on precipitation as a source for his fresh water supply. He used the roof of his house, and frequently his barn, for collecting water. A

32. Gregory, *Rural Social Areas in Missouri*, p. 23.

painted metal surface provided the cleanest water, and the metal roof was the easiest type surface to keep clean and serviceable for the purposes of collecting potable water. The Freistatt settlement, also on the uplands, which was established much later, relied on deep wells powered by windmills as a source of fresh water.

Lightning Rods. On several occasions, interviewees in the German areas commented on the presence of lightning rods as an indicator of German settlement in the Ozarks. According to data from the three traverse areas, there is some validity in this observation (Table 3–3). The continued use of the older style lightning rods, which are quite large and have a glass bulb near the base, is widespread in all three German areas. Their large size, and the presence of three or four on almost every sizeable farmstead structure, makes the lightning rod an obvious feature to passersby and makes the German farmer the subject of numerous jokes concerning his gullibility at the hands of enterprising lightning rod salesmen. However, the University of Missouri Extension Service continues to recommend lightning rods, although they caution that the older style rods still in use in the German areas are often more of a hazard than a help. The only explanation offered by the German farmers is that their lightning rods are still serviceable, and they believe lightning rods are functional.

Farmstead Location. On the whole, houses in the German areas are set back from roads a greater distance than are houses in the non-German areas (Figure 3–5). This can be partly explained by the greater age of houses in the German areas. At the time when most of the houses in the German areas were built, quick egress by way of an all-weather road was not an important factor. Additionally, Germans have remained on the farm to a greater degree than have the non-Germans and thus would be less concerned about immediate access to urban areas for employment and more concerned about retaining the old farmstead, which probably contained a number of serviceable structures in addition to the house. In the non-German areas, the house was often the only sizeable structure.

Attendant Features. Several general tendencies were observed that distinguished the German and non-German areas. The presence of such amenities as flowers and shutters is more common in the German areas and gives them a greater appearance of prosperity. Although gardens are commonplace in almost any rural area, the ones observed in German areas are unusually large, and virtually every house, village or farm, has one nearby. Gregory notes that there is a tendency in the German areas to produce for home consumption to a greater degree than in non-German areas.[33] Large gardens are one indication of a limited effort toward self-sufficiency. A curious feature of many of these gardens is the presence of grapes.

Double front doors are quite common on two very different house types. The linear style house in the German areas often has double front doors, as do the small, low-quality house type in the non-German areas. A common response to queries concerning the double front doors in the German areas is that the early German settlers, who built the house, planned two living rooms, each with its own entrance. No explanation can be found for the double front doors on small, low-quality houses.

Barns and Outbuildings. Differences were observed in several other areas relating to farmstead structures. The styles of barns observed represent a hodgepodge with no apparent pattern in either the German or non-German areas. However, Kniffen points out that barns were generally much more short-lived than houses, a fact that would account to some extent for the lack of patterns in barn types, such as those noted for houses.[34] Barn styles in the traverse areas represent more recent and varied influences than houses. A few barns of uniquely European styling are found, but their occurrence is rare (Figure 3–13). The most common style of barns in both the German and non-German areas is the transverse crib barn with an end-opening overhead hayloft. The roof design is normally the shallow A-frame type, but hip roofs are also quite common. Threshing barns with a side opening are encountered in the German areas, but they represent a small minority of all barns (Figure 3–14). Old dairy barns that have four to eight foot rock foundations are common in German areas in the Northern and Eastern Ozark Border regions but are almost totally absent elsewhere. No Pennsylvania German style barns exist in any of the traverse areas. Modern, low-profile metal barns are quite common in both the German and non-German areas.

Large, modern dairy barns with automated silos are encountered in the Freistatt traverse areas with a somewhat greater occurrence among the Germans than the non-Germans. They are also found, but to a lesser extent, in German areas in both the Ozark borders. This is partly explained by the fact that southwestern Missouri is

33. Ibid., pp. 22–23.
34. Kniffen, "Folk Housing," p. 552.

Figure 3–13.   European style limestone barn in Gasconade County.

Figure 3–14.   Side-opening threshing barn in Gasconade County.

a major dairying region, whereas the Northern and Eastern Ozark Border regions emphasize dairying to a lesser degree.[35]

The majority of barns in all three traverse areas is unpainted and metal roofed. Approximately one-fourth of the barns in the German areas, generally the larger ones in better condition, are painted usually white. Approximately one-third of the barns in the non-German areas are painted commonly white and red. A large proportion of the painted barns in the non-German areas is small, new barns, which appear almost as novelty items, and serve the purpose of machine sheds or garages.

Significant differences are noticeable in the size and number of barns in the German and non-German areas (Table 3–3). The average barn in the three traverse areas is medium sized. However, the German areas have a much higher percentage of large barns and a smaller percentage of small barns than the non-German areas. This is consistent with Sauer's findings in the Northern Ozark Border. He adds, "On the poor farms of the hill regions they [barns] are wretched sheds."[36] Of perhaps more significance is the average number of barns per farm. For all three traverse areas, the Germans average almost twice as many barns per farm as do the non-Germans. These differences can be partly accounted for by tradition. The Germans brought from the old country the habit of covering almost everything, as opposed to the Old Stock American who barely sheltered himself. It is not uncommon in the interior Ozarks to see farm machinery without cover. Such practices are less common in the German areas.

The larger number and size of barns in the German areas may also be an indication of the greater emphasis among the Germans on crop and dairy farming, as opposed to cattle and hogs in the non-German areas.[37] Related to the number and size of barns is the total number of outbuildings in addition to barns (Table 3–3). As with the barns, the German areas have a larger average number of outbuildings per farm than the non-German areas.

The overall condition of farmsteads for the three traverse areas indicates a marked and consistent difference in farmstead condition between the German and non-German areas (Table 3–3). In the Northern Ozark Border, these findings are consistent with

35. Milton D. Rafferty, Russel L. Gerlach, and Dennis J. Hrebec, *Atlas of Missouri*, p. 32.

36. Sauer, *Ozark Highland*, p. 206.

37. Marbut, *Soil Reconnaissance of the Ozark Region*, p. 50.

those of Cozzens and Collier. In particular, the core of German areas in northern Gasconade County and eastern Perry County stands out on the positive side, while the rougher sections of the non-German areas appear at the opposite extreme. In some instances, the differences noted can largely be accounted for by differences in land capability, usually favoring the German areas. Generally, the differences in overall farmstead condition vary significantly along ethnic lines irrespective of variations in land capabilities:

> The property of German farmers is likely to be distinguished by its neatness. Farm improvements are commonly superior to those found elsewhere in the area, and crop yields for a given soil type are likely to be higher in those communities which have a larger percentage of inhabitants of German origin. The German farmers have attained economic stability and moderate prosperity, whereas many neighboring groups of Anglo-Americans in similar physical settings eke out a precarious existence.[38]

In general, buildings in the German areas are in a better state of repair; fences are in more serviceable condition; and less clutter is observed near the farmstead. In the non-German areas, farmsteads appear to be in varying condition, ranging from excellent to almost total disrepair, with a majority tending toward the latter. Many outstanding farmsteads, appearing somewhat out of place in the Ozarks, are observed in the three German areas and, to a lesser extent, in the three non-German areas.

38. Cozzens, "Conservation in German Settlements," pp. 289–92; Collier, *Northern Ozark Border Region*, p. 52.

4. The Germans
Agriculture and Land Use

Germans were attracted to the Ozarks by promises of a good life and prosperity. Although some immigrants were motivated to leave Germany because of social injustices, the overwhelming majority was much more concerned in securing a living. Those Germans who settled in the Ozarks sought prosperity through agriculture; since most were farmers, their future lay directly in the land. They brought with them their Old World systems of agriculture. As much a cultural as an economic complex, German agriculture contrasted to varying degrees with the systems of agriculture already established in the Ozarks. The agriculture that evolved in the German settlements was influenced both by the Old World traditions the Germans brought with them and by the physical, economic, and cultural conditions in the Ozarks. To determine the character of the present farming of Germans and their non-German neighbors in the Ozarks, four sample areas containing German and non-German farmers were subjected to field investigation and analysis on a variety of measures relating to agriculture.[1]

The selection of the sample areas, including their number, size, and location, is based on a number of considerations. Each major area of German settlement in the Ozarks is represented in the sample areas, including the Northern Ozark Border, Eastern Ozark Border, and southwestern settlements. Both early German settlements (Gasconade and Perry counties) and later German settlements (Miller and Lawrence counties) are included. The sample areas include groups of differing cultural backgrounds, including religion, areas of birth and dwelling while in Germany, and group cohesiveness. Several types of farming are represented in the

---

1. Terry G. Jordan, *German Seed in Texas Soil*, p. 193; Walter M. Kollmorgan, "Immigrant Settlements in Southern Agriculture," pp. 74–76.

sample areas, including examples from (1) the Ozark border dairy and wheat region (Gasconade and Perry counties); (2) the southwestern fruit, dairy, and poultry region (Lawrence County); and (3) the Ozark meat production region (Miller County). Several geographic provinces of the Ozark Highland Region are represented in the sample areas, including (1) the Missouri River Border (Gasconade County); (2) the Mississippi River Border (Perry County); (3) the Springfield Plain (Lawrence County); and (4) the Osage-Gasconade river hills (Miller County).

The actual selection of sample areas was made on two sets of factors, and the sample areas were selected purposefully, rather than randomly. Each sample area includes comparable numbers of German and non-German farmers, who represent at least 90 per cent of the farmers in their portion of the sample area, and has similar conditions of soil, topography, and drainage, as much as was possible and practical. Each sample area is almost the size of a survey township. The data from the sample areas are summarized in Tables 4–1 through 4–6.

Table 4–1

Size of Farms and Cropland in the Sample Land-Use Areas, 1972

Area	No. of farms	Average size of farms (acres)	Average cropland per farm (acres)	Cropland as percentage of all land
German Areas				
Lawrence County	120	142.6	119.3	84.0
Miller County	48	211.8	65.4	30.9
Gasconade County	40	299.4	82.8	27.7
Perry County				
Lutheran	57	182.0	101.1	55.5
Catholic	67	152.0	114.0	75.0
All German Areas	332	180.2	102.9	57.1
Non-German Areas				
Lawrence County	86	96.7	71.1	73.5
Miller County	58	178.1	59.5	33.4
Gasconade County	55	212.6	100.9	47.4
Perry County	52	200.2	92.7	46.3
All Non-German Areas	251	162.3	79.4	48.9
All Areas	583	172.5	92.8	53.8

Source: A.S.C.S. records and field data.

General Relationships

From the data obtained on land use in the sample areas, the following generalizations concerning agriculture can be made:

1. The size of farms in the German and non-German areas differs in two respects. Overall size of the farms tends to be somewhat larger in the German areas, while the size of farms run only as full-time operations is larger in the non-German areas (Table 4–1).

2. The percentage of cropland differs little between the German and non-German areas (Table 4–1).

3. A higher percentage of land in the German areas is cleared of trees than in the non-German areas. A total of 66 per cent of land in the German areas are cleared, compared to a figure of 52 per cent for the non-German areas (Table 4–2).

Table 4–2

Land Use in Four Sample Areas, 1972: Woodland and Pasture

	Number of farms	Woodland Acres	%	Woodland Pasture Acres	%	Pasture* Acres	%
Perry County							
German Lutheran	57	2,934	28.7	162	1.6	3,835	37.4
German Catholic	67	1,764	17.2	–	–	5,087	49.7
Non-German	52	9,472	71.1	350	2.6	2,871	21.6
All Perry	176	14,170	41.9	512	1.5	11,793	34.9
Lawrence County							
German	120	781	5.9	447	3.4	5,265	39.6
Non-German	86	1,185	13.0	1,130	12.4	5,204	57.1
All Lawrence	206	1,966	8.8	1,577	7.0	10,469	46.7
Miller County							
German	48	5,365	53.6	643	6.4	2,918	29.2
Non-German	58	5,858	52.7	990	8.9	3,706	33.3
All Miller	106	11,223	53.1	1,633	7.7	6,624	31.4
Gasconade County							
German	40	7,490	73.1	393	3.8	1,120	10.9
Non-German	55	4,443	43.4	1,346	13.1	3,618	35.3
All Gasconade	95	11,933	58.3	1,739	8.5	4,738	23.1
Total German	332	18,334	34.0	1,645	3.1	18,225	33.7
Total Non-German	251	20,958	47.8	3,816	8.7	15,399	35.2
Total All Areas	583	39,292	40.2	5,461	5.6	33,624	34.4

*Includes all hay.
Source: Planimetric measurement of land-use maps.

4. The percentage of cleared pasture is similar for the German and non-German areas. However, woodland pasture is far more prevalent in the non-German areas, by a ratio of 2.9 to 1 (Table 4–2).

5. In both areas, wheat is the most important crop, exceeding feed grains by a ratio of 2.6 to 1 (Table 4–3).

Table 4–3

Land Use in Four Sample Areas, 1972: Crops

	Wheat and other small grains		Feed Grains		Soybeans		Plowed	
	Acres	%	Acres	%	Acres	%	Acres	%
Perry County								
German Lutheran	1,682	16.4	830	8.1	235	2.3	284	2.8
German Catholic	1,436	14.0	886	8.6	8	0.1	317	3.1
Non-German	205	1.5	189	1.4	44	0.3	24	0.2
All Perry	3,323	9.8	1,905	5.6	287	0.9	625	1.9
Lawrence County								
German	3,669	27.6	886	6.7	—	—	760	5.7
Non-German	742	8.1	252	2.8	—	—	131	1.4
All Lawrence	4,411	19.7	1,138	5.1	—	—	891	4.0
Miller County								
German	687	6.9	131	1.3	—	—	—	—
Non-German	292	2.6	16	0.1	—	—	—	—
All Miller	979	4.6	147	0.7	—	—	—	—
Gasconade County								
German	508	5.0	366	3.6	—	—	78	0.8
Non-German	292	2.9	155	1.5	—	—	24	0.2
All Gasconade	800	3.9	521	2.5	—	—	102	0.5
Total German	7,982	14.8	3,099	5.7	243	0.4	1,439	2.7
Total Non-German	1,531	3.5	612	1.4	44	0.1	179	0.4
Total All Areas	9,513	9.7	3,711	3.8	287	0.3	1,618	1.6

Source: Planimetric measurement of land-use maps.

6. A much higher percentage of land in the German areas is actually in crops. In the German areas, 23.7 per cent of all land are in crops, compared to a figure of 5.4 per cent for the non-German areas, or a ratio of 4.4 to 1, favoring the German areas (Table 4–4).

7. The rate of full-time farming is much greater in the German areas than in the non-German areas. Approximately half the

Table 4–4

Land Use in Four Sample Areas 1972: Summary

	Number of Farms	Woodland		Non-Agricultural and miscellaneous		Total Pasture[1]		Total Crop[2]		All Land	
		Acres	%	Acres	%	Acres	%	Acres	%	Acres	%
Perry County											
German Lutheran	57	2,934	28.7	278	2.7	3,997	39.0	3,031	29.6	10,240	100
German Catholic	67	1,764	17.2	742	7.3	5,087	49.7	2,647	25.8	10,240	100
Non-German	52	9,472	71.1	175	1.3	3,221	24.1	462	3.5	13,330	100
All Perry	176	14,170	41.9	1,195	3.5	12,305	36.4	6,140	18.2	33,810	100
Lawrence County											
German	120	781	5.9	1,472	11.1	5,712	43.0	5,315	40.0	13,280	100
Non-German	86	1,185	13.0	476	5.2	6,334	69.5	1,125	12.3	9,120	100
All Lawrence	206	1,966	8.8	1,948	8.7	12,046	53.7	6,440	28.8	22,400	100
Miller County											
German	48	5,365	53.6	261	2.6	3,561	35.6	818	8.2	10,005	100
Non-German	58	5,858	52.7	253	2.4	4,696	42.2	308	2.7	11,115	100
All Miller	106	11,223	53.1	514	2.5	8,257	39.1	1,126	5.3	21,120	100
Gasconade County											
German	40	7,490	73.1	285	2.8	1,513	14.8	952	9.3	10,240	100
Non-German	55	4,443	43.4	362	3.6	4,964	48.4	471	4.6	10,240	100
All Gasconade	95	11,933	58.3	647	3.2	6,477	31.6	1,423	6.9	20,480	100
Total German	332	18,334	34.0	3,038	5.6	19,870	36.8	12,763	23.6	54,005	100
Total Non-German	251	20,958	47.8	1,266	2.9	19,215	43.9	2,366	5.4	43,805	100
Total All Areas	583	39,292	40.2	4,304	4.4	39,085	40.0	15,129	15.4	97,810	100

Source: Planimetric measurement of land-use maps.
[1] Includes woodland pasture and pasture from Table 4–2.
[2] Includes wheat, feed grains, soybeans, and plowed from Table 4–3.

farmers in the German areas reported no income other than that received from farming, compared with a figure of 16 per cent for the non-German areas (Table 4–5).

Table 4–5

Full-Time Farming in the Sample Land-Use Areas, 1972

Area	Number of Farms	Full-Time Farmers		Part-Time Farmers	
		No.	%	No.	%
German Areas					
Lawrence County	120	29	24	91	76
Miller County	48	21	44	27	56
Benton County	75	68	91	7	9
Gasconade County	40	14	35	26	65
Perry County					
Lutheran	57	45	79	12	21
Catholic	67	37	55	30	45
All German Areas	407	214	53	193	47
Non-German Areas					
Lawrence County	86	8	9	78	91
Miller County	58	11	19	47	81
Gasconade County	55	9	16	46	84
Perry County	52	11	21	41	79
All Non-German Areas	251	39	16	212	84
All Areas	658	253	38	405	62

Source: A.S.C.S. records and field interviews.

8. The tenancy rate is low in all sample areas but is even slightly lower in the German than the non-German areas (Table 4–6).

9. The farmers in the German areas generally participate more in the various programs of the Agricultural Stabilization and Conservation Service (Table 4–7).

Viewed individually, these generalizations indicate some basic agricultural differences of the German and non-German farmers in the Ozarks. Viewed in their interrelationships, these generalizations suggest even stronger differences in the agriculture of the two groups.

These data reinforce findings in other regions of the United States that Germans as a group farm their land more intensively than others, especially in contrast to groups of Southern background. This is reflected both through their greater emphasis on crop agriculture and through their lower rate of off-farm employ-

Table 4–6

Tenancy in the Sample Land-Use Areas, 1972

Area	Number of Farms	Full Owners		Part Owners		Full Renters	
		No.	%	No.	%	No.	%
German Areas							
Lawrence County	120	108	90	10	8	2	2
Miller County	48	42	88	6	12	0	0
Benton County	75	69	92	5	7	1	1
Gasconade County	40	33	82	5	13	2	5
Perry County							
Lutheran	57	49	86	8	14	0	0
Catholic	67	55	82	7	10	5	8
All German Areas	407	356	88	41	10	10	2
Non-German Areas							
Lawrence County	86	70	81	11	13	5	6
Miller County	58	49	84	7	13	2	3
Gasconade County	55	47	85	6	11	2	4
Perry County	52	36	69	10	19	6	12
All Non-German Areas	251	202	80	34	14	15	6
All Areas	658	558	85	75	11	25	4

Source: A.S.C.S. records and field interviews.

ment. The percentages of land in crops vary from sample area to sample area, but in all cases, the German farmer averages a higher rate of cropping than does his non-German neighbor. This fact was frequently mentioned in conversation with officials of the University of Missouri Extension Service and the Agricultural Stabilization and Conservation Service on land use in the sample counties.

The rate for full-time farming varies widely from region to region, but, again, in all cases, the German farmer is more likely to be a full-time farmer than is his non-German neighbor. The actual rate is dependent on the quality of land, age of the farmers, and possibilities for off-farm employment. In secluded areas, as Perry and Benton counties, the overwhelming majority of German farmers has no income other than that received from farming. In the German settlement in Lawrence County, which is near Springfield, nearly two-thirds of the German farmers work off the farm. In the sample area in Miller County, where conditions for agriculture are generally poor, the full-time farming rate is somewhat lower than in the better areas.

Table 4–7

Participation in A.S.C.S. Feed Grain and Wheat Programs in the Sample Land-Use Areas, 1969–1971

Area	Number of Years Participating in Either or Both Programs							
	0 Years		1 Year		2 Years		3 Years	
	No. of farms	%	No. of farms	%	No. of farms	%	No. of farms	%
German Areas								
Lawrence County	25	21	15	12	35	29	45	38
Miller County	27	56	1	2	4	8	16	33
Benton County	13	17	12	16	20	27	30	40
Gasconade County	12	30	4	10	19	48	5	12
Perry County								
Lutheran	2	4	23	40	8	14	24	42
Catholic	3	4	27	40	9	14	28	42
All German Areas	82	20	82	20	95	24	148	36
Non-German Areas								
Lawrence County	43	50	14	16	10	12	19	22
Miller County	32	54	8	14	9	16	9	16
Gasconade County	20	36	7	13	24	44	4	7
Perry County	6	12	20	38	11	21	15	29
All Non-German Areas	101	40	49	19	54	22	47	19
All Areas	183	28	131	20	149	22	195	30

Source: A.S.C.S. records.

Perry County presents a striking contrast between the German farmer and his non-German neighbor, regarding full-time farming. Full-time farms are largest in the non-German sample area, averaging more than 320 acres. The comparable figures for the German Lutheran and German Catholic sample areas are 206 acres and 168 acres, respectively. Approximately two-thirds of the full-time farms in the German sample areas are less than 200 acres, and 15 per cent are less than 100 acres. In the non-German sample area, nearly two-thirds of the full-time farms are 300 acres or more (Table 4–8).

Table 4–8

Size of Farms Operated Full Time in Sample Land-Use Areas of Perry County, 1972

| | Total number of farms | Number of full-time farms (according to size by acres) | | | | | | | |
| | | 100 or less | | 101–200 | | 201–300 | | More than 300 | |
		No.	%	No.	%	No.	%	No.	%
German Lutheran	46	9	19.6	20	43.5	8	17.4	9	19.6
German Catholic	36	4	11.1	22	61.1	6	16.7	4	11.1
Non-German	11	0	0	1	9.1	3	27.3	7	63.6
Total	93	13	14.0	43	46.2	17	18.3	20	21.5

Source: A.S.C.S. records and field interviews.

The preference in the German settlements for small grains was noted in the samples of land use, as well as in interviews with government officials in these locales. Even in Miller County, where relatively little land is used for crops, the statement was made that the Germans stand out as the county's wheat producers. The preference for small grains among German farmers has been noted previously for the Ozarks and for other regions. Marbut refers to the German farmers in the Northern and Eastern Ozark Border regions as "natural-born grain growers rather than stock raisers."[2]

2. H. H. Krusekopf and H. G. Lewis, *Soil Survey of Cape Girardeau County, Missouri*, pp. 16–17; Jordan, *German Seed*, p. 193; Kollmorgan, "Immigrant Settlements," p. 74; Curtis F. Marbut, *Soil Reconnaissance of the Ozark Region of Missouri and Arkansas*, p. 21.

The tenancy rate is low for both German and non-German areas, although the figure for the non-German areas is somewhat higher. The high rate of ownership is consistent with the findings of other studies of German farmers. The low tenancy rate in the non-German areas is reflective of the Ozarks as a whole, where the renting of farmland is generally unprofitable.[3]

The level of participation in A.S.C.S. programs in the sample areas shows a rate favoring the German farmers. This is somewhat unexpected, considering the conservative nature of the German farmer. Twenty years ago, very few farmers in the German settlements of Perry County participated in government-sponsored programs of acreage control. This is confirmed for several other areas of German settlement through interviews with local officials.[4] All those interviewed, however, agreed that there has been a dramatic turnabout with the German farmers in the last ten years, who now participate at a somewhat higher rate than their neighbors.

On conservation practices, local officials frequently commented on the greater use of contouring and terracing in several of the German settlements. Such practices are highly visible and are observed more frequently in the German areas. However, such practices are needed more in the German areas, where more sloping land has been cleared and put into crops. Strip-cropping is also noted more frequently in the German areas.

Thus, one might hastily conclude that German farmers in the Ozarks are superior to their non-German neighbors in agriculture. Numerous references to this effect can be cited, whereas no negative references to German agricultural practices in the Ozarks can be encountered.[5] However, any such conclusion must be tempered by a knowledge of several factors that tend to favor the German farmer.

The German farmer in the Ozarks came with the skills of agriculture fresh in his mind. He put down the plow only long enough to cross the Atlantic. By contrast, the tradition of the Old Stock

3. Jordan, *German Seed*, p. 193; Kollmorgan, "Immigrant Settlements," p. 70; Cecil L. Gregory, *Rural Social Areas in Missouri*, p. 25.

4. A. B. Cozzens also noticed this tendency for Germans in Gasconade County in the 1940s, "Conservation in German Settlements of the Missouri Ozarks," p. 293.

5. Cozzens, "Conservation in German Settlements," p. 298; H. G. Lewis and F. V. Emerson, *Soil Survey of Miller County, Missouri*, p. 10; Sauer, *Ozark Highland*, p. 165; E. S. Vanatta and H. G. Lewis, *Soil Survey of Franklin County, Missouri*, p. 13; E. B. Watson and H. F. Williams, *Soil Survey of Cedar County, Missouri*, p. 14; and A. W. Haswell, *The Ozark Region: Its History and Its People*, vol. 1, p. 270.

American in the Ozarks was frequently a one-generation removal from the practice of agriculture. He was a pioneer, who lived by hunting and fishing, and, "for some time very little farming was done beyond that necessary to supply food and clothing."[6] It seems reasonable to conclude that the skills of agriculture cannot survive a generation or more of inactivity, without some loss in technique and proficiency.

The Old Stock American who emigrated from Appalachia to the Ozarks was drawn largely from the lower socioeconomic strata of that era. No amount of romanticizing can alter this fact. In a comparative sense, this illiterate, scrabble farmer, who also was a woodsman and hunter, was up against some of the most skilled farmers Europe had to offer. Nowhere was this distinction more important than in the selection of land. The German selected his land according to the quality of the soil:

> The ability of one group to select superior soils was a cultural factor of considerable significance at the very start. It is hard to picture eighteenth-century German peasants ever settling on some of the Southern lands occupied by the English and from which the Federal Government is today trying to remove their unfortunate descendants.[7]

The Old Stock American sought soils that were easy to work, which meant bottomlands and somewhat sandy uplands. Unfortunately for many of them, the soils they selected were inferior ones found in rocky and hilly terrain.

For example, the Germans in Lawrence County, who were latecomers, still got some of the best land in the county. They selected a prairie area north of Monett, which had been avoided by the earlier settlers who preferred the less fertile but wooded areas. Other considerations, certainly, must have influenced the German's selection of land; yet, the fact remains that a map showing the distribution of Germans in the Ozarks can also be a map of the better soils in the region.

Once established on the land, the German farmers demonstrated an ability to recoup maximum benefit from their soils. Two studies report German yields to be higher than those of their neighbors on the same soil. The German farmer in the Ozarks has been looked upon as an excellent interpreter of soils. In Cole County, German farmers were singled out for their uncanny ability to "suit each soil to a specific crop." Much of the German farmer's success

---

6. B. W. Tillman and C. E. Deardorff, *Soil Survey of Perry County, Missouri*, p. 9.
7. Richard H. Shryock, "British and German Farmers," p. 37.

traces back to his history of locational stability. Local officials often commented that the German farmer's soils are not necessarily, inherently more fertile, but rather, the German has upgraded his soils over a period of several decades to the extent that they are now more fertile than those of his neighbor.[8]

Regarding yield per acre, the gap between the German and non-German farmer in the Ozarks has narrowed considerably over the years. There are three possible explanations for this. First, the less able or less skilled farmer has been weeded out as part of the modernization of American agriculture. This process, undoubtedly, exacted a greater toll among non-German farmers in the Ozarks. Second, the quality of all farmers has been upgraded through educational programs sponsored by government agencies at the local, state, and federal levels. The non-German farmer has benefitted greatly from such programs. Third, and perhaps most importantly in the Ozarks, the non-German farmer has stopped cropping much of his marginal land and has confined his efforts to the smaller but more productive areas of the remaining land. The German, on the other hand, has continued to cultivate the slopes, as, for example, in Perry County.

Although the German farmer is often admired for his tenacity, in that he has not succumbed to the pressures that have driven most of the region's farmers partly or totally off the farm, he is as often criticized for his lack of modernization. For example, in all of the sample areas, the percentage of full-time farmers is greater among the Germans. There are two interpretations that explain this difference between the two groups. First, the Germans' higher rate of full-time farming is an indication of their superiority in agriculture over their neighbors. Second, and equally as plausible, the lower rate among the non-Germans is an indication that part-time farming is compatible with a full-time urban job, with the end result of a marked increase in one's standard of living.

The differences between the German and non-German areas in land in crops can be interpreted in the same manner. Is the fact that the Germans grow more crops a measure of their superiority in agriculture, or is it a measure of the fact that they must farm more intensively, because they have no other income to fall back on. In Perry County, the consensus among local officials, some of whom are of German descent, seems to favor the latter interpreta-

---

8. James E. Collier, *Geography of the Northern Ozark Border Region*, p. 52; Conrad H. Hammar, *Factors Affecting Farm Land Values in Missouri*, p. 47; A. T. Sweet and Robert Wildermuth, *Soil Survey of Cole County, Missouri*, p. 1507.

tion. They give the German full credit for his skills in agriculture and the care with which he handles his land. But, they pointed out that the German farms are too small; the slopes they cultivate are often too steep for safe use under even the best of techniques; and their return per acre is frequently marginal. As a result, one does not see many new and modern farm machinery in the German settlements, except in Lawrence County. What they do have is well kept, but, all too often, it is antiquated. The non-German areas are no better, but since they farm less intensively, they require less sophisticated machinery. Yet, the Germans refuse to accept the contention that alterations in their system of agriculture, such as those already made by their neighbors, would represent progress.

Perry County represents the extreme case of traditional attitudes in agriculture among the Ozark Germans, but the tendency in this direction is evident in all of the German settlements. What it seems to come down to in the final analysis is which of the following two interpretations one accepts: (1) the present situation reflects the superiority of the German's agricultural skills; or (2) the present situation reflects the refusal of the Ozark German to break with tradition. All of the evidence indicates that there is an element of truth in both interpretations.

5. The Germans
Social Characteristics

The German immigrant brought to the United States a substantial array of beliefs, attitudes, and traditions, which sharply contrasted with the prevailing Anglo-derived values of nineteenth-century America. The German immigrant spoke a different language, which he tenaciously clung to until the pressures of World War I forced him to accept English on, at least, a coequal basis with his German language. His religion represented a mixture of conservative to ultraliberal Protestantism and Catholicism, which carried the fear of popery and Rome. He also brought his reputation for intemperance, which conflicted with the Anglo bearers of the puritan and evangelical traditions, his attitudes of thrift, hard work, and conservatism. The German respected the values and traditions of the fatherland, and he made a concerted effort to preserve many of his Old World ways in a numerically superior culture demanding his conformity to the values of Anglo-America.

Religion

Areal patterns of religious groups are among the most effective and sensitive measures of the variable cultural landscape of the United States. This is particularly true with rural areas and ethnic groups. All three major religious groupings (British colonial groups, European immigrant groups, and native American groups) that are found in the United States are represented in the contemporary religious makeup of Missouri (Figure 5–1). As a whole, the dominance of Baptists in the Ozark Highland Region is overwhelming. The Baptists are outnumbered by European immigrant denominations only along the Northern and Eastern Ozark Border regions. The present distributional patterns of religious groups in the Ozarks are intimately tied to the region's settlement history.

The Roman Catholic church was the official church in the area of

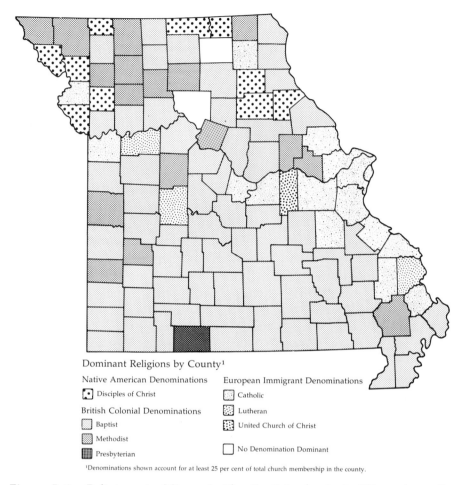

Dominant Religions by County[1]

Native American Denominations

[•] Disciples of Christ

British Colonial Denominations

[ ] Baptist

[▨] Methodist

[▦] Presbyterian

European Immigrant Denominations

[⋯] Catholic

[⋮] Lutheran

[⊞] United Church of Christ

[ ] No Denomination Dominant

[1]Denominations shown account for at least 25 per cent of total church membership in the county.

Figure 5–1. Religions in Missouri. The Baptists dominate Missouri areally. However, they are outnumbered by the Catholic, Lutheran, and United Church of Christ religions in regions with preponderantly ethnic populations. Sources: *National Atlas of the United States,* and Zelinsky, "An Approach to the Religious Geography of the United States. . . ."

Missouri, under both the French and the Spaniards. Other churches were forbidden to operate in Missouri, although the Spaniards did allow the Protestants limited privileges during the late years of their control of Missouri. However, it is probable that many people in Missouri during this period were not members of any particular church or at the most only nominally adherents to Catholicism. Because of the frontier conditions of pre-territorial Missouri, which were so demanding of the pioneer's time, and the isolation of the frontier, the early settlers had little opportunity for religious activities of any kind. With the passing of Louisiana to U.S. control, the situation gradually changed. The arrival of American settlers in large numbers from the East and South was "frequently accompanied and invariably followed by the settlement of some zealous minister in their midst."[1]

Religious bodies such as the Congregationalists and Presbyterians, who believed that a congregation must be organized before a minister could be called, did not succeed well on the frontier. Baptists and Methodists, on the other hand, were organized quite differently and were more successful in adjusting to the conditions of the frontier. The Baptists, with their form of local church government, did not stress formal education for their clergymen, and thus most of the early Baptist ministers were "farmer-preachers." Many of the Baptist ministers migrated along with the early settlers and made the presence of the church felt very soon after the settlers arrived. The Methodists succeeded in the frontier because of the availability of circuit-riding ministers, who were assigned to developing settlements. Thus, Methodist circuit-riders were able to keep up with the expanding frontier. As a result, these two religions were the dominant Protestant denominations in the Ozarks almost from the beginning of American settlement. The Methodist church declined in importance in the Ozarks in later years due to its opposition to slavery.[2]

Because life in the post-frontier period became organized and because preachers who emphasized fear in their "hell and damnation" sermons were less adapted to the conditions of settled life, some religious bodies changed practices such as camp meetings and revivals to be harmonious with more civilized conditions. Many of the varieties of Baptists and Methodists, as well as Pentecostal, Holiness, Assembly of God, Church of God, and other religious bodies, started as schismatic movements that either favored or opposed the post-frontier changes that had such an impact on religion in the Ozarks and elsewhere.[3] During the late nineteenth century, many new congregations were formed in the Ozarks by the various sect-type religious bodies then being organized. The number of religious bodies present today in the Ozarks is staggering.

The religious history of the Germans in the Ozarks is less com-

1. Carl E. Schneider, *The German Church on the American Frontier*, p. 42.
2. Lawrence M. Hepple, *The Rural Church in Missouri*, part 1, *Introduction*, pp. 8–9; Sydney E. Ahlstrom, *A Religious History of the American People*, p. 661.
3. Hepple, *The Rural Church*, part 1, *Introduction*, p. 9.

plicated. The German religious denominations present in the Ozarks are directly from three Old World religions: (1) Roman Catholic, (2) German Lutheran, and (3) German Reformed.[4] Undoubtedly, some of the early German settlers in the Ozarks who had come from the eastern United States did join non-German churches. However, those who arrived later in large numbers went directly to the Ozarks from Germany. In most cases, clergymen either accompanied the immigrants or followed soon after. Their large numbers and compact settlements facilitated the establishment of cohesive congregations at the time of initial settlement in the Ozarks. Their early dependence on the German language necessitated its use in church services, and this was possible only in the German churches. Thus, there was no period of religious adjustment in the German settlements, during which time non-German churches could have made inroads and established themselves in the German settlements.

Once established, the authority of German churches in the German areas went almost unchallenged. Since the Germans bought out their non-German neighbors almost immediately, the non-German and his church retreated in most of the German areas in the Ozarks. Numerous examples of abandoned non-German churches encircled by German landowners are encountered in the Ozark German settlements. Two active non-German rural churches were found in which more than 90 per cent of the landowners within a one-mile radius of both churches are German. These churches are near the edge of German settlements. Several active non-German rural churches of substantial age are found just beyond the boundaries of German settlements, suggesting that a portion of their rural hinterlands had been usurped by the expanding German settlements.

German and non-German churches differ in several respects, in addition to church doctrine. German churches are larger than non-German churches. Hepple reports that churches in rural German areas of Missouri averaged 160.2 members, while rural churches in the Ozarks, excluding most of the German settled areas, averaged 83.2 members. On the other hand, the frequency of distribution of rural churches is greater in the non-German areas. The average number of rural churches per township in all of Missouri is 5.1.[5]

4. The German Reformed Church has gone through several mergers. The most recent merger resulted in the creation of the United Church of Christ in 1957.

5. Lawrence M. Hepple, *The Rural Church in Missouri*, part 2, *Rural Religious Groups*, p. 43.

In a random sampling of twenty rural townships in the Ozarks, ten German and ten non-German, the average number of churches per township is 4.7.[6] The ten German townships average 2.6 churches, while the ten non-German townships average 6.7 churches.

These differences are the result of several factors. In the latter decades of the nineteenth century, competition among the various Protestant churches was intense in the Old Stock American areas in the Ozarks:

> There was . . . a large amount of competition among the four main religious bodies [in Missouri]. If the Baptists organized a congregation in a settlement, it was not long until the Disciples of Christ, the Methodists, or the Presbyterians started another in the same settlement. . . . This competition undoubtedly was a factor in getting a larger number of congregations organized than could possibly survive over a long period of time.[7]

Added to this competition among the various churches was the emergence of many small religious bodies in the Old Stock American areas in the Ozarks. In the Old Stock American areas, 40.7 per cent of the total congregations are classified as sect-type churches, compared to a comparable figure of 5.7 per cent for the German areas.[8]

The results of the proliferation of rural churches in the Old Stock American areas of the Ozarks are visibly manifested in the region's rural landscape. Churches tend to occupy small structures often not designed originally to serve as houses of worship. Many rural churches stand abandoned, and an equally large number remains active, but in a state of poor repair. Rural churches in the Old Stock American areas are clustered at crossroads, with as many as three to four visible from one vantage point. Occasionally, all but one of the churches in a cluster will be abandoned, with the remaining one serving as the "community church," or simply "union church." Two structures used for religious purposes in the Old Stock American areas but absent in German areas are the brush arbor, which appears to be on its way out, and the large tent used throughout the region during the warm months for revival meetings.

6. The data were obtained from land assessment and tax books in Carter, Douglas, Gasconade, Osage, Ozark, Perry, Ste. Genevieve, and Shannon counties between June and September of 1972.

7. Hepple, *The Rural Church*, part 1, *Introduction*, p. 11.

8. George T. Blume, "Spatial and Social Relationships of Rural Churches in Six Selected Areas of Missouri," p. 37.

Two observations made nearly a half century past concerning rural churches in the United States appear both relevant and valid for much of the Ozarks today. First, much of the region appears to be overchurched, and in Galpin's words, "It is undeniable that any honest student of conditions in rural churches is confronted by staggering and depressing statistics of overchurching . . . in some sections. . . . There are ten times as many churches for every thousand persons in some of the rural districts of the United States as there are in New York City. . . . It really seems that the fewer churches a county is able to afford, the more it is apt to have."[9]

The patterns of religious affiliation in the German areas in the Ozarks are quite different. There is usually one church per settlement. The religious homogeneity of individual German communities reflects the original homogeneity of the early settlers. As previously mentioned, there has been relatively little switching by the Germans to non-German denominations and from one German church to another. This is especially true of the two major German denominations in the Ozarks—Lutheran and Catholic. The doctrinal differences between the two are so great as to preclude any significant rate of defection from one to the other.

Osage and Perry counties reflect the religious homogeneity of the German settlements. In western Osage County, the Catholic church, dominated by Germans, remains supreme to this day. The Lutheran church is dominant in southeastern Perry County, while German Catholics dominate the south-central portion. The dominance of German Catholics carries north into Ste. Genevieve County, where every German settlement in the county is Catholic. In the western Ozark German settlements of Benton County, the Lutheran church is nearly as dominant. There is strong religious unity in the original and later German settlements of all four counties.

The boundaries separating the different German denominations are, occasionally, quite sharp. In Perry County, Federal Highway 61 is recognized as the boundary between Catholics to the west and Lutherans to the east. The recognition of the highway as a religious boundary may well have influenced the location of Catholics and Lutherans in the county since the turn of the century to the extent that it now represents an almost absolute religious divide. Interviews with farmers on both sides of the highway

9. Charles J. Galpin, *Empty Churches: The Rural Urban Dilemma*, p. 6.

elicited some comments to the effect that each group prefers to remain on its own side of the highway, and each hoped the other would do the same.

Gasconade County presents a somewhat different picture, with all three German denominations intermixed geographically within the county. However, the German settlements in Gasconade County were founded ostensibly on social and not religious grounds. This also holds true with areas to the east of Gasconade County. The railroad settlements in southwestern Missouri are also represented by all three German denominations. However, even with the railroad settlements there has been a degree of religious sorting out with passing time. The German settlement at Freistatt has evolved from an original minority of German Lutherans around the village of Freistatt to a 98 per cent majority within three miles of the village today.

These conditions, particularly the exclusiveness of territory, have resulted in few but large churches in the German areas of the Ozarks. The difference in the number of churches in the German and non-German areas is quite apparent in Gasconade County. Both Hermann, a German town at the northern end of the county, and Owensville, a largely non-German town in the southern part of the county, have similar populations (2,658 and 2,416 respectively), but the number of churches in each is quite different. Hermann has a total of four churches, or one for every 664.5 inhabitants, excluding rural parishioners. Owensville, by contrast, has fifteen churches, or one for every 160.8 inhabitants.

The large size of rural German churches in the Ozarks is a very visible feature in the landscape. Trinity Lutheran at Freistatt is immense in proportion to the village, which numbers only slightly more than 100 inhabitants (Figure 5–2). This particular church was voted one of the top twelve Protestant churches in the United States in 1950 in a poll of 100,000 ministers, who had taken into consideration things such as how well the church had served the community.[10] Similarly, the Evangelical and Reformed Church in Hermann is as prominent as the Gasconade County courthouse. Westphalia, a German village in Osage County, with a population of 332, contains only one church, in this case Catholic, and it, too, is of immense size for such a small village. These three churches are exceptionally large, but the average German church is still

10. "Great Churches in America: Trinity Lutheran, Freistatt, Missouri," *The Christian Century*, pp. 753–59.

Figure 5–2.   Trinity Lutheran Church in Freistatt.

considerably larger than the average non-German church in the Ozarks.

To determine if differences exist in the church structures in the German and non-German areas, data were collected on 276 rural churches (Table 5–1). Churches in the rural German areas tend to be in better condition than churches in the non-German rural areas. However, churches in both German and non-German rural areas are generally well kept when compared to farmsteads in the same localities. The difference in this regard between the German and non-German areas may well reflect the greater economic strain of the non-German churches. The construction material of the churches suggest the greater endurance of the German churches. The greater use of limestone and brick in church construction in the German areas may have also resulted partly from both the German preference for brick and their striving for permanence.

The frequency of abandoned churches is much higher in the non-German areas, and many rural non-German churches appear to be deteriorating to a state of abandonment. The higher rate of abandonment is probably due to the large number of already precariously small rural churches per unit of area in the non-German areas competing for a steadily diminishing rural popula-

Table 5–1

Characteristics of Rural Churches in the Ozarks for German and Non-German Traverse Areas

	German Areas	Non-German Areas
Total Number of Churches	102	174
*Condition**		
Good	96 (94%)	118 (68%)
Medium	6 (6%)	42 (24%)
Poor	0 (0%)	14 (8%)
*Construction Material**		
Frame	16 (16%)	132 (76%)
Brick, Limestone, and Block	86 (84%)	42 (24%)
Abandoned Churches	4 (4%)	40 (23%)

* Abandoned churches not included in calculations.
Source: Field data sheets.

tion. Gregory notes that a higher percentage of the ministers in the Old Stock American areas reported having an occupation in addition to preaching.[11]

Assessing any differences in the church's role in the life of the community in the German and non-German areas of the Ozarks is beyond the scope of this study. However, some observations based on interviews with clergymen and laymen, as well as a general feel for the areas under study, can be offered.

It appears that the German church, of whatever denomination, occupies a more central role in the life of the community than does the non-German church. German churches in the Ozarks have a substantial degree of continuity, in terms of both time and membership. The church, typically, has been in the community in nearly its present form since the early settlement, and its membership traces through at least several generations. In the non-German areas, where churches have come and gone to a much larger extent, membership in a given church is less permanent. The greater number of churches in a given community in the non-German areas would appear to weaken the influence on community life of any one church. The German church is more central to the life of the community, because it is commonly the only church in the community. Furthermore, in German areas, a relatively large

11. Cecil L. Gregory, *Rural Social Areas in Missouri*, p. 35.

proportion of the population is made up of church members, and attendance is high.[12]

The German church, particularly the Lutheran and Catholic churches, utilizes parochial schools in the majority of cases, thus gaining a greater influence over their membership. In Altenburg, all Missouri Synod-Lutheran children attend the parochial school through the eighth grade, which in its physical plant is far superior to the village's public school, which is attended only by children from the American Lutheran church. A rather unique situation regarding parochial education involved the German Catholic community of Westphalia in Osage County. Westphalia originally had only parochial schools. However, in the earlier part of this century, public schools were established in the village. From 1933 to 1951, the public schools in Westphalia were staffed largely by Catholic nuns, and the parochial schools were, in effect, funded with local tax money. Since there were only a few non-Catholic families in the vicinity, there were no recorded complaints about the situation.

The use of the German language in church services until recently in many German settlements placed the church as the preserver of the cultural traditions of the community.[13] No medium is comparable in carrying on culture in the non-German areas. German churches appear to be economically in a better position to assert themselves in community matters than are non-German churches.

In one rural German settlement, the pastor of a Lutheran congregation summed up the role of the church by noting that "virtually nothing happens in this community that does not in some way involve the church." Gregory notes in general that the churches in the German settlements, "probably furnish a more inclusive social program to their members than other denominations," and, "More of the social interaction would be expected to revolve around the church . . . than in areas where these denominations are less important."[14]

The status of the German church in the Ozarks today reflects many of the patterns previously discussed. The German church remains paramount in the older areas of German settlement. It has shown some growth, in the sense that new congregations have been formed, but it has not spread out into the interior Ozarks.

12. Ibid., p. 27.
13. Ibid., p. 25.
14. Ibid., p. 28.

Language

The widespread use of German as a functional language is largely a thing of the past in the Ozarks, as it is in most rural areas of the United States. The rise and demise of German as the primary language of Germans in the Ozarks parallels more than any other single factor the Americanization of all German-speaking peoples in the region.

In the early days of settlement, German was of necessity the language, and the only language, of most German immigrants in the Ozarks. In addition to being the spoken language among the Germans, it was used in church, school, newspapers, and periodicals. And, it was through the church, school, and printing press that later efforts were made to maintain the bilingual character of Germans in Missouri.

The role of the church in preserving German culture in the Ozarks, including language, varied with the different denominations. Protestant churches, on the whole, made a more conscious effort to isolate their members in order to maintain the European traditions of the church. In the case of Lutherans, "the German language was summoned to duty not only as a means of communication but also as a means of identification and preservation." The continuance of the German language in church services was facilitated by the constant flow of German Lutheran theological students to the United States until the end of the nineteenth century.[15]

The position of the Catholic church in the Ozarks, and in the United States, was somewhat different. First, Catholics were of diverse ethnic backgrounds, compared to the German Protestant denominations. German culture, and in particular language, was never seen as the bulwark supporting the church. There were many voices in the Catholic church during the nineteenth century who advocated an Americanization of all Catholics in the United States. The adoption of the English language in church services was a basic step in this direction. Of all Catholics, however, Germans were most fervently opposed to the Americanization of their church, and where their settlements were large, they were

15. Frederick C. Luebke, "The Immigrant Condition as a Factor Contributing to the Conservatism of the Lutheran Church—Missouri Synod," p. 19; Robert M. Toepper, "Rationale For Preservation of the German Language in the Missouri Synod of the Nineteenth Century," p. 156.

often able to retain the national or ethnic character of their parishes.[16]

The German Catholic in the nineteenth-century Ozarks found himself under additional pressure to Americanize. He was not only a "foreigner" to his neighbors, but he was also a member of a church thought to be controlled from foreign soil. In essence, he had to try harder to establish himself as a loyal American. One means of indicating his willingness to become a true American was to accept English as his language.

The Germans' attitude toward education was the same as that toward their religion. Generally, German Protestants were more insistent that their children be taught German than were Catholics. Therefore, it was necessary to establish parochial schools, although a few public schools in areas dominated by Germans did employ the German language to varying degrees. In 1870, there were approximately one hundred German schools in Missouri; half were Lutheran and half were Catholic. Officially, most Germans justified the parochial school system and the use of German on religious grounds; however, "Unofficially . . . many Missourians viewed the parochial school system primarily as an agency for the preservation of German culture." The use of the printing press as a means of resisting language assimilation among Germans in Missouri followed similar patterns. In 1870, approximately seventy German-language periodicals were being printed in Missouri. Finally, there were the various fraternal orders, lodges, and mutual aid societies, which encouraged the preservation of German culture, including language.[17]

The continuing acculturation and assimilation of Germans in the Ozarks, as well as pressures from World Wars I and II to be American, have exacted a heavy toll on the use of the German language in the Ozarks. Yet, German is still spoken in several areas of the Ozarks, and there are indications that it was quite widely spoken up to the 1950s.

For example, in 1937, a Dr. Rholeder erected a small hospital in Freistatt and named it "Das Klein Krankenhaus," suggesting that the language was still used to some extent.[18] In Ste. Genevieve County, it was reported that an interpreter was hired by the local

16. Ahlstrom, *A Religious History*, pp. 825–42.
17. Lewis W. Spitz, "The Germans in Missouri: A Preliminary Study," p. 106–8; Toepper, "Preservation of the German Language," p. 164.
18. *Lawrence County, Missouri, 1845–1970: A Brief History*, p. 63.

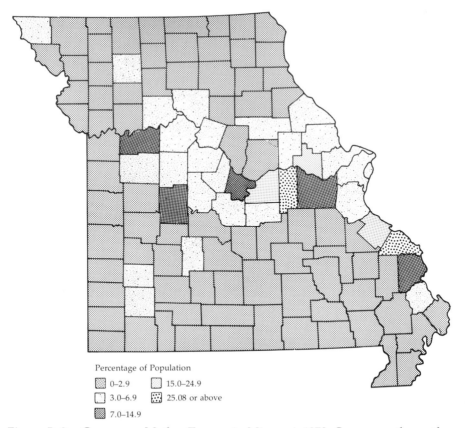

Percentage of Population

▨ 0–2.9   ▢ 15.0–24.9

▢ 3.0–6.9   ▨ 25.08 or above

▨ 7.0–14.9

Figure 5–3.   German as Mother Tongue in Missouri, 1970. German as the mother tongue is fading rapidly in the German settlements of Missouri. Only in the larger settlements (Perry, Ste. Genevieve, Gasconade, and Osage counties), has the German language survived to any extent. Source: *United States Census of Population, 1970.*

draft board during World War II to process the young men coming in from the Weingarten area.[19] Finally, a German Catholic priest, from Hungary, reported that his favorite pastime is to visit the barbershop in Altenburg, Missouri, where he said the most perfect High German dialect he has ever heard is spoken.

The extent to which German is spoken in the Ozarks today is indicated in Figure 5–3.[20] The two areas where the German lan-

19. This story was confirmed by interviews with several people. Apparently, the young men all spoke some English but needed help in taking the written examinations.

20. *Mother tongue* is defined by the U.S. Census Bureau as the language of early childhood.

guage has fared best are the two most concentrated German areas: (1) Gasconade-Osage counties; and (2) Perry-Ste. Genevieve counties. The figures in Figure 5–3 are based on total population, which for most counties was not entirely made up of Germans. Table 5–2 presents the same information for selected counties but excludes the non-German portion from the calculations. The aforementioned core areas are still apparent; however, several additional counties emerge as strongholds of spoken German.

Table 5–2

German as Mother Tongue of German-Descended Population for Selected Ozark Counties, 1970

County	Approximate percentage of county's population of German descent*	German as Mother Tongue	
		Percentage of total population	Percentage of German-descended population
Benton	30%	13.5	44.9
Cole	50%	10.2	20.4
Osage	70%	18.5	26.5
Gasconade	85%	27.0	31.8
Ste. Genevieve	65%	16.2	25.0
Perry	70%	25.6	36.6
Warren	90%	18.1	20.1
Lawrence	15%	3.2	24.6

* Estimates based on familiarity with the areas involved.
Source: *1970 Census of Population, General Social and Economic Characteristics,* Table 119, pp. 423–32.

Many factors contribute to the significant percentage of the population of areas in the Ozarks where the German language is still registered as the mother tongue. These areas originally had a large German-speaking population and were dominated by the Old Lutheran and Roman Catholic churches employing parochial schools as a means of retaining the German language.

In the core of the Northern and Eastern Ozark Border regions, the Germans came early and in large numbers. They viewed themselves as co-founders, rather than guests in a well-established commonwealth. They came at a time when their language was competing for large-scale coexistence with English. At the time, it did not seem unrealistic to hope that Missouri might emerge as a bilingual state, at least with regard to education.

Several other factors affected the success of maintaining the German language in the Ozarks. St. Louis had emerged as the spiritual capital for both orthodox Lutherans and Catholics of German extraction and thus exerted a positive influence in the efforts made to preserve everything German in the Ozark settlements. The Old Lutherans and Roman Catholics employed their own school systems. They differed in one important respect, however. Almost from the beginning, the Catholic church stressed the bilingual aspect of parochial education, while the Lutherans tried tenaciously to preserve the predominance of German over English within their schools. In addition, the Old Lutherans carried the doctrine of "Language Saves Faith" further than any other denomination.

The degree of linguistic homogeneity, in terms of number of dialects, affected the success of efforts at language maintenance. The greater the variety of dialects, the greater the linguistic instability. The settlements in the Northern Ozark Border, particularly the Hermann area, represent mixtures of different dialects. This is also true of most of the German Catholic settlements. In Hermann, five different dialects have contributed to the German spoken today, commonly referred to as "Hermann German." In the Catholic settlements in the Eastern Ozark Border, Badish, Bavarian, and High German are among the dialects commonly represented within a single parish. The purest settlements, from a linguistic point of view, are the Lutheran settlements, and particularly the Saxon settlements in Perry County.

In eastern Perry County, virtually everyone is a Saxon and speaks a Saxon dialect very similar to High German. In addition, the Saxons use their own schools almost exclusively. The area is also somewhat isolated, and, to this day, few outsiders spend much time there. As a result, the Lutherans in Perry County stand far above the other German settlements in the retention of their native tongue. In 1930, nearly 80 per cent of church services were still being conducted in German. Today, Altenburg is one of only two communities in the Ozarks still offering German church services on a regular basis. Frohna and Wittenberg, also in Perry County, discontinued German services on a regular basis, because they could not secure a pastor capable of conducting services in German.

The percentage of the population listing German as the mother tongue in Perry County is approximately one-fourth of the total population and one-third of all Germans. However, the percentage for only the Saxon area in eastern Perry County is somewhere between 66 and 75 per cent. Field data were collected on the degree to which German is still spoken in several residencies in eastern

Perry County. Although the figures are not exact, it was concluded that approximately 60 per cent of the residents still speak fluent German. Included are many older people whose accent was a tip-off to their mother tongue and, surprisingly, many younger people of pre-school age on up. Although German is still spoken to some extent in all of the German settlements, Perry County is the only area where German is used to any degree in the conduct of day-to-day business.

It should be added that German is on the decline in Perry County, as it is elsewhere. There are efforts being made through the church to slow the rate of language assimilation. And in Hermann, students in most grades are again studying the German language in an effort to revive its usage among younger people in that community.[21] However, not one person that was interviewed in any of the German settlements was optimistic about the future of the German language in the Ozarks. Apparently, two or perhaps three generations remain before the German language will not be spoken in the Ozarks.

Attitudes on Temperance

The German's appetite for alcoholic beverages, particularly beer, is a legend and needs little elaboration. The beer garden was a basic cultural institution the German brought with him to the United States. As a result of his attitudes on temperance, the German was accused of bringing an increase in both taverns and drinking to the United States.[22] The German's intemperance represented an extreme social deviation in the Missouri Ozarks, a region dominated by Baptists representing some of the most fundamentalist religious beliefs of all Old Stock Americans.

From the earliest days, the brewing of beer and the making of wine in the Ozarks have been dominated by people of German background. Of the 131 breweries using family names that existed in Missouri between 1810 and 1971, 93 per cent were owned and operated by Germans. Their distribution shows an overwhelming correlation with areas of German settlement. Some of the old breweries are still intact, although the majority of them did not reopen following the repeal of prohibition (Figure 5–4). In addition to the brewing of beer, the Ozark Germans developed a large-scale

21. Samuel F. Harrison, *History of Hermann, Missouri*, p. 5.
22. Hildegard Binder Johnson, "The Location of German Immigrants in the Middle West," p. 12; Edward A. Ross, *The Old World in the New*, p. 228.

Figure 5-4.   Anheuser-Brenner Brewery in Wittenberg.

winemaking industry, particularly along the Northern Ozark Border, as well as a widespread development of small-scale winemaking throughout the Ozarks at an early date. Sauer attributes the continued German immigration into the Northern Ozark Border settlements after 1848 to the prosperity brought by the conversion of grapes into wine. At one time, Stone Hill Winery at Hermann was the second largest winery in the United States, and, at the turn of the century, Hermann exported more wines than any other town (Figure 5-5).[23]

The passage of the Eighteenth Amendment instituting prohibition confirmed the differences in attitudes regarding temperance of Old Stock Americans and Germans in the Ozarks (Figure 5-6). Methodists, Baptists, and Presbyterians in the Ozarks strongly supported prohibition, whereas the Germans as strongly opposed it.[24] The election results for the Twenty-first Amendment repealing prohibition showed the same basic patterns of continued support for prohibition over much of the Ozarks, with the German areas as obvious exceptions. Interviews with longtime German residents of the Ozarks indicated that even during prohibition the brewing of beer simply shifted in the German areas from a commercial operation to a home industry.

    23. *Missouri Breweries, 1810–1971;* Carl O. Sauer, *The Geography of the Ozark Highland of Missouri,* p. 170; *Held's Stone Hill Winery, Hermann, Missouri.*
    24. Ernest Cherrington, *Anti-Saloon League Yearbook, 1909,* pp. 212–15.

Figure 5–5.   Stone Hill Winery in Hermann.

The current patterns of beer consumption in the Ozarks continue to reflect the ethnic divisions of the region. However, the pattern is somewhat confused now by the lake regions of south-central and southwestern Missouri, which cater largely to tourists on a seasonal basis. The brewing of beer is now confined to the larger urban centers, with St. Louis vying for preeminence with Milwaukee as the nation's leading brewing center. There has been something of a rebirth of winemaking in the Ozarks. The Old Stone Hill Winery at Hermann was reopened in 1960, and several other small wineries in the German areas are again in operation.

The tavern itself is a different institution in the German and non-German areas of the Ozarks. O'Conner's observation that, "The German saloon was as respectable a place, as family oriented as the corner grocery," holds true for the Ozarks.[25] Most taverns in the German areas of the Ozarks serve meals and are frequented by entire families. By contrast, the tavern in the Old Stock American areas of the Ozarks is basically a male-oriented institution, and children, in particular, are rarely seen in such places.

The fact is that drinking is an accepted part of German culture, and no stigma whatsoever is attached to it; although the observa-

25. Richard O'Conner, *The German-Americans: An Informal History,* p. 293.

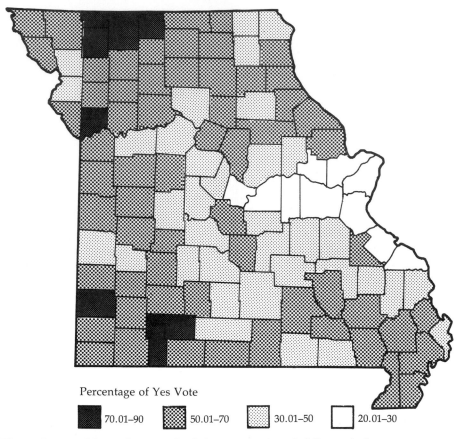

Percentage of Yes Vote

■ 70.01–90   ▨ 50.01–70   ▨ 30.01–50   ☐ 20.01–30

Figure 5–6.   5 November 1915 Prohibition Election. In Missouri, the vote on prohibition was greatly affected by ethnic affiliation. The central and eastern Europeans strongly opposed prohibition while native Americans in Missouri generally
favored the ban on drinking. Source: State of Missouri, *Official Manual*, 1917–
1918.

tion frequently seen in the literature that despite their drinking
Germans rarely become intoxicated and unruly is perhaps ques-
tionable. By contrast, drinking openly and in public places, in
particular, is not an accepted part of Ozark culture. This is reflected by the amount of public drinking, as evidenced by the
frequency of taverns in these areas and by the clientele frequenting
them.

Hyphenism Today

To the casual observer, the German in the Ozarks is distinctive
not so much through his agriculture, architecture, or religion, but

rather through his Teutonic place names and through his efforts to make his cultural heritage known to others by festivals and tourist-generating activities. Very often the German was the first to settle a locale and, therefore, claimed the honor of selecting its name. Place names of distinctly German origin are quite common in the Northern and Eastern Ozark Border regions.

Most German communities in the Ozarks commemorate their heritage through some type of organized festival or celebration. Most are local and not widely advertised. However, the "Maifest" and "Octoberfest" held annually at Hermann are quite widely advertised, and large crowds from Missouri as well as neighboring states attend. Hermann is well suited for such activities in two respects. First, Hermann has the physical appearance of a German village along the Rhine, including the hills, architecture, and town vineyards (Figure 5–7). Second, Hermann is near St. Louis, with its large German population insuring both financial support and crowds. The Hermann festivals have been patterned after those held annually in Frankenmuth, Michigan, and their success grows annually.

Similar efforts in Perry County to commemorate its German heritage have been both more somber and less successful than in

Figure 5–7. Mozart Street in Hermann, reflecting the hilly terrain in the bluff land along the Missouri River.

Hermann. Most of the activities in Perry County have been in the Saxon area and have been centered primarily on the Saxons as the founders of the Missouri Synod of the Lutheran Church. Unlike Hermann, the Saxon area in Perry County is remote, lying one hundred miles south of St. Louis and twelve miles east of the interstate on a road that dead ends at the Mississippi River, although there is a small ferry at Wittenberg that crosses the Mississippi. There is a billboard on the old highway, which has since been superseded by the interstate, that invites the passing tourist to visit the Saxon settlements. For the tourist who does visit eastern Perry County, numerous historic points of interest have been marked by signs, and the log-cabin seminary, Saxon Memorial, and Lutheran churches are there for his inspection. The East Perry County Historical Society would like to have a festival comparable to those in Hermann, but they lack the funding needed to restore buildings and otherwise "prepare" the area. However, for the student of Lutheran history and German culture, eastern Perry County has much to offer, including the only German coronet band in Missouri.

The number of German festivals in or near the Ozarks has increased over the past several years, as have community festivals of all types. To accommodate larger crowds, the German festival held annually at Belleville, Illinois, has been moved to the St. Louis waterfront. The small German community of Lockwood initiated an annual "Strassenfest" in 1973. And Hermann, encouraged no doubt by the success of the "Maifest," has inaugurated an "Octoberfest" and an annual wine festival. The increase in community festivals during the past decade appears to be a response to the large number of tourists now going to the Ozarks. Although the tourist's prime interest in the Ozarks might be fishing, water sports, or just camping, he might also have the time, money, and interest to visit a broiler festival, bluegrass festival, Kewpie doll festival, copperhead hunt, or German festival. The themes the various festivals are patterned on are really of secondary importance. If the community is ethnic, that may well provide the theme; however, once the decision is made to stage a community festival, the potential themes to be selected from are innumerable.

To his neighbor, there are more subtle indications of the Ozark German's hyphenated character. Approximately fifty non-German farmers in Perry County were asked for their impressions of their German neighbors. The interviews were casual and, although hardly scientific, were revealing. Most all of those interviewed are aware of their neighbors' German extraction, and most attach some significance to it. Some typical comments supposedly reflective of their neighbors' German ancestry are:

"They don't throw anything away."

"If you're not one of them, forget it."

"They take more pride in their barns than their houses."

"They still speak broken English."

"They are Germans all right."

"You know they won't go to public schools."

"They live in the past too much."

"They still call us English."

"They won't listen to anybody but their own kind."

"They give the whole county a German flavor."

"They don't make much money, but they live good."

"They like their flowers and gardens."

"They are very honest, but clannish."

"You won't find any welfare over there."

The German's attitude toward his own ethnicity varies, but as one might expect, his attitude is a favorable one. Virtually all those interviewed are proud of their German background. There is much disagreement among them as to the degree to which their present character reflects their ethnic background. It appears that their neighbors attach more significance to their ethnic background than they themselves do. However, each community seems to have one zealot who sees his life's work as the preservation of the community's German heritage. As one farmer put it, "They are trying to preserve today what we tried so hard thirty years ago to forget." One would have to conclude that as of today the Ozark German sees himself as an American and not as a hyphenated German-American.

6. Other Europeans

In contrast to the Germans in the Ozarks, whose settlements are large and often dominate entire townships, the other European settlements in the Ozarks are mainly small and are generally dispersed in such a way that they constitute a minority even in their core areas. Their history differs from that of the Germans. Because most non-German European settlements were small, and established at a late date, they were, on the whole, rather easily absorbed into the dominant Anglo society around them. There are exceptions. The French at Old Mines, who came early, have managed, more through neglect than by choice, to retain certain aspects of their French culture. The Italians at Rosati are distinctive through their viticulture. The Poles at Pulaskifield retained use of their national language until quite recently.

On the other hand, although one rarely encounters a Frenchman in Ste. Genevieve, the long lots south of the village indicate the old French stronghold there. A highway sign in Swedeborg suggests a community of Swedes, but its residents proclaim they are Ozarkians.

Processes and Patterns

Non-German ethnic groups settled in the Ozarks around 1860, except for the early French. The Germans settled in the Ozarks in the early 1840s. This difference of approximately two decades in the date of settlement of these groups is very important. During this period, the population of Missouri more than tripled, from 387,702 to 1,182,012.[1] The Germans came early for the purpose of settlement and saw themselves as co-founders, whereas the remaining ethnic groups came when society was organized and values were already established in the Ozarks.

During the period of the early German settlements, the forces

1. *Fifteenth Census of the United States, 1930: Population,* vols. 1, 2.

of societal organization were not well developed. The settler was not tied to the state nor to any established system of cultural values and norms, since, stated simply, none existed. By the time a value system reflecting the majority's attitudes had evolved, the German had his own and resisted new ideas.

The later Europeans faced very different conditions. Society was now organized, and there were rules that newcomers, ethnic or nonethnic, were expected to conform to. By this time — the 1860s — there was relatively little opportunity of escaping the pressures of the dominant society through isolation. The best land was long since settled, and the remaining large tracts offered limited economic possibilities. While the Philadelphia Society had its choice of location, and the Saxons were able to virtually shut the rest of the world out, those who came later had to settle among and amidst a dominant nonethnic population. The result was that these European groups were pressured to conform, or Americanize, from the day they came into the Ozarks.

The less compact nature of the later European settlements can be seen in the contrast between the Swedish settlement at Verona and the German settlement at Freistatt (Figure 6–1). With a few exceptions, there is no indication that the later European ethnic settlements placed a high value on exclusiveness of territory, or compact group settlement. To some extent, this could have been done in time by buying out nongroup members, as the Freistatt Germans did. Therefore, the higher rate of dispersion of the later European settlements has resulted from both an inability to establish compact settlements early and a reluctance to pursue compact settlement as a long-range goal.

The small size of the later European settlements further contributed to their rapid absorption into the Anglo-dominated society of the Ozarks. Most of these settlements numbered about twenty-five to fifty families. Very few were enlarged through subsequent immigration, such as the chain migration that continually enlarged the German settlements. It would have been impossible to conduct primary relations within the ethnic group under such conditions. In general, their small size was not reinforced by neighboring groups of similar backgrounds. As a result, if the group chose to attempt to preserve its Old World cultural values and traditions, it received no support — direct or psychological — from neighbors, none of whom shared their predicament of a cultural identity. Such a condition favored assimilation at the expense of group co-

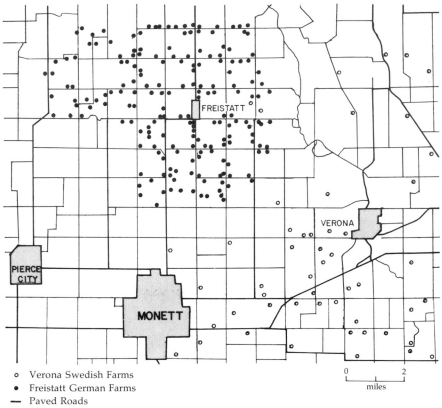

o Verona Swedish Farms
• Freistatt German Farms
— Paved Roads
— Unpaved Roads

Figure 6–1. Location of Swedish and German Farmers in Lawrence County, 1972. The German settlement at Freistatt is a typical compact German agricultural settlement. The Swedish settlement at Verona represents the more dispersed pattern typical of the later European settlements.

hesion.[2] This is not to say that all aspects of the group's culture had to be abandoned. Their methods of agriculture, crop, livestock associations, and settlement characteristics could survive without being culturally at odds with those of their neighbors, if they were adaptable to conditions in the Ozarks.

To some extent, leadership, or the presence of "elites," was also fundamental in determining group cohesion. With such leadership, a group, regardless how small, can often resist the pressures to assimilate.[3] This was the case with the Germans who had, perhaps,

2. Frederick C. Luebke, *Immigrants and Politics: The Germans of Nebraska, 1880–1900*, p. 44.

3. S. N. Eisenstadt, "The Place of Elites and Primary Groups in the Absorption of New Immigrants in Israel," pp. 222–31.

too many leaders. Among the smaller European settlements, this leadership was usually lacking. Several groups mentioned this lack of leadership as a major factor in their inability, or lack of interest, in establishing a group focus. Because of this lack of cultural leadership, no effort was made among most of the smaller European settlements to preserve their native language. In fact, the opposite often happened; the children of the immigrants were encouraged to speak English, even at home. It certainly would have been impractical to attempt to retain their native language for all purposes among such small settlements. Generally, with the passing on of the original settlers, their native language fell into almost total disuse.

This process was partly accelerated by the necessity to conduct day-to-day business in English. Since most of the merchants and others with whom they had daily dealings were not group members, they had little choice in the matter. In some cases, this carried over to religion, where those who were members of ethnically mixed religions, as the Methodists, had to adopt a language acceptable to all, which was English. In other cases, those who joined nonethnic churches — and many did become Baptists — were forced to convert to English at an early date.

The attitude of most of these groups, which was often one favoring rapid assimilation, led to marriage outside the group and relegated the group's ethnicity to a level of low importance. The important point here is that these activities are primary in the sense that they affect the values and traditions of the group at the most basic level and go beyond the measures required simply to exist in an alien culture. As time passed, the role of these groups regarding their ethnicity passed from a sense of participational identification to one of historical identification.[4]

Case Studies

To further, and more specifically, explore the general findings on the previous pages, six ethnic groups were singled out for detailed treatment. They have been selected to demonstrate the various degrees of assimilation and the major factors involved therein. The French Waldensians at Monett and the Swedes at Verona represent the groups approaching nearly complete assimilation. The Swiss near Hermann represent the groups who settled amidst

4. Milton M. Gordon, *Assimilation in American Life: The Role of Race, Religion, and National Origins*, p. 32.

other ethnic groups—usually Germans—and underwent assimilation on two levels. The Poles at Pulaskifield represent a high level of material assimilation, but with a high degree of ethnic awareness still present. The Italians at Rosati represent a substantial loss of ethnic character, but with certain aspects of their ethnic heritage still detectable in the landscape. Finally, the French at Old Mines represent the retardation of the processes of assimilation through both isolation and poverty.

The method used to analyze the evolution of the cultural expression of these groups is similar to, and adopted from, that developed by Bjorklund.[5] The analyses will focus on how these groups perceived, evaluated, and acted with regard to the problems and circumstances that confronted them after settling in the Ozarks, with particular reference to how these matters affected their ethnic character. The emphasis in each case will be on the processes of cultural appraisal and will involve, but not be limited to, innovation, selection, and continuation.

Swedish Immigrants at Verona

The Swedish settlement near Verona exists in the sense that descendents of the original colonists still live in the vicinity and, in many cases, operate the original farms. However, there remains very little ethnic identity among them. Other than a natural pride in their ancestry, very few of those interviewed attach any significance to their Swedish background. A few older residents representing the few remaining members of the second generation can still speak Swedish, but they pointed out that they rarely have occasion to do so. Several interviewees mentioned that Swedish farmers in the area are involved in dairying and that represents their link with the past. By all significant measures, this group would be classified as completely assimilated.

The factors that led to the assimilation of the Verona Swedes are numerous, but all seem to be related to one central issue: there never was a serious effort made to prevent their assimilation. There is even some question as to whether or not the group viewed the perpetuation of their ethnic character in the Ozarks as desirable. Considering the makeup of the colony, this is not really surprising. The Swedes were assembled in New York City by the Frisco Railroad and transported to Missouri in three contingents over a two-year period. They were not a homogeneous group; many had never

5. Elaine M. Bjorklund, "Ideology and Culture Exemplified in Southwestern Michigan," pp. 227–41.

met before coming to the Ozarks. They were of several religions, and some converted to nonethnic churches shortly after their arrival in the Ozarks.

They apparently had no cultural or religious leader, or, at least, no one alive today recalls ever hearing a mention of one. Although three of their churches were referred to as Swedish, one was, in fact, organized and served by a German minister from nearby Freistatt.[6] Some older residents recalled hearing of Swedish services, but, apparently, they were short-lived. Although they resent to some extent to be stereotyped as Ozarkian, as do many residents of the Springfield Plain, those interviewed could recall no restrictions in their interpersonal relations that were based on ethnic considerations.

The disinterest in establishing a cohesive ethnic colony is seen in their settlement pattern (Figure 6–1). Their farms are quite dispersed because, according to interviews, settlers considered establishing a compact ethnic colony as secondary to obtaining good land. Furthermore, many did not even stay in the Verona vicinity. Quite a number soon moved to Springfield, where a Swedish church was established.[7] Some Swedish farmers, apparently from the Verona settlement, are scattered for a radius of thirty miles around Verona. This, again, suggests that the original colony was not very cohesive.

It appears that the Verona Swedes accepted the advise of John Quincy Adams, who said in 1818 of the then incoming European immigrants:

> They must cast off the European skin, never again to resume it. They must look forward to their posterity rather than backward to their ancestors; they must be sure that whatever their own feelings may be, those of their children will cling to the prejudices of this country.[8]

French Waldensians at Monett

The French Waldensians differ significantly from the Verona Swedes, yet there are certain similarities between the two groups. The Waldensians were a more cohesive group at the time of settlement, and their settlement had a sense of colony about it. Yet today, they are as fully assimilated as their Swedish neighbors.

The cohesive character of the Waldensians stemmed from their

6. A. W. Haswell, *The Ozark Region: Its History and Its People,* vol. 2, pp. 16–17.
7. Johnathan Fairbanks and Clyde E. Tuck, *Past and Present of Greene County, Missouri,* p. 607.
8. Quoted in Gordon, *Assimilation in American Life,* p. 268.

long history as a distinct but small religious minority in France. The persecution they had suffered in their native homeland undoubtedly intensified their sense of group identity. In this respect, and through their migrations to flee religious persecution, they resemble other Anabaptist groups.

Upon arriving in the Ozarks, the members purchased farms in close proximity to the Frisco. At that time, the only member of the group who could speak English was its minister. The colony was enlarged over the next decade by the arrival of new families from Europe. Although some were Waldensians, most were French and French-speaking Swiss who were affiliated with other Protestant sects. Many were referred to the Monett settlement by the minister of a French evangelical church in New York City.

As a result of both their small number and their mixed religious character, the Waldensians affiliated with the Presbyterian Church in the United States. The period that followed was one of religious unrest. They could not keep a minister, and there were several defections from the colony, with some leaving the area, and others joining different churches in the area, including the Baptist and Mormon churches. Religion, which had been their original basis of unity, had become a bone of contention.

The French language was originally spoken in the settlement. However, the various ministers who served the settlement prior to 1910 spoke either French or English. While a French-speaking minister was in residence, French was the language of the settlement. When he left, the settlement went back to English. This pattern of events occurred five times during their first twenty years in the Ozarks. The American parishioners must have been at a distinct disadvantage when French was the language of the church. Finally, in 1910 French was discontinued in church services. The reasons are that the children lacked proficiency in French, as did the American parishioners, who were becoming more numerous.

Their agriculture was not notably different from their neighbors. They emphasized small grains, with a lesser emphasis on potatoes and corn. They quickly adopted the "free range" method of livestock grazing, which was then prevalent in the Ozarks. Their farms were large for the area, averaging 160 acres. But most of the Waldensians had sufficient capital to purchase large farms. Some of the colonists had been "winegrowers" in France, but viticulture did not develop beyond a few rows of grapes on a number of farms.

Today, the French Waldensian community is still intact. In fact, they have increased their landholdings to some extent in their core area. As a result of their affiliation with the Presbyterian church, intermarriage has become quite common, and no significance is attached to it. There are reminders of their French heritage. French names such as Arnaud, Bertalot, Courdin, Lauteret, and Planchon abound. However, the pronunciation of most has been anglicized. Their church and cemetery, in which 90 per cent of the names are French, are still located in the center of the settlement. A few examples remain of their early architecture, which is unique to the area and bears some similarity to styles in their native Cottian Alps. However, all those interviewed agreed that these are only reminders of the past and are of little practical significance today. They echoed the sentiments of Watts:

> The visitor to the Monett [Waldensian] colony is impressed with its apparent prosperity and its almost complete Americanization. One hears but little French around the Waldensian Church. Some of the older citizens still greet each other in the dialects of the valleys, but all speak English with little or no trace of foreign accent. The Waldenses of Barry County have not clung to their old Waldensian customs, traditions, and celebrations.[9]

Swiss Immigrants near Hermann

The Swiss are among a number of nationalities that settled among the Germans in the Northern and Eastern Border regions. Their settlements were generally small, completely encircled, and often intermixed with the Germans. The Swiss settlement in Gasconade County is located nine miles south of Hermann around the hamlet of Swiss. The Swiss in Gasconade County number more than 300 people, with approximately a third settled among themselves, a third settled in Hermann, and one-third dispersed among the German settlers in the northern half of the county. The Swiss came early to Gasconade County. Swiss immigrants were represented in the Philadelphia Society that founded Hermann. By 1860, the Swiss settlement was well established, and very few Swiss came to Gasconade County thereafter.

The Swiss pattern of assimilation is a double one. First, they were far outnumbered and were encircled by a similar cultural group, the Germans. The differences between a Swiss and a German are no greater than the differences between a Rhinelander and a Hannoverian. In this sense, the Swiss in Gasconade

9. George B. Watts, *The Waldenses in the New World*, pp. 61–73.

County are in no sense "ethnic" in relation to the dominant group. Added to this is the fact that many of the Swiss identified closely with the Germans, as indicated by their presence in the Philadelphia Society. There are no distinctly Swiss churches in Gasconade County. The Swiss attend several of the German churches, which represent all of the German denominations. The Swiss blended into the German-dominated society of Gasconade rather easily and quickly. They became German-Swiss, and, in a sense, willingly rode the cultural coattails of the Germans.

The second level of assimilation involved the Swiss relative to Anglo society. Although there has been significant assimilation in this direction, it has undoubtedly been retarded by the identification of the Swiss with the larger German society around them. Compared to the cultural distance separating the Swiss from the Germans, the distance between the Swiss and Anglo society was indeed great. Without the presence of the Germans forming a cultural buffer zone, the Swiss would probably have been unable to resist quick absorption into Anglo society.

Today, the Swiss in Gasconade County are indistinguishable from the Germans around them. They have intermarried freely with the Germans for more than a century, and more live out among the Germans now than in their own settlement. Many of those interviewed identified themselves as German-Swiss, a condition not uncommon in the old country. Many are of actual German-Swiss ancestry, but the cultural distinctions exist for all. These Swiss are, then, double hyphenates — Swiss-German-Americans.

Poles at Pulaskifield

Compared to the previous ethnic groups, the small Polish settlement at Pulaskifield has retained a remarkable degree of its ethnic character. Polish ethnicity is closely linked with the Catholic church and has been for some time. Repeatedly invaded, dismembered, or partitioned out of existence, and constantly menaced by Protestant Germany or Orthodox Russia, Poland has linked its national identity with Roman Catholicism for centuries. Thus, the parish church and the parochial school in the Ozarks became a substitute for the national existence that had been denied them for so long in Europe. For first-generation immigrants, the Polish language "became the cornerstone that maintained solidarity. They firmly believed that when the language was lost — all was lost." For these reasons, they were willing to make great sacrifices in order to maintain their cultural heritage.[10]

These considerations help explain how a small and poor Polish settlement nearly two hundred miles away from other Polish settlements could retain for a century so much of its national heritage and pride. An example of the intense pride of these Polish settlers was recounted by an elderly Polish farmer from Pulaskifield. In 1896, Archbishop Glennon of St. Louis was about to leave Pierce City on a visit to Pulaskifield, some five miles to the south, when he was approached by forty Polish men riding white horses. The men took their positions and bared their heads while the leaders fired a royal salute. Then they formed two lines and escorted him to the church. It was essential that they have a Polish priest, and until recently they were able to retain them through a seminary in Michigan that assists Polish congregations in such matters.

The Poles have preserved their culture through their church in Pulaskifield. According to interviews with parishioners, the church exerted strong leadership in this area until recently. Their parochial school taught Polish up to 1952, and in 1968 the school was closed. Polish was used in church services until 1955, and 90 per cent of confessions were in Polish up to the mid-1960s. The community remains to this day very close knit and church centered. However, in areas such as settlement characteristics there is nothing to distinguish the Polish farmers at Pulaskifield from their neighbors.

Recently, the rate of assimilation affecting this settlement has increased substantially. In the early 1960s, the Catholic church in the United States withdrew its support from the perpetuation of national or ethnic parishes on the grounds that such institutions forced parishioners into an uncomfortable situation of maintaining dual loyalties. To implement its decision, the church transferred many priests out of ethnic parishes and replaced them with non-ethnic priests. This was the case at Pulaskifield, where the Polish priest was transferred to nearby Pierce City. In his place a priest of non-Polish background and with little interest in preserving Polish culture was assigned to Pulaskifield. Both the Polish priest and his former Polish parishioners viewed the decision regretfully. Undoubtedly, they say, the settlement will rapidly lose any significant vestiges of its already fading Polish character.

10. Sydney E. Ahlstrom, *A Religious History of the American People*, p. 1000; Aloysius J. Wyeislo, "The Polish Catholic Immigrant," p. 183.

Italians at Rosati

The Italian settlement at Rosati is one of the more recent ethnic settlements in the Ozarks, dating only to 1900. In many respects, it has progressed on the continuum of assimilation to a point approaching complete Americanization. Yet, through the vineyards established by the original Italian colonists, Rosati is distinctive.

The cultural decline in the Rosati settlement is not very different from the previously discussed ethnic groups. The settlement is small, having a population of sixty families at its maximum. Perhaps of greater significance, the settlers were destitute at the time of their settlement in Missouri, and their first few years were a struggle to survive.[11] Under such conditions, the fostering of ethnic ways was probably a secondary consideration.

At the time of their settlement in Missouri, most of the colonists spoke only Italian. Since their location was somewhat isolated from American settlers, they were under little pressure to speak English. However, they made only limited efforts to maintain their own language, and today only a few older residents are able to converse in their native tongue. A critical factor was probably the lack of an ethnic cultural leader, like Father Bandini, who accompanied an Italian group in Arkansas. And, Rosati "had no leader like Father Bandini."[12]

The Italians at Rosati are all Catholic, but their religion does not serve them well on ethnic matters. Unlike the Poles who identify their national character directly with and through the church, the Italians view their attachment to the church with much less fervor. In the specific case of Rosati, the church has been of virtually no significance on ethnic matters:

> Rosati never did have an Italian parish priest. While the Catholic faith and the church have remained part of the total culture of the Italians, the priests of the two parishes [Rosati and Tontitown] do not feel themselves an integral part of the two communities. They provide service while remaining on the margin of the community which is Catholic in their eyes, but Italian and social in the eyes of the people.[13]

Velikonja observes several lingering ethnic traits that are still recognizable in the Rosati settlement. He notes their tendency for

11. "Family Reunion at Rosati Recalls Town's Early History," *St. Louis Post Dispatch*.
12. Joseph Velikonja, "The Italian Contribution to the Geographic Character of Tontitown, Arkansas, and Rosati, Missouri," p. 12.
13. Ahlstrom, *A Religious History*, p. 999; Velikonja, "The Italian Contribution," p. 19.

aggregate settlement in a region dominated by dispersed settlement as a deviation from the American norm. Their methods of land use and their attitudes toward the land contrast with normal practices in the Ozarks. Their practices of intensive agriculture and small farms are suggestive of their Mediterranean background. Their practices reflect both a striving for permanence and locational stability:

> Their neighbors took note of the differences, of the methods of cultivation which were unknown to them, and of practices which were considered strange. The Italians leveled the land clearing out brush and forest, at the same time introducing poplars and willows; they planted fruit trees whose economic value was not immediate. Land for the Italians was more than its superficial productivity. It became a symbol of their independence. Most of the land is still in the hands of the original families and of their descendants.

Their agriculture apparently is distinctive in a qualitative sense also, and one writer, who likened the Italians to the Germans farther north, refers to the Rosati settlement as an "oasis of self and family maintenance in a veritable desert of relief." Hewes characterizes the agriculture of the Italians at Tontitown, Arkansas, who were part of the same original group of Italians, in similar terms.[14]

On a more subtle level, Velikonja characterizes the Rosati Italians as possessing a consciousness to "be different," and he maintains that this feeling has persisted. He cites the "sense of village" and a community spirit as examples, which he attributes to the areas of their origin. One of the few remaining residents of the original settlement concurred with these sentiments but pointed out that the Italians at both Rosati and Tontitown lost this sense to be different sometime around World War II. The lessening of this sense to be different, in the case of Rosati, has resulted from both unrestricted intermarriage and the large emigration of the community's younger population.[15]

The viticulture developed at Rosati by the Italian colonists and perpetuated by their descendents represents the most distinctive aspect of their culture. Their presence is particularly apparent in a region where vineyards are uncommon. The Rosati area contains approximately 1,000 acres of vineyards, or 600,000 individual

14. Velikonja, "The Italian Contribution," p. 15; Conrad H. Hammar, "Institutional Aspects of Ozark Decline," p. 845; Leslie Hewes, "Tontitown: Ozark Vineyard Center," pp. 137–38.
15. Velikonja, "The Italian Contribution," pp. 17–27.

vines.[16] About half of this acreage is in the hands of descendents of the original Italian colonists.

There is some confusion as to how the Italians got started in the raising of grapes at Rosati. Initially, they grew fruits and vegetables for the St. Louis market, probably at the suggestion of the Frisco, which as the colonizing agent had a definite interest in furthering the economic success of the fledgling Italian colony. The colony also supported itself by exploiting trees in the forests, which were used for both mine props and Frisco railroad ties. A very probable explanation of the idea to grow grapes is that grapes were traditional with them and were introduced for sentimental reasons. Some of the colonists had been involved with viticulture in Italy, but they represented a small minority. Without question, their familiarity with viticulture made them more receptive to its introduction, regardless how this was accomplished.[17]

According to one story, the Italian colonists acquired the idea and their first cuttings from a small group of Frenchmen who grew Concord grapes a few miles west of Rosati. It is not clear how the French acquired the idea to grow grapes. Another story that was told by one of the original colonists states that large grapes were growing wild in the Rosati area when the Italians settled there, and this stimulated their interest in starting vineyards. Finally, Velikonja suggests that Rosati's vineyards were a direct result of the success of similar activities at Tontitown.[18]

The soils in the area are not ideal for grapes, but they are even less suited for other crops. The primary use of the land in Rosati is for forests and some pastures. However, the soils are adaptable to fruit culture.[19] The colony is located on a low ridge separating the Meramec and Gasconade Drainage Basin regions, which facilitate cold air drainage, and this has become an important factor in the success of their viticulture. The climate is not ideal; late freezes often occur; hail is a problem; and droughts are not uncommon. Yet, considering all factors, the area is considered well suited to viticulture.

The initial production of grapes at Rosati was modest. Grapes

16. The Rosati area is not considered to be of national significance in the production of grapes. For more information see Clarence W. Olmstead, "American Orchard and Vineyard Regions," pp. 189–236.

17. Velikonja, "The Italian Contribution," p. 12; Joseph R. Castelli, "Grape Growers of Central Missouri," p. 115.

18. Castelli, "Grape Growers," p. 115; "Family Reunion at Rosati Recalls Town's Early History," *St. Louis Post Dispatch;* Velikonja, "The Italian Contribution," p. 12.

19. Castelli, "Grape Growers," p. 114.

were sold locally and used in winemaking for the community. By 1910, every family in the settlement owned a vineyard of at least one-half hectare in size.[20] Non-Italian growers, many of whom were of German ancestry, appeared early in the Rosati area. Acreage devoted to grape cultivation expanded up to the time of prohibition. At that time, the entire industry in the United States, including the Rosati growers, suffered a setback.

It was extremely difficult to find a market for grapes. Facing uncertain conditions, the growers formed the Knobview Fruit Growers Association in 1920. The association handled the picking, processing, and marketing of the grapes. This seems to have been a turning point for the colony. Grape production and acreage increased steadily up to World War II (Table 6–1). The loss of local

Table 6–1

Acreages of Grapes in the Rosati Area, 1910–1975

Year	Acres of Grapes
1905	first plantings
1910	250 (estimate)
1934	800
1945	1,500
1960	1,000
1970	1,000
1975	1,200

Sources: Data were drawn from several sources; their approximate accuracy was confirmed through interviews with older producers.

labor during World War II reduced the grape acreage. Following the war, the labor shortage persisted. Facing total disaster, the growers began selling the crop on the vine to the Welch Company out of Springdale, Arkansas. Welch provided labor for picking the grapes, as well as a guaranteed market for the growers. In 1952, 4,500 growers, including those at Rosati, purchased the Welch Grape Juice Company and established the National Grape Cooperative Association, Inc. Acreage in the Rosati area increased by approximately 20 per cent between 1970 and 1975. More than half of the approximately 100 growers in the area are of Italian descent. Judg-

20. Velikonja, "The Italian Contribution," p. 12.

ing from the age of their vines, the majority of the non-Italian growers in the area have only recently entered viticulture as a result of a program conducted by the Missouri State Fruit Experiment Station at Mountain Grove to expand the industry in the Rosati area since World War II. The acreage was to reach 5,000; however, this figure was never realized.[21]

Viewed regionally, the Rosati area is the leading grape-producing locality in the Missouri Ozarks and ranks second in the entire Ozark region only to Tontitown, Arkansas (Figure 6–2). In the Missouri Ozarks, grape production outside the Rosati area is spotted. The vineyards in southwestern Missouri are old and

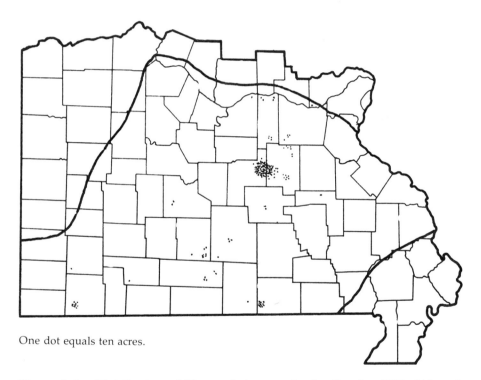

One dot equals ten acres.

Figure 6–2. Distribution of Vineyard Acreage in the Ozarks, 1972. Although grapes are grown throughout the Ozarks, the Italian growers and their non-Italian neighbors at Rosati clearly dominate in the Missouri Ozarks. Sources: Ozark Grape Growers Coop, Missouri State Fruit Experiment Station, and National Grape Cooperative.

21. Knobview was the original name of the Italian settlement. The name was changed to Rosati in the 1920s in honor of Bishop Rosati of St. Louis. Judd Wyatt, "History of the Knobview Fruit Growers Association"; Castelli, "Grape Growers," p. 116; "Ozark Vineyards: Fresh From the Hills," *Chicago Tribune*.

associated with the northwestern Arkansas grape region. The grapes near Hermann are of recent origin and are associated with the reopening of the Old Stone Hill Winery at Hermann. In addition, the Hermann winery purchases approximately 260 tons of grapes per year from the Rosati area. The cluster of dots in the south-central Ozarks is centered around the Missouri State Fruit Experiment Station at Mountain Grove. The experiment station has forty acres of grapes and has encouraged several farmers in the area to plant grapes.[22]

A rather novel vineyard in this region is in Douglas County, where a Trappist Monastery was established in 1959. The monks operate a vineyard of approximately fifteen acres. Much like the Italians, the monks market their grapes at Springdale, Arkansas. The vineyards in the extreme southern Ozarks are of very recent origin. A large St. Louis winery has contracted with a grower in Oregon County to produce 800 tons of grapes per year. A total of more than one-hundred acres of grapes is involved.[23]

Ninety per cent of the grapes in the Missouri Ozarks are of the Concord variety. Other varieties are grown in small amounts, which are primarily used in winemaking. Most of the grapes are marketed at Springdale, Arkansas, by the National Grape Cooperative.

In an effort to broaden the economic base of the community and strengthen the position of viticulture in the area, commercial winemaking has been reintroduced to Rosati. The Italians at Rosati had tried commercial winemaking before. A winery with a capacity of 120,000 gallons annually was operated for several years during World War II. However, due to improper winemaking techniques, it was closed in 1945.[24] With Interstate Highway 44 bisecting the vineyards, it was felt that a return to winemaking might be profitable. Two wineries were started: one Italian funded but operated by a German immigrant, and the other non-Italian owned and operated. The latter is on the site of the original Rosati winery. Both are doing quite well, selling primarily to tourists. Their success has led to optimism concerning the future of grapes in the area. The interstate, with its fenced-in right-of-way, has all but

22. Hewes, "Ozark Vineyard Center," pp. 141–42. The grapes purchased by the Hermann winery are among approximately 200 acres of grapes in Rosati not contracted to the National Grape Cooperative at Springdale, Arkansas.

23. Dale Freeman, "Ozark Trappists: The Happy People . . ."; "Wine Grapes in the Ozarks?" *Springfield Leader and Press.*

24. Charles De La Haye, "Grape Stands Return to Rosati as Vineyards Stage a Comeback."

eliminated the roadside grape stand. The annual grape festival, first held in 1953, is still staged at the completion of the grape harvest each August. Referred to as "feste d'Vendemmix," or "Wintage," the festival was moved to St. James, five miles to the west, and has been greatly expanded under the leadership of a largely non-Italian chamber of commerce.

French Immigrants at Old Mines

The story of the French in the Ozarks, from a cultural point of view, has been a sad one. Sauer enumerates nine respects in which the French proved inferior to the Americans, including agriculture, mining techniques, standard of living, individual initiative, and enterprise. He adds that the development of French stock should have been parallel to that of the American and later of the German immigrants, but "for the most part, the French have retrograted with time."[25] In an intermixed culture, the French either easily assimilated or retreated. It is only in areas where the French did not intermix culturally that they have retained any sense of their ethnicity.

Fifty years ago, Sauer recorded several remaining French outposts in the Ozarks; most were remote, and all but one was small.[26] The only sizeable French stronghold was the Old Mines barite district in Washington County. Today, the Old Mines area is the only remaining French stronghold in the Ozarks, and it is fast fading into oblivion.

The French occupy almost solidly an area of fifty square miles, which is centered on the village of Old Mines, north of Potosi (Figure 6–3). The area includes the northern half of one of the leading barite deposits in the United States. Originally, the French were drawn to the area by the lead deposits. At one time there were twenty lead smelters operating in Washington County, and only one decaying stack remains (Figure 6–4).[27]

After the lead was exhausted, many French miners turned to farming; some continued to work the surface lead deposits that the companies had considered too meager for their needs; and few left the area. The economy of the region was depressed. When the lead mines were almost forgotten, it was discovered that the heavy multicolored spar that had been a nuisance to the lead miners was valuable. This material was barite, or tiff, as it is called locally. It is

25. Carl O. Sauer, *The Geography of the Ozark Highland of Missouri*, pp. 93–95.
26. Ibid., p. 94.
27. Ruth F. Van Doren, "A Tough Life—Mining Tiff," p. 19.

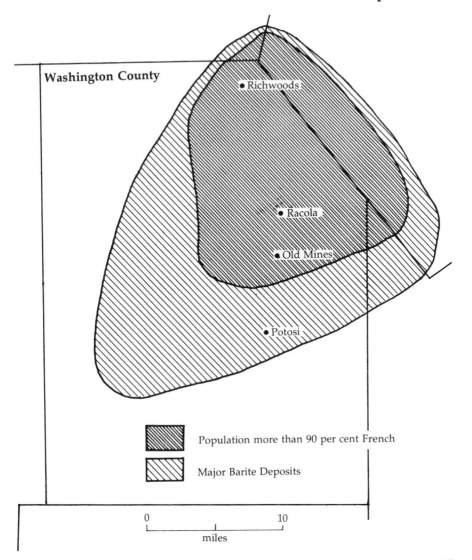

Figure 6–3. Barite Deposits and French Settlement, Washington County. The French occupy almost solidly an area of fifty square miles in northern Washington County. Sources: *Atlas of Missouri* and field data.

used in paint, oil-well drilling, and as a source of barium. The mining of tiff became the new industry in northern Washington County, and virtually the entire population became involved in its production and processing.

The method used to mine barite was crude and primitive. The barite was hand dug by individuals with little or no organiza-

Figure 6–4.   Remains of the last lead smelter at Old Mines in Washington County.

tion in the production end. The essentials of tiff mining are vividly portrayed:

> A primitive type of mining equipment is used to get the tiff from the rocky clay ground. It consists of a windlass made from scrap lumber, a short length of peeled log, a rope and a bucket or tub with improved bail. A handle at one end of the log enables a miner to lift a bucket full of the heavy tiff from the hole with little effort. . . . The holes are seldom more than 20 feet deep.
>
> Tiff is cleaned with "tiff hatchets" . . . a "rattle box" . . . is also used to clean tiff. This box is operated by filling it with tiff and shifting the box, on its two center legs, to the right and left by an upright handle on the side of the box. The dirt falls through the holes punched in the tin bottom of the box. Some of the boxes are made entirely of wood slats and resemble vegetable crates.
>
> Picks, shovels, and crow-bars complete the crude mining equipment.[28]

The miner hauled his tiff to the processing and reloading point where it was crushed and shipped out by rail. Very few people were attracted to the mining of barite deposits. The pay was low, and the work was extremely difficult and dangerous. This was the primary method of mining tiff up to the mid-1930s, and some miners were still hand digging in the late 1940s. The hand-dug holes are still present and are often hazardous to cattle being pastured in these areas.

Beginning in the 1930s, the landowners began replacing the miners with power shovels. Some of the former hand miners secured employment in the new mechanized tiff industry; many simply retired to live on welfare or no income at all. The new mechanized industry proceeded to scour the hills, leaving behind a scene even more bleak than that left by strip mining, which, at least, leaves somewhat uniform scars. The area lapsed into an economic depression from which it has not yet recovered. In one apt appraisal of the situation it was said, "The land became so exhausted after the mechanized mining a crow had to bring his own food in order to fly over it." This situation holds true today. In 1930, prior to the mechanization of tiff mining in Washington County, the population density in Union Township, which includes more than 90 per cent of Old Mines parish, was 43.0 people per square mile. In 1970, the population density in Union Town-

---

28. Ruth Fitch Hopson, "Barite Mining in Southern Missouri," p. 107.

ship was 40.4 per square mile, only a slight decrease from the 1930 figure.[29]

The French community at Old Mines totals approximately 1,400 people, or 400 families. All of the French at Old Mines are Roman Catholics. Their church in which they take great pride was founded in 1828 and is one of the oldest Catholic churches west of the Mississippi River and east of the Rocky Mountains. There are a few non-French residents in the area, including several local businessmen. However, approximately 95 per cent of the population in the Old Mines parish is French. The growth of the population increased naturally, as opposed to immigrational increase from other areas. There is some indication that a few French from other areas in the Ozarks, and possibly Illinois, came to Old Mines in the mid-nineteenth century to escape Americans and stay among their own kind; however, they were probably few in number. In addition, there was little out-migration from the Old Mines area until quite recently. Such conditions are conducive to the preservation of old cultural ways.[30]

The extent to which population growth at Old Mines increased naturally within the group was best stated by Sauer, "The isolation of the settlement resulted in consanguinity, which possibly had deleterious effects."[31] It is widely believed in the area today that excessive inbreeding, which some say is still a problem, has had such deleterious effects on the population of the Old Mines settlement. For example, there are fifty-seven families of one surname in the community, and only one person with this surname has married outside the community since the turn of the century. It is literally true that, with the exception of the few outsiders now living in the area, everyone at Old Mines is related, and most are at least third cousins.

The isolation of the Old Mines settlement has contributed to the preservation of old ways in much the same way isolation has contributed to the general backwardness of other isolated areas in the Ozarks. Isolation is relative and never complete in any populated area. Old Mines has been effectively isolated from the outside world in two ways. First, until 1949, when the road to St. Louis

29. *Fifteenth Census of the United States, 1930: Population*, vol. 3, part 1, p. 1386, Washington, D.C.: Government Printing Office, 1971; *Census of Population, 1970: Characteristics of the Population, Missouri*, p. 152.

30. Parish register, 1972; Mark G. Boyer, *St. Joachim*, p. 19; Oliver F. Fink, "Missouri's Old French Pocket"; Lauren C. Post, "Acadian Ethnology; Material Culture on the Prairies of Southwest Louisiana," p. 2.

31. Sauer, *Ozark Highland*, p. 93.

was paved, it was difficult to get to and from the area. Second, few people from outside have had reason to go to Old Mines; it is a bleak and poverty-stricken area offering little to either the person seeking a new home or the person out to "see the sights." On the other hand, the people of Old Mines have had little desire to leave the area, and many still choose unemployment to moving from the community. For some of the older people who live back in the hills, the occasional trip to either Old Mines or Potosi is the extent of their travel. The physical isolation is now all but gone, and the social isolation, much of which has been self-imposed, is beginning to break down.

To the passerby, the poverty of the Old Mines area is perhaps the most noticeable characteristic of the settlement. It is not only noticeable, it is persistent and chronic. The French in this locale have apparently always been poor; however, they have been poorer at some times than others. During the period of hand-dug tiff, economic conditions were relatively stable. With the mechanization of the barite industry, conditions grew worse. In the period following World War II, unemployment among adult males in the settlement was estimated to be between 65 and 75 per cent.[32] By 1949, malnutrition was a serious problem, and it affected the majority of the area's population.

Such problems are less acute today because of the various forms of government and church assistance available and the availability of some jobs in nearby towns and St. Louis. Yet, there are still many indications of poverty in this area. The habitations of the majority of the population are of low quality. Twenty-one vintage log cabins that are still occupied were encountered in traverses along side roads. Many of the rural dwellings are on company land, and the inhabitants are, in effect, squatters. Approximately half of the dwellings in the settlement have no indoor plumbing, or running water. Some people travel as far as two miles to secure drinking water from an approved well, and the practice of obtaining drinking water from creeks is diminishing but has not ceased. Obviously, much of the community is assisted by government programs.[33] The standard of living is low throughout rural Wash-

32. Boyer, *St. Joachim*, p. 84.

33. Efforts were made to obtain statistics of welfare for the Old Mines area, but the government agencies involved would not release the data. According to the *Census of Population, 1970: Missouri* (p. 482), 24.8 per cent of all families in Washington County reported incomes below the poverty level. This is substantially higher than for surrounding counties.

ington County. However, in the vicinity of Old Mines, conditions among the neighboring non-French appear to be much better in a relative sense. Low-quality habitations, although present, are encountered less frequently in the areas surrounding Old Mines.

The high rate of welfare or assistance programs in the Old Mines area is associated with a low educational level among the adult population. A report published in 1968 stated that males of thirty-five years of age and over in the Old Mines area are largely uneducated and neither read nor write. From a socioeconomic point of view, such a condition is, of course, discouraging. But, from a cultural point of view, "A low educational level perpetuates cohesion . . . a tendency to keep aloof from American life, and to perpetuate institutions and customs that preserve the traditions and values common in their former homelands." However, it is not suggested that ignorance or poverty are good or beneficial because they appear to greatly reduce the rates of acculturation and assimilation.[34]

In a more positive vein, the French possess a strong sense of family. This characteristic has been ascribed to rural French in southern Louisiana as well. This sense of family is a factor that distinguishes the French from their neighbors. Young adult members in the French settlement are reluctant to leave the community to secure employment. Many who do leave, return shortly, apparently preferring the poverty of Old Mines to the economic betterment offered elsewhere. One effect, which Kollmorgan noted in Louisiana and is also evident in Old Mines, has been a "pyramiding" of people on land that cannot offer adequate support for them, rather than searching for new land. The population density in Old Mines parish is approximately forty people per square mile, more than three times the average rural population density for Washington County.[35]

Their strong sense of family is also demonstrated in a more striking manner. The French at Old Mines are still quite dispersed over the countryside, and they have settled in hollows. Through the years, the hollows have become settlements, or compounds. A hollow may have anywhere from three to ten units of one extended family living in what appears to be a small hamlet. Fifteen of these compounds containing at least three nuclear family units of a larger extended family can be seen.

34. "Old Mines Project," p. 2; Heinz Kloss, "German-American Language Maintenance Efforts," p. 210.
35. Walter M. Kollmorgan and Robert W. Harrison, "French-Speaking Farmers of Southern Louisiana," p. 156; Census of Population, 1970: Missouri, p. 152.

The French language is no longer the spoken language in the Old Mines area. However, in the mid-1930s, 90 per cent of the population were still employing a broken French in daily conversation. In the 1950s, French was still said to be in common usage, but most of the French said they preferred to speak "American." Today, only the elderly residents can speak French, and they rarely do so any more. It is interesting that the French in the Old Mines area have preserved a French dialect for so long, considering their obstacles. The language has not been used in the church since the latter decades of the nineteenth century. It appears that no conscious effort was made to preserve French. There is no indication that there has been any leadership on ethnic matters among the Old Mines French.[36]

The French are still described by those who know them well as being distinctive in character. They are devout Catholics, although the church is not involved in any way with preserving their French culture. They are described as being superstitious and emotional. They marry at a young age, with nearly half marrying within one year following graduation from high school. They still prefer to marry within their group and rarely marry someone outside the community. They tend to have large families, with at least a dozen families in the parish having ten children or more. These characteristics may well be French, but they may also well be the characteristics of a very conservative, traditional, and isolated people.

The French, like many other ethnic groups in the Ozarks, commemorate their heritage through various activities suggestive of their French origins. One of the most colorful activities is a New Year's Eve custom, called "La Guignolee" (or Gaie-anne), which had its origin in the Middle Ages in France. According to custom, a small band of singers visits neighbors, and at a nod from their leader, they begin singing. They are invited in the home where they finish their singing. They receive a treat and later gather for a ball with the treats they have collected.[37] The song of "La Guignolee" is still sung in French, but other songs are now sung in English. The same custom is celebrated in Ste. Genevieve, but there it is staged, whereas at Old Mines it is still spontaneous, and, in a word, authentic.

This custom may be of significance; however, the French culture is rapidly declining at Old Mines, and many do not regret its de-

36. Ward Allison Dorrance, *The Survival of French in the Old District of Ste. Genevieve*, p. 8; Fink, "Missouri's Old French Pocket."
37. "La Guignolee," *Independence Journal.*

cline. They hope that the passing of French ways will mean, at last, an entry into the mainstream of American life.

Summary

The case studies indicate the wide range of experiences the smaller non-German European settlements have had in the Ozarks. The Swedes at Verona, the French Waldensians at Monett, and the Swiss near Hermann are representative of the majority of the small European settlements in the Ozarks. Their cultural landscapes are not distinctive when compared with those of their neighbors or when placed in a regional context. In this sense, the Poles at Pulaskifield, the Italians at Rosati, and the French at Old Mines are atypical of the majority. The Poles at Pulaskifield did not create an ethnic landscape in the Ozarks. On the contrary, there is little in the cultural landscape of the Poles that distinguishes them from their neighbors. Yet, they have retained a strong sense of ethnic identity. The Italians at Rosati lack this strong sense of ethnic identity, but through their preference for viticulture, their landscape has continued to reflect their ethnic heritage. The French at Old Mines are perhaps the most distinctive of all of the non-German European settlements, both in the details of their landscape and through their sense of ethnic identity. It is somewhat ironic that the distinctive character of the French at Old Mines is more a result of isolation and poverty than a conscious effort to retain a traditional way of life.

7. Amish and Mennonites

Introduction

The Amish and Mennonites who have settled in the Ozarks are for the most part ethnic, although some of the more liberal Mennonite groups have attracted through time members of varying ethnic backgrounds. Yet, they are basically of German, Swiss, and Dutch background, and they remain conscious of this fact. However, their distinctiveness is generally accorded to their unusual religious beliefs and the effects these beliefs have had on shaping a landscape that is both distinct and identifiable. The more personal characteristics of these groups have been adequately described elsewhere and will not be emphasized here, except to the extent that such matters aid in interpreting Amish and Mennonite landscapes in the Ozarks.[1] Emphasis here will be on the less personal aspects of occupance, including settlement, agriculture, and patterns of interaction.

Considering the distinct character and appearance of the more traditional Amish and Mennonite groups in the Ozarks, a brief assessment of the religious and social climate of the region is necessary to place a proper perspective on this matter. The Ozarks region is commonly characterized as possessing a quite traditional and conservative outlook on matters relating to social conduct and religion. As such, Ozarkians are said to be intolerant of both that which is new and different. To exist without continual confrontation, the Amish and Mennonites would logically avoid such an adverse social climate as that typified in the Ozarks. Yet, in interviews

1. Numerous accounts of the life style and religious beliefs of these groups are available. The Amish, in particular, are among the most studied of all rural groups in the United States. An Amish farmer in Pennsylvania commented that during the last fifty of his seventy-eight years he had been interviewed by someone purporting to be doing research at least once a year if not more often. In addition to the references cited in Chapter 2, two very descriptive and vivid accounts of the life styles of these groups are by John A. Hostetler, *Amish Life* and *Mennonite Life*.

with the Amish and Mennonites who did settle in the Ozarks, it was pointed out that, despite the outward appearance of intolerance, the social climate of the Ozarks is actually quite tolerant toward divergent religions, particularly those of a more fundamentalist nature such as the Amish and Mennonites.

As discussed earlier, the Ozarks are, in many respects, a religious shatter belt. All of the standard denominations are represented in the region, as well as the myriad religions. In fact, the Amish and Mennonites are by no means the only or even the most unconventional religious groups in the Ozarks. It is probable that even the Old Order Amish are not considered any more unordinary than the Holiness Church, whose members have been known to handle poisonous snakes in connection with their worship, or the Order of Zion of the Sons of Levi, who follow communism along lines similar to practices of the kibbutz in Israel. Religious groups such as those mentioned along with the Amish and Mennonites are not considered to be out of place in the Ozarks. Because of their long association with regions such as the Ozarks, they are perhaps more tolerated in the Ozarks than in less conservative and more enlightened areas.

Settlement Patterns

The majority of the Amish and Mennonite settlements in the Ozarks is new, with three–fourths having settled in the last decade and over half in the last five years. As a result, it is probably too early to adequately assess their imprint on the landscape of the Ozarks. They will undoubtedly pass through a period of adjustment and transition to the new and different conditions that have confronted them in the region. If the Amish and Mennonite groups adjust favorably to the conditions in the Ozarks, then, more groups may come into the region. If, on the other hand, they cannot adjust, they may leave, as they have left a number of Southern states.[2] Assuming they remain in the Ozarks, and there has been no indication that those now in the Ozarks plan to leave, a landscape reflective of their cultural adjustment to the region will evolve. Whether or not their landscape will be distinctive is a matter

2. James E. Landing, "The Failure of Amish Settlements in the Southeastern United States: An Appeal for Inquiry," pp. 376–88. The avoidance of Southern states had been a characteristic of most immigrant groups to some extent. For more on this see Wilbur Zelinsky, *The Cultural Geography of the United States*, pp. 28–33.

for speculation. However, even at this early date, a number of general tendencies are apparent, and given the caution that these are tendencies and are thus somewhat tentative, an appraisal of presently discernible patterns has been offered.

Settlement Distribution

Amish and Mennonite settlements in the Ozarks are generally dispersed to the extent that they constitute a majority of landowners nowhere, even at the center, or core, of their settlements. In all cases, the inholdings of the "English," as the Amish and Mennonites call their neighbors, are extensive. This can be partially explained by the fact that the Amish and Mennonites buy that land that is currently being offered for sale, and only rarely would large blocks of land fall into this category.

Yet, their patterns of landholdings are influenced by several additional factors. Even in the older strongholds of Amish and Mennonite settlement, such as Pennsylvania and Ohio, this pattern of mixed landholdings is quite common.[3] This suggests that even though they may desire a very compact settlement, they are willing to tolerate nongroup members in their midst. The reasons are more economic than intrinsic. They simply are not willing to pay the price to establish compact settlements.

The price of land in the areas of Amish and Mennonite settlement in the Ozarks has inflated considerably in the years since these groups established their original settlements. Once the groups begin moving in, many locals near the center of the new settlement will put their land on the market at grossly inflated prices, hoping that the group will pay more to obtain a solid core of land. In many cases, the price of land near Amish and Mennonite settlements has doubled within weeks of the news that these groups are buying land, and several instances have been found where the price of land has tripled. The causes of the inflation are threefold: (1) their neighbors mistakenly believe that the Amish and Mennonites will pay almost any price to establish compact settlements; (2) their neighbors believe that those using horse-and-buggy transportation must settle in fairly close proximity out of practical necessity; and (3) there are always rumors that the first settlers are the advance element of much larger groups that plan to move to the Ozarks, which is rarely true.

The Amish and Mennonites are aware of the inflation in land

3. Maurice A. Mook and John A. Hostetler, "The Amish and Their Land," p. 25.

prices that occurs almost wherever they settle. They have a strategy, so to speak, to overcome this situation. Several instances are found where members of an Amish or Mennonite group would come in and very discreetly scrutinize an area and leave without giving any indication they are interested in buying. Several months later, they would return and buy land for the whole group at one time. In one case, a group bought four thousand acres for twenty families.

After the settlement is well established, and presumably successful, more land will be purchased but generally in small amounts and after the land boom has lessened. Still, they feel they are forced to pay unfair prices in subsequent purchases. If practical, they will buy land bordering their current holdings and through time attempt to consolidate the settlement. But this is not an overriding consideration. For groups using automobiles, it is of relatively minor significance. For those using horse and buggies, dispersed settlement does create problems. A small Amish settlement at Latham with thirteen families operates three schools for the settlement to avoid excessive buggy rides to and from school. The Seymour Amish, who now send their children to public school, pointed out that if they established one school and located it in the center of their settlement, the outlying families would have a daily six-mile buggy ride each way.

In the two areas where several Amish and Mennonite groups are somewhat clustered (Moniteau and Webster counties), the individual settlements are geographically separate from neighboring settlements. In Moniteau County, there was some intermingling at the time of settlement, but through land trading, the different groups were concentrating their settlements relative to each other. There is some significance in this matter of separation of settlements, particularly among the more conservative groups. They view their religious differences with other Anabaptist factions as highly significant and interact very little with each other. Their desire to be separated from other Amish and Mennonite groups is at least as great as their desire to be separated from the English. This point was made clear by the Seymour Amish who could send their children to a Mennonite school nearby but instead have chosen the public schools. They say the public schools, at least, will not involve their children in the church doctrine, as would other Anabaptist groups.

The settlement patterns discussed involve other perceived and actual factors. The variables involved in site selection include practical considerations of land quality as well as the efforts by these groups to establish compact settlements. In most cases, those interviewed indicated that they would not purchase land simply because it bordered land of other group members or because it would increase the compactness of the settlement. In a region such as the Ozarks, where land quality can vary greatly within short distances, tracts of quality land are often interspersed with larger tracts of low-quality land. The advantages to group cohesion offered by compact settlement must be balanced against the quality of land involved. It appears that these groups are willing to sacrifice some loss in land quality to have group cohesion, but by no means do they carry this point to extremes.

Only one case can be found where land quality was almost totally disregarded and subordinated in favor of social considerations. A small Mennonite settlement of the Stauffer affiliation, similar to the Old Order Amish but continually plagued by disunity among themselves, settled in a remote and sparsely populated area of northeastern Dallas County. The land on which they settled is among the poorest in quality in the entire Ozark region, but it is remote and offers social isolation. Only one county road leads into the area, and it dead-ends at the Niangua River. As a result, very few people enter the area for any reason. When asked why they picked such a desolate location a spokesman commented, "We want to be left alone."

Structural Occupance Features

The Mennonite settlements that have been in the Ozarks for some time are more liberal groups and are almost indistinguishable from their neighbors in most matters relating to occupance. The newer groups, most of which are more conservative, however, are distinguishable in certain aspects of their occupance. Most of them settled on farmsteads that had previously been occupied. The Old Order Amish would immediately tear out the electrical wiring, plumbing, disconnect central heating systems, and replace these with kerosene lamps, outhouses, hand pumps, windmills, and wood-burning stoves. However, excepting these changes, they have maintained the old farmsteads in most cases.

In addition, several groups have built new farmsteads that are distinctive. The Seymour Amish have built fourteen new farmsteads. The house they build, and most of the styles are the same, is a large two-story frame, box style house, which is always covered with gray roll-type siding (Figure 7-1). Large houses are built to accommodate their large families and their church services, which

Figure 7–1. New Amish farmstead in Seymour.

are held in the home. The Elkland Amish also have built several new farmsteads, but they are quite different from those built by the Seymour Amish. Their houses are of a contemporary style with simple design and include indoor plumbing but no electricity. The Latham Amish have also built several new farmsteads that are still different. Their houses are either basement houses with no above ground portion or block houses built into the side of a hill.

Whether or not new farmsteads are built, and the form they take, is a matter of both culture and affluence. The Seymour Amish, whose farmsteads are the most impressive, have an equal number of younger and older families. Apparently, the older families were considerably wealthy, which allowed them to build elaborate farmsteads. The Elkland Amish are similar but not as wealthy. The Latham Amish, on the other hand, are mostly young families and can spare little to build elaborate farmsteads. The Seymour Amish paid $400,000 in cash to purchase their land, whereas the Latham Amish had to retire a heavy land debt.[4]

The Amish and Mennonites in most cases have also used existing barns and other farm buildings. When they build a new barn,

4. "Amish in the Ozarks: The Old Days Returneth," *Springfield Leader and Press.*

it is usually larger than would be normal for the area. The only distinguishing feature of Amish barns in the Ozarks is an over bay at one end under which buggies are parked. Amish barns are generally unpainted, but that is not a distinguishing feature in the Ozarks. In addition, the presence of windmills, outdoor toilets, and assemblages of horse-drawn farm machinery are commonly associated with Amish farms. In summary, the Amish farms in the Ozarks are reminiscent of times past, whereas Mennonite farms are often indistinguishable from those of their neighbors.

Agriculture and Land Use

The Amish and Mennonites who have settled in the Ozarks were by tradition crop farmers. Because they were well aware of the limited productivity of the soils there, however, they have been willing to adjust to the less intense livestock-oriented economy. The more conservative groups have even planned to rely exclusively on their incomes from swine and cattle, although some occupations outside the farm do not conflict with their religious practices. Particularly with the Amish, a rural way of life is a must, and farming is the preferred occupation.

Several groups, including the Amish, are raising poultry. Nearly every Amish farm at Seymour, Elkland, and Buffalo has a large poultry barn. The poultry barns of the Old Order Amish are of frame construction and are without electricity. The Amish-Mennonites, who are modernized in their agriculture, have built their poultry barns, which are usually automated, of metal. The raising of poultry and the production of eggs is an advantage for the Amish who are able to employ their large families who are not effectively utilized in the raising of livestock. Most of the poultry are raised under contract with a large poultry and feed company. Other activities that supplement normal farm income are cheesemaking and selling products made of wood, including charcoal. The bulk of their income, however, comes from the raising of cattle and swine and the selling of grade-B milk.

The Amish, and the more conservative Mennonite groups, produce a greater variety of crops than is typical for the Ozarks, including oats, barley, and broomcorn, as well as a wide variety of vegetables, in addition to corn, wheat, and grain sorghum. This is partly done in an effort to become self-sufficient. As an indication of their self-sufficiency, one Amish farmer commented when asked how much he spends for commercial food, "We don't spend over

$10 a month for such things as sugar and salt."[5] However, all of the Amish and Mennonite settlements in the Ozarks are involved in commercial agriculture rather than primarily in subsistence production.

The Amish are up to date in their agriculture, although they have retained many of their traditional practices. They use commerical fertilizers, feed supplements, dairy testing, and soil testing. Some of the Amish are even enrolled in short courses through the University of Missouri Extension Service, although none will accept financial assistance from any governmental agency. The Mennonites, on the other hand, use the most modern methods of agriculture, including machinery. One case can be found involving a conservative Mennonite group where tractors are used, but to insure that they are not used for pleasure, the wheels on the tractors are metal rimmed.

To determine if there are significant differences in use of the land, two of the more conservative groups, the Seymour Amish and the Buffalo Amish-Mennonites, are examined. The Seymour Amish have been in the Ozarks for five years, and the Buffalo Amish-Mennonites have been in the Ozarks for nine years. Both groups devote a larger percentage of their land to crops than do their neighbors. This is particularly evident with the Old Order Amish at Seymour, who crop one-fourth of their land compared to one-twentieth for their neighbors. There are two reasons for this difference. First, since the Amish are by tradition more crop oriented than their neighbors, they feel that their soils can be upgraded to a moderate level of productivity through time. They are more concerned about the long-range improvements that will insure subsistence of future generations on the farms than with low yields and immediate income. Second, because the Amish came to the Ozarks intending to produce some crops, they bypassed land that offered little possibility for cropping.

Besides the emphasis on crops, the Amish and Mennonites do not differ greatly from their neighbors in agriculture. Their practices appear to be on the same level than those of their neighbors. Their philosophy regarding agricultural trends and practices is similar to that of any farmer. Other than in those areas where religious restrictions prevent innovation, they are as progressive as the next farmer. In fact, many of the Old Order groups are either

5. Frank Farmer, "The Contrast of Half a Century."

converting to modern machinery or renting machinery to perform more difficult tasks, such as brush hogging and land clearing. If there is one overriding difference between the more conservative groups and their neighbors, it is one of attitude. The Old Order groups feel that they must be successful in agriculture because they cannot depend on part-time or full-time employment in non-farm occupations. The greater emphasis on crops by the Seymour Amish, as compared to both their neighbors and the Amish-Mennonites at Buffalo, reflects this difference in attitude. The more liberal groups, on the other hand, will accept most types of nonfarm employment, although most do adhere to a rural way of life.

Social Patterns

Religion

The religious imprint of the Amish and Mennonites, as evidenced in the landscape, is not truly distinctive in the Ozarks. Their church structures are simple and functional with minimal ornamentation. Churches of the more liberal groups are similar in appearance to small fundamentalist churches throughout the Ozarks. Churches of the more conservative groups often bear no resemblance to the typical church structure. The Amish conduct church services in their own homes.

The more liberal groups have their church services performed in English and openly invite their neighbors to worship with them. The more conservative groups, especially the Amish, speak German both in church and among themselves. Although they do not openly exclude nonmembers from their worship services, their use of German has that effect. Since the German language, and the dialect of Pennsylvania Dutch, forms an effective cultural barrier between the more conservative groups and the broader society around them, it is significant that two groups stopped speaking German upon arriving in the Ozarks. Both groups stated that the German language is neither practical nor necessary any longer. This represents a quite liberal attitude and may have been a factor in their decision to leave their old homes and settle in the Ozarks.

Several of the groups that settled in the Ozarks do represent schisms, or break-off groups. In some cases, those who settled in the Ozarks were in the process of liberalizing, while others migrated to escape liberalizing influences in the old settlement. They differed on the issues of drinking, electricity, cars, powered farm machinery, plumbing, and Sunday schools. One group since coming to the Ozarks has split, with half of the members staying in the Ozarks and the other half going farther south into Arkansas. A second group is also splitting over the issue of powered farm machinery.

Education

A matter of great importance to the more conservative Anabaptist groups is the education of their children. They believe that formal education for their children should concentrate on the three Rs and be terminated at the conclusion of the eighth grade. They do not necessarily insist on their own schools, but they do insist that the public schools their children attend be conservative and avoid topics such as sex education. Almost ironically, they are sympathetic with the ban on religious activities in public schools imposed by the Supreme Court. They prefer to handle all religious matters strictly within the group. The groups will make use of public schools that can meet these conditions, and they especially like the convenience offered by busing, which makes lengthy buggy rides unnecessary. However, when these conditions cannot be met by the public schools, the Amish and conservative Mennonite groups will, almost without exception, establish their own schools.

The conditions surrounding education in the Ozarks are generally favorable to the needs of the Amish and Mennonites. The rural public schools in the Ozarks are quite conservative, and topics objectionable to the Amish and Mennonites are frequently also objectionable to the local population as a whole. Twelve of the sixteen Amish and Mennonite settlements in the Ozarks, including all of the more liberal ones, currently send their children to public schools. Several of the groups stated that this is being done only on an interim basis, and eventually they will have their own schools.

The Amish and Mennonite children do not attend high school, except for the more liberal groups who accept education beyond the eighth grade. School officials have not questioned the groups on this matter. The Amish and Mennonites received some support on this controversy in the 1972 decision by the Supreme Court in the case of *Wisconsin* v. *Yoder*, which, although a specific and not general decision, upheld the right of these groups to educate their own children as they see fit.[6] This decision makes it unlikely that this issue will be raised in Missouri.

The four groups using their own schools have also had very few problems with local or state officials. They do not have certified teachers or even high school graduates in their schools. To avoid a confrontation, they all have separate buildings that are used solely as schools. Some of the buildings are very simple, while others are not very different in appearance from the typical rural elementary school of twenty years ago. In all, the Amish and Mennonites in the Ozarks view the circumstances surrounding all aspects of education in the Ozarks favorably.

Miscellaneous Considerations

The unique style of dress, old-fashioned buggies, horse-drawn farm machinery, or black chromeless cars of the Amish, and some of the more conservative Mennonites are what make them most distinctive to those who encounter them. It is not uncommon to see an Amish family of ten or twelve members doing their shopping in the urban areas near their settlements or to see them at zoos and farm sales. They have definitely, though unintentionally, made their presence known to others.

They do interact with their neighbors in several ways. First, the groups using buggies depend on their neighbors for transporting themselves and their produce any great distance. Normally, some retired farmer in the vicinity supplements his income through services rendered to the Amish and Mennonites as a chauffeur. They also frequently hire their neighbors to perform difficult tasks requiring machinery, which their religion prohibits them from owning or operating. And, despite their original intention of working only on the farm, many are now working off the farm, primarily in construction. The interaction of the Amish and Mennonites with their neighbors is quite extensive on economic and social matters, but only rarely does it extend to matters of religion.

Problems in the Ozarks

In an overall view, the Amish and Mennonites have adjusted quite well to conditions in the Ozarks. The very fact that they are not leaving the region and that more are coming is an indication

6. "The Right to be Different," *Time.*

that they find conditions tolerable, if not to their liking in all cases. Of course, several groups have been in the Ozarks for nearly a century and have made their adjustments satisfactorily. However, a number of problems, some anticipated and some not, now confront the Amish and Mennonite settlements in the Ozarks.

Traveling is frequently hazardous under the best of conditions for the Amish and Mennonites who use buggies as their prime means of transportation. In the Ozarks, the problems of safe movement by buggy are compounded by irregular topography, winding, narrow roads with little or no shoulder area to drive on, and the absence of parallel side roads, which would enable them to move about without using busy roads. In most cases, the groups came from areas where conditions were far more favorable to safe buggy transportation than in the Ozarks. Although only one serious accident has occurred to date, several families have left the Ozarks because of unsafe road conditions.

Second, and perhaps most important, the land is not producing as they had anticipated it would. With the exception of the liberal groups, very few envisioned the necessity for off-farm employment at the time they settled in the Ozarks. The Seymour Amish stated in 1969 that they had no intention of seeking nonfarm employment. By mid-1972, half of the men in this settlement were working at least halftime in nonfarm occupations, primarily construction. The Amish-Mennonites at Buffalo have experienced similar circumstances, but they have solved their problem differently. To avoid sending their young men out to work in a worldly environment, they established their own construction company to erect metal barns. They are able to secure the income from off-farm employment without the corrupting influences they have feared would result by working for others. Several other groups have had to face similar circumstances. Some have not fared well in this regard because off-farm employment is not available everywhere.[7]

The only animosity the Amish and Mennonites have faced in the Ozarks is the result of their off-farm employment. They are good carpenters, and they work for relatively low wages. In the Seymour area, where several Amish and Mennonite groups compete directly for local jobs, they are accused of undercutting the longtime area residents for jobs that are already scarce. However, in most areas,

7. Milton D. Rafferty, "Persistence Versus Change in Land Use and Landscape in the Springfield, Missouri, Vicinity of the Ozarks," p. 194; Timothy Guse, "Quick Way to Build a Barn," p. 4.

their neighbors find them strange but pleasant. One farmer noted that anyone who can add a little stability to the area should be considered a welcome addition.

A third problem they face in the Ozarks, and one that most had not faced previously, is the remoteness of the Ozarks from the major areas of Amish and Mennonite settlement. They need to interact with others of their culture for a number of reasons. On a purely social basis, it is difficult for a small settlement to exist. The young often find it impossible to marry within the settlement either due to the problem of consanguinity or simply the lack of potential mates. They are forbidden to marry outside their religion. In some cases, mate selection is handled by mail, and, in others, a return to their previous area of settlement is required, which is both time-consuming and expensive. For equipment that is not available locally, such as buggies, they are dependent on distant areas. In general, locating in a region with few Anabaptist settlements creates some serious problems.

Very little research has been done on the impact the size of Amish and Mennonite settlements has on their effective functioning.[8] It would seem that the size of individual settlements is less significant than the aggregate size of all settlements in a given area. The settlements in the Ozarks are in a very critical stage. The present settlements do suffer from small size and remoteness. As they grow, which is by no means guaranteed, both small size and remoteness should become of less significance. The group members today are, in effect, pioneers. The success of their pioneering efforts depends on whether or not their individual settlements are reinforced. One Amish farmer stated that many would like to leave the older, more crowded areas in favor of new areas in the Ozarks, but they want assurances that the new settlements will be both successful and prosperous. To date, relatively little reinforcement of individual settlements has occurred, although the number of settlements is still increasing.

The future of these groups in the Ozarks is very much a matter of speculation. However, several facts are clear. The more conservative groups, in particular, who have high rates of population growth, and who desire very much to maintain agriculture as their occupation, must find land for expansion or new places to settle. Second, they need land that will both produce and, yet, is not prohibitively expensive. There are many possible places where

8. Landing, "The Failure of Amish Settlements," p. 376.

such conditions exist, including some outside the United States, but the Ozarks is definitely one possibility.

The first phase in the process of Amish and Mennonite settlement has occurred in the Ozarks and is nearing completion. The second phase, which overlaps the first, is the evaluation of the suitability of the area for their specific needs. This phase, which is currently underway, involves the consideration of the desirability and feasibility of expanding settlement efforts in the region. In this connection, it is important to point out that the price of land that initially attracted many has inflated substantially throughout the Ozarks in the past few years and may no longer give the Ozarks a competitive edge over other areas. The third and most critical phase could take several forms. First, those now in the Ozarks could pull up stakes and head back to the old area or to some other new area that promised greater rewards. Second, word could filter back to the old areas of settlement that conditions in the Ozarks are favorable to their settlement, which could result in a sizeable migration of Amish and Mennonites to the Ozarks. Third, the situation could remain in a state of uncertainty regarding the future in which case the more liberal groups could probably survive, but the more conservative groups would either be forced to merge with the liberal groups or emigrate, as has happened in a number of Southern states.[9]

9. Ibid., pp. 376–88.

8. Conclusions

The three objectives that were laid down as the purpose of this study are: (1) to map the past and present ethnic population of the Ozark region in Missouri; (2) to determine the degree of ethnic retention of the various ethnic groups; and (3) to ascertain the occupance characteristics of both ethnic and nonethnic populations.

The comparative study of ethnic and nonethnic populations in the Ozarks has revealed a number of similarities and differences. Undoubtedly, the differences noted were greater in past years, and the similarities will be greater in the future. Yet, significant variations between the populations in the Ozarks are found in agriculture, occupance features, religion, and other social variables. In some cases, the differences are overwhelming while in others the differences are only a matter of degree. In some instances, Old World traits are directly transplanted to the Ozarks and sharply contrast with the region as a whole. However, more often the differences stem from varying perceptions of the ethnic groups of what would and would not work in the Ozark environment. Frequently, Old World traits were dropped completely, and innovation or imitation occurred. Thus, the cultural landscapes in the ethnic areas of the Ozarks reflect an intertwining of the old and the new, frequently resembling a hybrid of both the Old World practices and the ways of the Ozarks.

Are ethnic landscapes in the Ozarks distinctive? The answer is both yes and no. For the larger German settlements, particularly the core areas, and for the Amish and Mennonites, especially the more conservative groups, the answer is definitely yes. For the other small European settlements, on the other hand, the answer is, in most cases, no.

The most apparent contrasts in the cultural landscapes in the Ozarks are in settlement patterns and, specifically, structural occupance characteristics. The French architecture of Ste. Genevieve, which may well be the most authentic and complete representation of French colonial styles in the United States, is a vivid reminder of the early presence of the French in the Ozarks. To the astute observer, the remnants of both the French and Spanish systems of land subdivision suggest the areal extent of the early French occupation of the Ozarks. The presence of French in the Ozarks today is marked not by the opulence of Ste. Genevieve but by the poverty of the tiff-scarred landscape of Old Mines. The landscape in Old Mines is distinctive, but, with the possible exception of the family compounds tucked back in the hollows, it is not truly French.

Germans, of all the region's ethnic groups, have made the deepest imprint on the cultural landscape of the Ozarks, through both the areal patterns of their settlement and the structures they built. German farmsteads are more evenly distributed on the land. They have concentrated very little along all-weather roads, compared to their neighbors. German string-like villages, of which there are approximately a dozen in the Ozarks, have no counterpart in the non-German areas of the region. Examples of European architectural styles are especially prevalent in the German villages in the Ozarks. However, German houses and barns are distinctive through their large size in a region known best for the modesty of the architecture. German houses are old but well built. Despite their age, they are generally in excellent condition.

Although a minor feature in the total landscape, the German church is a visible indicator of the cultural contrast between the German and non-German. The German church in the Ozarks is usually large and almost opulent in appearance when compared with the small frame rural church typical of the entire region.

The Amish, among the Anabaptist groups, most visibly reflect their different way of life through their settlements. Their assemblages of horse-drawn farm machinery, their buggies, and their fashions of dress are part of the landscape. Their farmsteads are distinctive and reflect their traditions. The more liberal groups, however, do not differ greatly in the outward expression of their settlement patterns.

Significant differences are found in the agriculture of several ethnic groups. The German farmer is distinctive through his greater emphasis on crop agriculture. In general, German agriculture in the Ozarks appears to reflect a greater intensity of production in all types of land use than is evident among neighboring groups. Viticulture indicates the presence of Italians in the central Ozarks. However, there is an equal number of Italian and non-Italian grape growers in the Ozarks today. The Amish are similar to the Germans in their emphasis on a combination of crops and livestock. The remaining ethnic groups are not distinctive in their agriculture.

Reminders of the region's ethnic heritage are evident through other less prominent features of the rural landscape. Place names, admittedly a minor feature, indicate the presence of many ethnic groups, although not always in proportion to their numbers. The Ozarks are well endowed with French place names. The Northern and Eastern Ozark Border regions abound with German place names. Many other ethnic groups gave their settlements names reflecting their ancestry, such as Rosati, Swiss, Swedeborg, Krakow, and Pulaskifield.

Most ethnic groups are distinctive through their religious beliefs. The Lutheran and Evangelical churches in rural areas of the Ozarks are closely associated with Germans. The Catholic church is still an ethnic church in the rural Ozarks, with French, Germans, Poles, and Italians comprising the bulk of its membership. The Mennonite church in the Ozarks is perhaps the most exclusive of all.

The contrast in social attitudes between the European, particularly the German, and the Old Stock American can occasionally be detected in the landscape. Breweries and wineries are only seen in ethnic areas of the Ozarks. The tavern, an indicator of the attitude toward alcoholic beverages, is encountered with a far greater frequency in ethnic settlements.

Locational stability varies widely between ethnic and nonethnic settlements in the Ozarks, being greater generally in the former. Although not directly reflected in the landscape, locational stability has influenced landscape features in the Ozarks. The German, coming from a tradition of locational stability, built his home and improved his land as part of a long-range goal of establishing a permanent home for himself and his children after him. The Old Stock American was traditionally more footloose. His more limited improvements on the land, as compared to the German, partly reflect this fundamental difference in attitude.

The differences found between the landscapes of ethnic and Old Stock American populations in the Ozarks have been the result of numerous variables. It can be assumed that the ethnic group in its early years in the Ozarks did attempt to create a landscape reminiscent of the old country. To assume otherwise would be to deny the influence of culture in the shaping of cultural landscapes. Many factors favored the introduction of Old World cultural traits during the first years of settlement in the Ozarks. Perhaps the most basic of these was cultural inertia. The very fact that a trait was known to a group, in the sense that it had traditionally been a part of their culture, gave it an initial advantage over some unknown or poorly understood new trait. It would seem illogical to abandon the familiar for the unfamiliar without first trying the former.

There are also many factors that resulted in either the alteration or abandonment of numerous European cultural traits. As time passed, memories of the old country undoubtedly began to fade. The European who settled in the Ozarks experienced a cultural shock. Without question, the Ozark environment presented sharp contrasts to the environment of Europe. Although the European settled in the Ozarks of his own free will, his perception of the region prior to his arrival did not always accord with reality. Many thousands were misled by Duden and others into believing that conditions in the Ozarks were ideal for their way of life. It is doubtful that they were prepared for the physical and cultural conditions that confronted them when they did arrive.

The European who settled in the Ozarks was forced to experiment and improvise, and he either continued or discarded his European traits through trial and error. He undoubtedly watched his non-European neighbor closely and adopted and modified non-European traits that were both workable and culturally acceptable to him.

There is some indication that ethnic groups in the Ozarks did attempt to preserve their ethnic character through conscious efforts intended to inhibit interaction with neighboring populations. Early examples of this include settlement in remote areas and attempts to establish exclusive control of most of the land. Although the initial barriers to interaction were often physical and related to accessibility, changes that reduced the effect of physical barriers did not necessarily lead to greater interaction. New barriers of a social and cultural nature would often replace the declining physical barriers.[1]

The phenomenon referred to as cultural rebound, in which ethnic groups develop a sense of group consciousness sometime after settlement in a new area, may well be a manifestation of the substitution of social barriers for physical barriers. For example, many immigrants who had little association with the ethnic church in the old country, all of a sudden, rediscovered religion in the rural

1. James O. Wheeler and John A. Jakle, "The Dutch in Kalamazoo, Michigan: A Study of Spatial Barriers to Acculturation," pp. 253–54.

ethnic settlements in the United States.[2] This factor may also account for the apparent homogeneity that developed among the Germans in Gasconade County, who are, in fact, a heterogeneous group by any reasonable standard.

On the other hand, there were many Europeans who showed little interest in creating an ethnic landscape in the Ozarks. First, there were many rapid assimilators whose ethnic identity was quickly forgotten. The rapid assimilator tended to play down his obvious ethnic characteristics, and his numbers have probably been underestimated. There are many factors that tend to produce a willingness among ethnic groups to acculturate and eventually assimilate. If ethnic identity threatens the financial well-being of an immigrant, he will often abandon his ethnic identity in favor of his financial security. Generally, the wealthy, as a group, assimilated rapidly. Higher levels of education generally stimulate rapid assimilation. Handlin sums up the advantages of assimilation when he observed that the price of ethnic retention is often social stagnation and detachment from the forces that shape the rest of the nation. However, other studies have concluded that a failure to assimilate does not necessarily mean social stagnation. An ethnic group can progress and be receptive to change and, at the same time, retain important aspects of its ethnic culture.[3]

Every ethnic group in the Ozarks faced these opposing forces. On one hand, sentiment strongly favored ethnic retention, and, on the other hand, many advantages awaited those who chose to break with their ethnic past. In Rosenthal's words, it was a matter of "push and pull."[4] The "push" represents the external forces operating on the group to acculturate, and the "pull" represents the internal forces operating within the group to resist accultura-tion. In any given situation, it is the relative balance of these forces that determined the extent to which a group is assimilated.

In assessing ethnic landscapes in the Ozarks, one final matter

2. Frederick C. Luebke, *Immigrants and Politics: The Germans of Nebraska, 1880–1900*, p. 45.

3. Luebke, *Immigrants and Politics*, pp. 35–38; J. T. Borhek, "Ethnic Group Cohesion," p. 43; Oscar Handlin, "Historical Perspectives on the American Ethnic Group," p. 223; Elaine M. Bjorklund, "Ideology and Culture Exemplified in the Southwestern Michigan," p. 241; Matti Kaups and Cotton Mather, "Eben: Thirty Years Later in a Finnish Community in the Upper Peninsula of Michigan," p. 70.

4. Erich Rosenthal, "Acculturation Without Assimilation? The Jewish Community of Chicago, Illinois," p. 277.

deserves mention. The distinctiveness of any immigrant landscape is partially dependent on the extent of the differences between the immigrant group and the native population among whom they settled. If the cultural context in which an immigrant group locates is one of general similarities to the existing population, their landscapes are apt to be not very distinctive. This is found to be the case among the Mennonites in southeastern Iowa and the Dutch in southeastern Nebraska. This is also the case among several European groups that settled among the Germans in the Northern and Eastern Ozark Border regions.[5]

If the cultural context in which the immigrant group locates is one in which their culture contrasts sharply with that of the existing population, their landscapes are apt to be distinctive. For example, the European immigrants who settled in areas of Southern agriculture are quite distinctive, whereas these same immigrants in the northern United States would probably not appear out of place.[6]

The culture of the Ozarks is a combination of Appalachian and Southern character, which contrasts sharply with the culture of the Europeans. In addition to being Appalachian and Southern in origin, the productive economy of the Ozarks is, so to speak, a "backwash" of traditionalism, and progress in most areas had been minimal. The Ozark region is characterized by poverty of material culture. The differences between the European immigrant and the Old Stock American in the Ozarks provide a "built-in" contrast, which is, no doubt, reflected in the contemporary landscapes of both groups.

It would be somewhat arbitrary to attempt a ranking of the ethnic populations of the Ozarks on the basis of ethnic retention. However, there are groups that are clearly more assimilated than other groups. For the Germans, a broad analogy can be drawn with Meinig's classification of the Mormon culture region.[7] St. Louis, much like Salt Lake City, would be the core. St. Louis was long the leading center of German culture in the lower Midwest. It was to St. Louis that most German immigrants to the Ozarks first came. But, like

5. Carla Lowenburg, "The Historical Analysis of the Mennonite Cultural Landscape of Franklin Township, Lee County, Iowa," pp. 127–34; Phillip Vogel, "The Holland, Nebraska, Locality: A Comparative Study of Dutch and Non–Dutch Occupance," p. 111.

6. Walter M. Kollmorgan, "A Reconnaissance of Some Cultural-Agricultural Islands in the South," pp. 409–30, and "Agricultural-Cultural Islands in the South—Part II," pp. 109–17; Terry G. Jordan, German Seed in Texas Soil, pp. 200–201.

7. D. W. Meinig, "The Mormon Culture Region: Strategies and Patterns in the Geography of the American West, 1847–1964," pp. 191–220.

any large urban industrial complex, St. Louis is much more than a center of German culture in the Midwest. It is the domain where German culture is truly dominant. The domain of German culture in the Ozarks would include northern Gasconade County, central Osage County, and southern Perry County. In these areas, over 90 per cent of the population are German, and the remnants of German culture are most pronounced. The sphere would include the remaining areas of German settlement in the Ozarks, where Germans coexist with contrasting cultures, and where the process of acculturation has progressed to nearly total assimilation.

The remaining ethnic settlements in the Ozarks have largely undergone acculturation to the point of near complete assimilation, with the few exceptions previously noted. The French at Old Mines, the Italians at Rosati, and the Poles at Pulaskifield represent the few non-German European settlements where ethnic identity has been retained to any significant degree. And then, of course, the Amish and Mennonites have added to the Ozarks a new ethnic element, distinctive in its own right.

The ethnic landscapes of the Ozarks have been described; the processes that produced them have been analyzed; and some suggestions of the causes of the differences between ethnic and nonethnic landscapes have been made. Yet, much more remains to be said of the peoples and cultures of the Ozarks. Even on the limited subject of ethnic groups in the Ozarks, this investigation is by no means complete. This study does suggest, however, that the old hypothesis that the United States is an ethnic melting pot is not applicable to the rural Ozarks. This writer concurs with Glazer and Moynihan, who observe:

> The American nationality is still forming: Its processes are mysterious, and the final form, if there is ever to be a final form, is as yet unknown.[8]

---

8. Several recent studies have reached this same conclusion for the United States as a whole, including Melvin Steinfield, *Cracks in the Melting Pot*, p. xiii; Nathan Glazer and Daniel P. Moynihan, *Beyond the Melting Pot: The Negroes, Puerto Ricans, Jews, Italians, and Irish of New York City*, p. 315; Karl B. Raitz, "Ethnic Settlements on Topographic Maps," p. 30.

Appendix

Population Origins in the Rural Ozarks

This information is a summary of material presented and referred to elsewhere in this study. For each county in the Ozarks, the origin of the rural population is summarized in two categories: Old Stock Americans in 1860 and ethnic groups for all periods. The same information is shown in less detail in Figure 2–11 (Nativity of the Old Stock American Population of the Ozarks, 1860), Figure 2–14 (Ethnic Railroad Settlements and Major Rail Lines), Figure 2–16 (Amish and Mennonite Settlements in the Ozarks of Missouri, 1972), and Figure 2–17 (Ethnic Settlements in the Ozarks). For the location of places mentioned in the tables, a standard highway map of Missouri should suffice.

Old Stock Americans by County, 1860

The states listed for each county are those that contributed the largest number of settlers up to 1860. The top five contributing states for each county are listed. The states in boldface contributed at least 25 per cent of the native-born population.

Barry County: **Tenn.,** Ky., Ill., N.C., Va.
Benton County: Tenn., Ky., Va., Ohio, Ill.
Bollinger County: **Tenn.,** Ky., N.C., Ill., Ohio
Boone County: **Ky.,** Va., Tenn., Ohio, Ill.
Butler County: **Tenn., Ky.,** Ill., N.C., Va.

Calloway County: **Va., Ky.,** Tenn., Ind., S.C.
Camden County: **Ky., Tenn.,** Va., Ind., N.C.
Cape Girardeau County: **Tenn.,** Ky., N.C., Ill., Va.
Carter County: **Tenn.,** Ky., Ill., S.C., Ala.
Cedar County: **Tenn.,** Ky., Va., Ind., N.C.
Christian County: **Tenn.,** Ky., Va., Ark., N.C.
Cole County: Ky., Va., Tenn., Ohio, N.C.
Cooper County: **Ky.,** Va., Tenn., Ohio, N.C.
Crawford County: **Tenn.,** Ky., N.C., S.C., Va.

Dade County: **Tenn.,** Ky., Va., N.C., Ill.
Dallas County: **Tenn.,** Ky., Ohio, Ill., Ind.
Dent County: **Tenn.,** Ky., N.C., Ind., Ohio
Douglas County: **Tenn.,** Ind., Ky., N.C., Ill.

Franklin County: Ky., Va., Tenn., Ohio, Ill.

Gasconade County: Va., Tenn., Ill., Ind., Ky.
Greene County: **Tenn.,** N.C., Ky., Va., Ill.

Henry County: Ky., Ill., Va., Ohio, Tenn.
Hickory County: **Tenn., Ky.,** Va., Iowa, N.C.
Howell County: **Tenn.,** Ark., Ky., N.C., Ind.
Howard County: **Ky., Va.,** Tenn., Ohio, N.C.

Iron County: **Tenn.,** Ky., Ill., Pa., Va.

Jasper County: **Tenn.,** Ky., Ind., Va., N.C.
Jefferson County: Ky., Tenn., Va., N.C., Ind.

Laclede County: **Tenn.,** Ky., Ill., Ind., N.C.
Lawrence County: **Tenn.,** Ky., N.C., Ill., Va.

Madison County: **Tenn.,** Ky., N.C., Va., Ill.
Maries County: **Tenn.,** Va., Ky., Ill., N.C.
McDonald County: **Tenn.,** Ky., Ind., Va., N.C.
Miller County: **Ky., Tenn.,** Va., Pa., Ind.
Moniteau County: **Ky.,** Tenn., Va., N.C., Ohio
Montgomery County: **Va.,** Ky., Tenn., Ind., Ohio
Morgan County: **Ky.,** Tenn., Va., Ind., Ill.

Newton County: **Tenn.,** Ill., N.C., Ind., Ky.

Oregon County: **Tenn.,** N.C., Ark., Va., Ky.
Osage County: **Tenn.,** Ky., Va., Ohio, Ill.
Ozark County: **Tenn.,** Ark., Ill., Ky., Ind.

Perry County: **N.C.,** Tenn., Ky., Ill., Ohio
Pettis County: **Ky.,** Va., Iowa, N.C., Ill.
Phelps County: **Tenn.,** Ind., Ky., Va., Ill.
Polk County: **Tenn.,** Ky., Va., N.C., Ind.
Pulaski County: **Tenn., Ky.,** Ill., Va., N.C.

Reynolds County: **Tenn.,** Ky., Ill., Va., Miss.
Ripley County: **Tenn.,** Ky., Ga., Ark., Ala.

St. Charles County: Va., Ky., Tenn., Ohio, Ill.
St. Clair County: **Tenn.,** Ky., Va., Ohio, Ind.
St. Francois County: **Tenn.,** Ky., Va., N.C., Ill.
Ste. Genevieve: **Tenn.,** Ohio, Va., Ky., N.C.
St. Louis County: Va., Ky., Ohio, Iowa, N.C.
Saline County: **Ky., Va.,** Tenn., Iowa, Ill.

Shannon County: **Tenn.,** Ala., Ky., Ind., Va.
Stone County: **Tenn.,** Ky., Va., N.C., Ind.

Taney County: **Tenn., Ky.,** Ark., N.C., S.C.
Texas County: **Tenn.,** Ky., Ill., N.C., Ind.

Warren County: **Ky.,** Va., Tenn., Ill., Ohio
Washington County: **Tenn.,** Ky., Va., Ohio, N.C.
Wayne County: **Tenn.,** N.C., Ala., Va., Ky.
Webster County: **Tenn.,** N.C., Ky., Va., Ill.
Wright County: **Tenn.,** Ky., Va., Ind., N.C.

Ethnic Population by County

For each county, all ethnic settlements are listed along with their locations within the county. Where appropriate, some additional information is included. In cases where the information is readily available elsewhere in the study, the appropriate references are included.

Barry County: **German**—near Stone's Prairie (see Table 2–1); **French**—near Monett (see Table 2–1); **Polish**—in Pulaskifield (see Table 2–1).
Benton County: **German**—in the northern part of the county, extending beyond the Ozarks boundary, especially concentrated around Cole Camp and Lincoln.
Bollinger County: **German**—concentrated in the eastern third of the county; **Dutch**—small settlement located east of Leopold on into Cape Girardeau County.
Boone County: **German**—in the extreme southern part of the county, near Hartsburg.
Butler County: **German**—a few settlements in the extreme southeastern portion of the county, west of Glennonville (see Table 2–1); **Hungarian**—small settlement near Poplar Bluff (see Table 2–1); **Yugoslavian**—small settlement extending from Harviell to Naylor in Ripley County (see Table 2–1).

Calloway County: **German**—extreme southern part of the county.
Camden County: No significant ethnic population.
Cape Girardeau County: **German**—large settlement, especially in the western two-thirds of the county. The settlements extend south beyond the Ozark escarpment to Illmo, Kelso, New Hamburg, and Diehlstadt; **Swiss**—small settlement around Dutchtown; **Dutch**—see Bollinger County; **Austrian**—small settlement near Pocahontas.
Carter County: **Irish**—extinct settlement in southwestern corner of the county; **Mennonite**—near Grandin (see Table 2–2).
Cedar County: **German**—small settlement near Jerico Springs.
Christian County: **German**—near Billings (see Table 2–1).

Cole County: **German**—spread over most of the county, especially in the north; **Belgian**—small settlement at Taos.

Cooper County: **German**—spread over the northern and western portions of the county, extending beyond the Ozark escarpment.

Crawford County: **Austrian**—near Steelville (see Table 2–1).

Dade County: **German**—at Lockwood (see Table 2–1); **Swiss**—south of Lockwood (see Table 2–1); **Moravian**—two extinct settlements.

Dallas County: **Amish-Mennonite**—near Buffalo (see Table 2–2).

Dent County: No significant ethnic population.

Douglas County: **Mennonite**—near Dogwood (see Table 2–2).

Franklin County: **German**—especially in northern two-thirds of the county; **Polish**—near Krakow and Clover Bottoms; **Bohemian**—near Japan; **Swedish**—near St. Clair (see Table 2–1).

Gasconade County: **German**—dominant in northern two-thirds of the county; **Swiss**—small settlement around the village of Swiss; **Bohemian**—in the southeastern part of the county (see Franklin County).

Greene County: **Swiss**—near Highlandville (see Table 2–1).

Henry County: **German**—in the southeastern portion of the county.

Hickory County: **Amish** and **Mennonite**—three extinct settlements.

Howell County: **German**—small settlement south of Mountain View and small settlement west of Thayer; **Mennonite**—near Mountain View (see Table 2–2).

Howard County: **German**—southwestern portion of the county.

Iron County: **German**—small settlement north of Pilot Knob; **Hungarian**—small settlement near Pilot Knob.

Jasper County: **German**—near Sarcoxie (see Table 2–1); **Amish** and **Mennonite**—two extinct settlements.

Jefferson County: **German**—in the northwestern portion of the county; **Hungarian**—small settlement west of House Springs; **Bohemian**—in the northwestern corner of the county.

Laclede County: **German**—near Rader (see Table 2–1); **Moravian**—small settlement at Lebanon.

Lawrence County: **German**—at Freistatt (see Table 2–1); **Swedish**—at Vernon (see Table 2–1).

Madison County: **German**—small settlements in the northern part of the county.

Maries County: **German**—in the extreme northwestern corner of the county.

McDonald County: No significant ethnic population.

Miller County: **German**—in the northeastern portion of the county around Marys Home, St. Anthony, and St. Elizabeth.

Moniteau County: **German**—in the northern portion of the county; **Swiss**—

small settlement near California; **Amish** and **Mennonite**—three settlements near Latham (see Table 2–2).

Montgomery County: **German**—in the southern portion of the county around Rhineland.

Morgan County: **German**—in the northwest corner of the county; **Amish** and **Mennonite**—three settlements east of Versailles (see Table 2–2) and one extinct settlement.

Newton County: **German**—small settlement south of Sarcoxie (see Table 2–1).

Oregon County: **German**—small settlement west of Couch (see Table 2–1).

Osage County: **German**—spread over most of the county; **French**—small settlement at Bonnets Mill.

Ozark County: No significant ethnic population.

Perry County: **German**—in the southeastern half of the county; **Belgian**—small settlement at Belgique; **French**—small settlement near Perryville.

Pettis County: **German**—spread through the eastern portion of the county.

Phelps County: **German**—small settlement south of Rolla; **Swiss**—near Rolla (see Table 2–1); **Swedish**—near Rolla (see Table 2–1); **Danish**—near Rolla (see Table 2–1); **Austrian**—near Rolla (see Table 2–1); **Italian**—at Rosati (see Table 2–1); **French**—at Dillon (see Table 2–1).

Polk County: **Bohemian**—near Bolivar (see Table 2–1); **Amish-Mennonite**—see Dallas County.

Pulaski County: **Swedish**—at Swedeborg (see Table 2–1).

Reynolds County: No significant ethnic population.

Ripley County: **German-Polish**—near Doniphan (see Table 2–1); **Yugoslavian**—see Butler County; **Moravian**—one extinct settlement.

St. Charles County: **German**—spread throughout the Ozark portion of the county.

St. Clair County: No significant ethnic population.

St. Francois County: **Austrian**—small settlement near Farmington; **Russian**—small settlement at Desloge; **Greek**—small settlement at Desloge.

Ste. Genevieve County: **German**—spread throughout the eastern two-thirds of the county; **French**—once concentrated in and around the town of Ste. Genevieve, few settlements left today.

St. Louis County: **German**—spread throughout the Ozark portion of the county; also concentrated in St. Louis City.

Saline County: **German**—in the eastern portion of the county, extending west beyond the Ozark escarpment.

Shannon County: **German**—small settlement near Summersville; **Mennonite**—near Birch Tree (see Table 2–2).

Stone County: No significant ethnic population.

Taney County: No significant ethnic population.

Texas County: **German**—small settlement at White Rock.

Warren County: **German**—spread throughout the southern portion of the county; **Mennonite**—one extinct settlement.

Washington County: **French**—large settlement at Old Mines.

Wayne County: **German**—small settlement west of Coldwater.

Webster County: **Amish**—two settlements, Elkland and Seymour (see Table 2-2); **Mennonite**—near Seymour (see Table 2-2).

Wright County: No significant ethnic population.

Bibliography

Books

Ahlstrom, Sydney E. *A Religious History of the American People.* New Haven, Conn.: Yale University Press, 1972.

Bek, William G. *The German Settlement Society of Philadelphia and Its Colony, Hermann, Missouri.* Philadelphia: American Germanica Press, 1907.

Bender, Harold S., ed. *Mennonite Encyclopedia.* 4 vols. Scottdale, Penn.: Mennonite Publishing House, 1955–1959.

Boyer, Mark G. *St. Joachim.* De Soto, Mo.: Roop Printing Company, Inc., 1972.

Brown, Miriam Keast. *The Story of Pierce City, Missouri, 1870–1970.* Pierce City, Mo.: Miriam K. Brown, 1970.

Brunhes, Jean. *Human Geography.* New York: Rand McNally & Company, 1920.

Burt, Henry J. *Population of Missouri: A General Survey of Its Sources, Changes, and Present Composition.* The University of Missouri Agricultural Experiment Station Research Bulletin No. 188. Columbia: University of Missouri, 1933.

Caldwell, Dorothy J., ed. *Missouri Historic Sites Catalog.* Columbia: The State Historical Society of Missouri, 1963.

Carr, Lucien. *Missouri: A Bone of Contention.* New York: Houghton Mifflin Company, 1888.

Cherrington, Ernest, ed. *Anti-Saloon League Yearbook, 1909.* Chicago: Anti-Saloon League of America, 1909.

Christian County: Its First 100 Years. Ozark, Mo.: Christian County Centennial, Inc., 1959.

Collier, James E. *Geography of the Northern Ozark Border Region.* The University of Missouri Studies, vol. 26, no. 1. Columbia: University of Missouri, 1953.

Dorrance, Ward Allison. *The Survival of French in the Old District of Ste. Genevieve.* The University of Missouri Studies, vol. 9, no. 2. Columbia: University of Missouri, 1935.

Dyck, Cornelius J., ed. *An Introduction to Mennonite History.* Scottdale, Penn.: Herald Press, 1967.

Emerson, Frederick V. *Geography of Missouri.* University of Missouri Bulletin, Educational Series, vol. 1, no. 4. Columbia: University of Missouri, 1912.

Erickson, Charlotte. *American Industry and the European Immigrant, 1860–1885.* New York: Russell & Russell, Publishers, 1957.

Fairbanks, Johnathan, and Tuck, Clyde E. *Past and Present of Greene County, Missouri.* Indianapolis: A. W. Brown and Company, 1915.

Faust, Albert B. *The German Element in the United States.* 2 vols. New York: The Steuben Society of America, 1927.

Finley, John. *The French in the Heart of America.* New York: Charles Scribner & Sons, 1915.

Forster, Walter O. *Zion on the Mississippi.* St. Louis, Mo.: Concordia Publishing House, 1953.

Franzwa, Gregory M. *The Story of Old Ste. Genevieve.* St. Louis, Mo.: Patrice Press, Inc., 1967.

Galpin, Charles J. *Empty Churches: The Rural Urban Dilemma.* New York: The Century Company, 1925.

Glazer, Nathan, and Moynihan, Daniel P. *Beyond the Melting Pot: The Negroes, Puerto Ricans, Jews, Italians, and Irish of New York City.* 2d ed. Cambridge, Mass.: The M.I.T. Press, 1970.

Gordon, Milton M. *Assimilation in American Life: The Role of Race, Religion, and National Origins.* New York: Oxford University Press, Inc., 1964.

Gregory, Cecil L. *Rural Social Areas in Missouri.* The University of Missouri Agricultural Experiment Station Research Bulletin No. 665. Columbia: University of Missouri, 1958.

Hammar, Conrad H. *Factors Affecting Farm Land Values in Missouri.* The University of Missouri Agricultural Experiment Station Research Bulletin No. 229. Columbia: University of Missouri, 1935.

Harrison, Samuel F. *History of Hermann, Missouri.* Hermann, Mo.: Historic Hermann, Inc., 1966.

Haswell, A. W., ed. *The Ozark Region: Its History and Its People.* Springfield, Mo.: Interstate Historical Society, 1917.

Hepple, Lawrence M. *The Rural Church in Missouri.* 7 parts. part 1: *Introduction;* part 2: *Rural Religious Groups;* part 3: *Clergymen in Rural Missouri;* part 4: *Index of Religious Group Action;* part 5: *Rural-Urban Churches Compared;* part 6: *Spatial and Social Relationships;* part 7: *What Rural People Think of Church.* The University of Missouri Agricultural Experiment Station Research Bulletin No. 633 A-G. Columbia: University of Missouri, 1957–1961.

Hostetler, John A. *Amish Life.* Scottdale, Penn.: Herald Press, 1952.

————. *Mennonite Life.* Scottdale, Penn.: Herald Press, 1954.

————. *Amish Society.* Rev. ed. Baltimore, Md.: The Johns Hopkins University Press, 1968.

Hostetler, John A., and Huntington, Gertrude Enders. *Children in Amish Society: Socialization and Community Education.* Case Studies in Education and Culture. New York: Holt, Rinehart and Winston, Inc., 1971.

Houck, Louis. *A History of Missouri.* 3 vols. Chicago: R. R. Donnelley & Sons Co., 1908.

———. *The Spanish Regime in Missouri.* 2 vols. Chicago: R. R. Donnelley & Sons Co., 1909.

Huebener, Theodore. *The Germans in America.* Philadelphia: Chilton Book Company, 1962.

Hutton, F. Z., and Krusekopf, H. H. *Soil Survey of Ripley County, Missouri.* Washington, D.C.: USDA, Bureau of Soils, 1915.

Jordan, Terry G. *German Seed in Texas Soil.* Austin, Tex.: University of Texas Press, 1966.

Kloss, Heinz. "German-American Language Maintenance Efforts." *Language Loyalty in the United States,* edited by Joshua A. Fishman. The Hague: Mouton & Co., 1966.

Konnyu, Leslie. *Hungarians in the United States: An Immigration Study.* St. Louis, Mo.: The American Hungarian Review, 1967.

Krusekopf, H. H., and Lewis, H. G. *Soil Survey of Cape Girardeau County, Missouri.* Washington, D.C.: USDA, Bureau of Soils, 1912.

Laughlin, Sceva Bright. *Missouri Politics During the Civil War.* Salem, Oreg.: S. B. Laughlin, 1930.

Lawrence County, Missouri, 1845–1970: A Brief History. Mt. Vernon, Mo.: Lawrence County Historical Society, 1970.

Lewis, H. G., and Emerson, F. V. *Soil Survey of Miller County, Missouri.* Washington, D.C.: USDA, Bureau of Soils, 1914.

Luebke, Frederick C. *Immigrants and Politics: The Germans of Nebraska, 1880–1900.* Lincoln: University of Nebraska Press, 1969.

Marbut, Curtis F. *Soils of the Ozark Region.* University of Missouri Agricultural Experiment Station Research Bulletin No. 3. Columbia: University of Missouri, 1910.

———. *Soil Reconnaissance of the Ozark Region of Missouri and Arkansas.* Washington, D.C.: USDA, Bureau of Soils, 1914.

Meyer, Duane. *The Heritage of Missouri-A History.* Rev. ed. Hazelwood, Mo.: State Publishing Company, Inc., 1970.

Miller, Levi, ed. *Mennonite Yearbook and Directory.* vol. 63. Scottdale, Penn.: Mennonite Publishing House, 1972.

Miner, H. Craig. *The St. Louis-San Francisco Transcontinental Railroad.* Lawrence: The University Press of Kansas, 1972.

Missouri, Office of the Secretary of State. *Official Manual.* Jefferson City, Mo.: Mid-State Printing Company, 1880–1971.

Mottaz, Mabel Manes. *Lest We Forget: A History of Pulaski County, Missouri, and Fort Leonard Wood.* Springfield, Mo.: Mabel Manes Mottaz, 1960.

Nelson, Lowry. *The Mormon Village.* Salt Lake City: University of Utah Press, 1952.

Newcomb, Rexford. *Architecture of the Old Northwest Territory.* Chicago: University of Chicago Press, 1950.

O'Conner, Richard. *The German-Americans: An Informal History*. Boston: Little, Brown and Company, 1968.

Roblee, Melvin B., ed. *Historical Review of Franklin County, Missouri*. Union, Mo.: Franklin County Sesqui-Centennial Corporation, 1968.

Ross, Edward A. *The Old World In the New*. New York: The Century Company, 1914.

Rothan, Emmet H. *The German Catholic Immigrant in the United States (1830–1860)*. Washington, D.C.: The Catholic University of America Press, 1946.

Rothensteiner, Rev. John. *History of the Archdiocese of St. Louis*. 2 vols. St. Louis, Mo.: Rev. John Rothensteiner, 1928.

Sauer, Carl O. *The Geography of the Ozark Highland of Missouri*. The Geographical Society of Chicago Bulletin No. 7. Chicago: University of Chicago Press, 1920.

————. *Geography of the Pennyroyal*. Frankfort, Ky.: The Kentucky Geological Survey, 1927.

Schlarman, J. H. *From Quebec to New Orleans*. Belleville, Ill.: Buechler Publishing Company, 1929.

Schneider, Carl E. *The German Church on the American Frontier*. St. Louis, Mo.: Eden Publishing Co., 1939.

Schoolcraft, Henry Rowe. *Schoolcraft in the Ozarks*. Reprint of a Journal of a Tour into the Interior of Missouri and Arkansas in 1818 and 1819, edited by Hugh Park. Van Buren, Ark.: Press-Argus Printers, 1955.

Schroeder, Walter O. *The Eastern Ozarks*. National Council for Geographic Education Special Publication No. 13. Normal, Ill.: Illinois State University, 1967.

Smith, Charles Henry. *The Story of the Mennonites*. Berne, Ind.: Mennonite Book Concern, 1941.

Steinfield, Melvin. *Cracks in the Melting Pot*. New York: Glencoe Press, 1973.

Sweet, A. T., and Wildermuth, Robert. *Soil Survey of Cole County, Missouri*. Washington, D.C.: USDA, Bureau of Soils, 1920.

Sweet, A. T., and Knobel, E. W. *Soil Survey of Barry County, Missouri*. Washington, D.C.: USDA, Bureau of Soils, 1916.

Tillman, B. W., and Deardorff, C. E. *Soil Survey of Perry County, Missouri*. Washington, D.C.: USDA, Bureau of Soils, 1915.

Turner, Frederick Jackson. *The Frontier in American History*. New York: Holt, Rinehart and Winston, Inc., 1920.

Vanatta, E. S., and Lewis, H. G. *Soil Survey of Franklin County, Missouri*. Washington, D.C.: USDA, Bureau of Soils, 1913.

Von Grueningen, John Paul. *The Swiss in the United States*. Madison, Wis.: Swiss-American Historical Society, 1940.

Watson, E. B., and Williams, H. F. *Soil Survey of Cedar County, Missouri*. Washington, D.C.: USDA, Bureau of Soils, 1911.

Watts, George B. *The Waldenses in the New World*. Durham, N.C.: Duke University Press, 1941.

Wyeislo, Aloysius J. "The Polish Catholic Immigrant." *Roman Catholicism and the American Way of Life,* edited by Thomas J. McAvoy. Notre Dame, Ind.: University of Notre Dame Press, 1960.

Young, A. J. *History of Dade County and Her People.* Greenfield, Mo.: A. J. Young Publisher, 1917.

Zelinsky, Wilbur. *The Cultural Geography of the United States.* Englewood Cliffs, N.J.: Prentice-Hall, Inc., 1973.

Journal Articles

Anderson, Hattie M. "Missouri, 1804–1828: Peopling a Frontier State." *Missouri Historical Review* 31 (January 1937): 150–80.

Bek, William G. "The Followers of Duden." *Missouri Historical Review* 16, 17 (October 1917–April 1919).

————. Trans. "Gottfried Duden's Report, 1824–1827." *Missouri Historical Review* 12, 13 (October 1917–July 1919).

Beveridge, Tom. "Look at the Ozarks." *Interface* 3 (January 1972): 3–9.

Bjorklund, Elaine M. "Ideology and Culture Exemplified in Southwestern Michigan." *Annals of the Association of American Geographers* 54 (June 1964): 227–41.

Borhek, J. T. "Ethnic Group Cohesion." *American Journal of Sociology* 76 (July 1970): 33–46.

Bratten, Samuel T., and Langedoerfer, Martha. "The Hermann, Missouri, Region." *Bulletin of the Geographical Society of Philadelphia* 29 (1931).

Castelli, Joseph R. "Grape Growers of Central Missouri." *Rocky Mountain Social Science Journal* 1 (April 1964): 113–18.

Cozzens, A. B. "Conservation in German Settlements of the Missouri Ozarks." *Geographical Review* 33 (April 1943): 286–98.

Crisler, Robert M. "Missouri's 'Little Dixie'." *Missouri Historical Review* 42 (January 1948): 130–39.

Dickinson, Robert E. "Rural Settlement in the German Lands." *Annals of the Association of American Geographers* 39 (December 1949): 239–63.

Eisenstadt, S. N. "The Place of Elites and Primary Groups in the Absorption of New Immigrants in Israel." *American Journal of Sociology* 57 (November 1951): 222–31.

Francis, E. K. "The Nature of the Ethnic Group." *American Journal of Sociology* 52 (March 1947): 393–400.

Garraghan, Gilbert J. "The Mission of Central Missouri." *St. Louis Catholic Historical Review* 2 (October 1920): 157–82.

Gates, Paul W. "The Railroads of Missouri, 1850–1870." *Missouri Historical Review* 26 (January 1932): 126–41.

Gerlach, Russel L. "Geography and Politics in Missouri: A Study of Electoral Patterns." *Missouri Geographer* 18 (Fall 1971): 27–36.

————. "Spanish Land Grants in Missouri." *Missouri Geographer* 20 (Fall 1973): 11.

Goodwin, Cardinal L. "Early Exploration and Settlement of Missouri and Arkansas." *Missouri Historical Review* 14 (April–July 1920): 385–425.

Gordon, Milton M. "Assimilation in America: Theory and Reality." *Daelalus* 90 (Spring 1961): 263–85.

"Great Churches in America: Trinity Lutheran, Freistatt, Missouri." *The Christian Century* 67 (June 1950): 753–59.

Guse, Timothy. "Quick Way to Build a Barn." *Today's Farmer* (August 1971): 6–9.

Hammar, Conrad H. "Institutional Aspects of Ozark Decline." *Journal of Forestry* 33 (October 1925): 843–50.

Handlin, Oscar. "Historical Perspectives on the American Ethnic Group." *Daelalus* 90 (Spring 1961): 220–32.

Hart, John Fraser. "The Middle West." *Annals of the Association of American Geographers* 62 (June 1972): 258–82.

Heintze, R. W. "Religious Organization in Missouri Before 1839." *Concordia Historical Institute Quarterly* 1 (January 1929): 91–94.

_____. "The Religious Situation in Missouri up to 1839." *Concordia Historical Institute Quarterly* 2 (October 1929): 69–75.

Hewes, Leslie. "Cultural Fault Line in the Cherokee Country." *Economic Geography* 19 (April 1943): 136–42.

_____. "Tontitown: Ozark Vineyard Center." *Economic Geography* 29 (April 1953): 125–43.

Hopson, Ruth Fitch. "Barite Mining in Southern Missouri." *Explosives Engineer* 14 (April 1936): 107–13.

Jinks, Michael W. "Some Aspects of Regional Delimitation: The Western Ozarks—A Case Study." *The Geographical Bulletin* 3 (November 1971): 19–29.

Johnson, Hildegard Binder. "The Location of German Immigrants in the Middle West." *Annals of the Association of American Geographers* 41 (March 1951): 1–41.

Jordan, Terry G. "German Houses in Texas." *Landscape* 14 (Autumn 1964): 24–26.

_____. "The Texan Appalachia." *Annals of the Association of American Geographers* 60 (September 1970): 409–27.

Kaups, Matti and Mather, Cotton. "Eben: Thirty Years Later in a Finnish Community in the Upper Peninsula of Michigan." *Economic Geography* 44 (January 1968): 57–70.

Klein, Ada Paris. "Ownership of Land Under France, Spain, and the United States." *Missouri Historical Review* 44 (April 1950): 274–94.

Kniffen, Fred B. "Louisiana House Types." *Annals of the Association of American Geographers* 26 (June 1936): 179–93.

_____. "Folk Housing: Key to Diffusion." *Annals of the Association of American Geographers* 55 (December 1965): 549–77.

Kollmorgan, Walter M. "A Reconnaissance of Some Cultural-Agricultural Islands in the South." *Economic Geography* 17 (October 1941): 409–30.

————. "Agricultural-Cultural Islands in the South-Part II." *Economic Geography* 19 (April 1943): 109–17.

————. "Immigrant Settlements in Southern Agriculture." *Agricultural History* 19 (April 1945): 69–78.

Kollmorgan, Walter M., and Harrison, Robert W. "French-speaking Farmers of Southern Louisiana." *Economic Geography* 22 (July 1946): 153–60.

Konnyu, Leslie. "Hungarians in Missouri." *Missouri Historical Review* 46 (September 1952): 257–61.

Kretzmann, P. E. "Saxon Immigration to Missouri, 1838–1839." *Missouri Historical Review* 33 (January 1939): 157–70.

Landing, James E. "Amish Population Changes, 1947–1964." *Mennonite Historical Bulletin* 31 (October 1970): 4.

————. "The Failure of Amish Settlements in the Southeastern United States: An Appeal for Inquiry." *The Mennonite Quarterly Review* (October 1970): 376–88.

Luebke, Frederick C. "The Immigrant Condition as a Factor Contributing to the Conservatism of the Lutheran Church—Missouri Synod." *Concordia Historical Institute Quarterly* 38 (April 1965): 19–28.

Lynch, Russell W. "Czech Farmers in Oklahoma." *Economic Geography*, 20 (January 1944): 9–13.

Lynch, William O. "The Westward Flow of Southern Colonists Before 1861." *The Journal of Southern History* 9 (August 1943): 303–27.

Meinig, D. W. "The Mormon Culture Region: Strategies and Patterns in the Geography of the American West, 1847–1964." *Annals of the Association of American Geographers* 55 (June 1965): 191–220.

Miller, E. Joan Wilson. "The Ozark Culture Region as Revealed by Traditional Materials." *Annals of the Association of American Geographers* 58 (March 1968): 51–77.

Mook, Maurice A., and Hostetler, John A. "The Amish and Their Land." *Landscape* 6 (Spring 1957): 21–29.

Olmstead, Clarence W. "American Orchard and Vineyard Regions." *Economic Geography* 32 (July 1956): 189–236.

Piehl, Charles K. "The Race of Improvement: Springfield Society, 1865–1881." *Missouri Historical Review* 67 (July 1973): 484–521.

Rafferty, Milton D. "Population and Settlement Changes in Two Ozark Localities." *Rural Sociology* 38 (Spring 1973): 46–56.

Raitz, Karl B. "Ethnic Settlements on Topographic Maps." *Journal of Geography* 72 (November 1973): 29–40.

Rosenthal, Erich. "Acculturation Without Assimilation? The Jewish Community of Chicago, Illinois." *American Journal of Sociology* 66 (November 1960): 275–88.

Saalberg, Gloria. "The New Madrid Land Claims in Howard County, Missouri." *Missouri Mineral Industry News* 7 (May 1967): 69–79.

Sauer, Carl O. "Geography and the Gerrymander." *The American Political Science Review* 12 (August 1918): 403–26.

———. "The Morphology of Landscape." *University of California Publications in Geography* 2 (October 1925): 19–54.

Schmidt, Joseph H. "Recollections of the First Catholic Mission Work in Central Missouri." *Missouri Historical Review* 5 (January 1911): 83–93.

Shoemaker, Floyd C. "Missouri's Tennessee Heritage." *Missouri Historical Review* 49 (January 1955): 127–42.

———. "Cape Girardeau: Most American of Missouri's Original Five Counties." *Missouri Historical Review* 50 (October 1955): 49–61.

Shryock, Richard H. "British and German Farmers." *American-German Review* 4 (June 1938): 36–38.

Spencer, J. E. "House Types in Southern Utah." *Geographical Review* 35 (July 1945): 444–57.

Stone, K. H. "The Development of a Focus for the Geography of Settlement." *Economic Geography* 41 (October 1965): 346–55.

"The Right to be Different." *Time* (29 May 1972): 67.

Toepper, Robert M. "Rationale for Preservation of the German Language in the Missouri Synod of the Nineteenth Century." *Concordia Historical Institute Quarterly* 41 (February 1968): 156–67.

Van Doren, Ruth F. "Myth—History of the Irish Wilderness." *Shannon County Historical Review* (July 1965): 6.

———. "A Tough Life—Mining Tiff." *The Ozarks Mountaineer* 21 (March 1973): 19.

Viles, J. "Population and Extent of Settlement in Missouri Before 1804." *Missouri Historical Review* 5 (July 1911): 189–207.

Violette, E. M. "Early Settlements in Missouri." *Missouri Historical Review* 1 (October 1906): 38–52.

Wheeler, James O., and Jakle, John A. "The Dutch in Kalamazoo, Michigan: A Study of Spatial Barriers to Acculturation." *Tjidschrift voor Economische Sociale Geografie* 60 (July–August 1969): 249–54.

Willibrand, W. A. "A Forgotten Pioneer of Westphalia, Missouri." *American-German Review* (April 1943): 7–9.

Zelinsky, Wilbur. "An Approach to the Religious Geography of the United States: Patterns of Church Membership in 1952." *Annals of the Association of American Geographers* 51 (June 1961): 139–93.

Pamphlets

Bethel Mennonite Church, 1867–1967, Fortuna, Missouri. 1967.

Centennial of Immanuel Lutheran Church, Rader, Missouri. 20 June 1971.

Centennial Remembrance of St. Joseph's Parish at Apple Creek, Missouri, 1828–1928. 1928.

De Paul Hospital. *Old Mines Project.* Mimeographed. De Soto, Mo., 1968.

Detwiler, Mary I. *History of the Berea Mennonite Church.* Birch Tree, Mo., 1954.

Diamond Jubilee, 1874–1949: Trinity Lutheran Church, Freistatt, Missouri. 1949.

Held's Stone Hill Winery, Hermann, Missouri. N.d.

History of Hermann, Missouri: Home of the Maifest. Hermann, Mo., 1953.

Hueber, Rev. S. P. *The Centennial History of Perry County, Missouri, 1821–1921.* 1921.

Knox, Willis. *A History of the Brazeau Presbyterian Church, Brazeau, Missouri, 1819–1970.* 1970.

Mt. Zion Mennonite Church, Versailles, Missouri, 1871–1971. 1971.

Rehm, Elinor. *Jefferson County: Its Settlers, Origin, and Development.* Mimeographed. N.d.

Sister Teresa. *The Eye, Arm, Spine of the Wilderness.* Mt. St. Joseph Ursuline Convent, 1957.

Souvenir of the Centennial Celebration of St. Joseph's Parish, Westphalia, Missouri, August 6, 1935. 1935.

Zahorsky, John, Jr. *The Austrian Immigration of Crawford County.* N.d.

Census Materials

U.S. Department of the Interior. Bureau of the Census. *The Seventh Census of the United States, 1850.* Washington, D.C.: Robert Armstrong, Public Printer, 1853.

———. Bureau of the Census. *Eighth Census of the United States, 1860: Preliminary Report.* Washington, D.C.: Government Printing Office, 1862.

———. Bureau of the Census. *Eleventh Census of the United States, 1890: Report on Statistics of Churches.* Washington, D.C.: Government Printing Office, 1894.

U.S. Department of Commerce. Bureau of the Census. *Fifteenth Census of the United States, 1930: Population,* vol. 1. Washington, D.C.: Government Printing Office, 1932.

———. Bureau of the Census. *Fifteenth Census of the United States, 1930: Agriculture,* vol. 2, part 1. Washington, D.C.: Government Printing Office, 1932.

———. Bureau of the Census. *Census of Agriculture, 1969: Area Reports, Missouri,* vol. 1, part 17, sec. 1. Washington, D.C.: Government Printing Office, 1971.

———. Bureau of the Census. *Census and Population, 1970: General Social and Economic Characteristics,* vol. 1, part 27. Washington, D.C.: Government Printing Office, 1972.

———. Bureau of the Census. *Census of Population, 1970: Characteristics of the Population, Missouri,* vol. 1, part 27. Washington, D.C.: Government Printing Office, 1972.

United States Census. Manuscript schedules of population for 1860 and 1870 for counties in study area are available on microfilm at the Springfield, Missouri, Public Library.

United States Census. *Census of Housing: 1970.* Tapes of small area returns provided by the Public Affairs and Information Service, University of Missouri–Columbia.

Maps, Atlases, and Aerial Photography

Aerial Photography. U.S. Department of Agriculture, Commodity Stabilization Service photographic coverage from 1964 to 1968 for the following Ozark counties. Scale 1:7,920: Dallas County: Gasconade County: Lawrence County: Miller County: Perry County: Polk County: Webster County.

Campbell, R. A. *Campbell's New Atlas of Missouri.* St. Louis, Mo.: R. A. Campbell, Publisher, 1875.

County Land Ownership Plat Maps. Published by the counties and dated from 1960 to 1970 for the following counties: Barry County: Cape Girardeau County: Dallas County: Franklin County: Gasconade County: Lawrence County: Maries County: Miller County: Osage County: Perry County: Polk County: Ste. Genevieve County: Washington County: Webster County.

Friis, Herman R. *A Series of Population Maps of the Colonies and the United States, 1625–1790.* Rev. Mimeographed and offset publication, no. 3. New York: American Geographical Society, 1968.

General highway maps for all counties in the study area. Prepared by the division of highway planning, Missouri State Highway Department, in cooperation with the Bureau of Public Roads. U.S. Department of Commerce. Scale 1:63,360.

Gerlach, Arch C., ed. *The National Atlas of the United States.* Washington, D.C.: U.S. Department of the Interior, Geological Survey, 1971.

Illustrated Atlas of Perry County, Missouri. Chicago: George A. Ogle, 1915.

Missouri Breweries, 1810–1971. St. Louis, Mo.: Falstaff Brewing Corp., 1971.

Missouri: Official Highway Map. Jefferson City, Mo.: State Highway Commission, published annually.

Paullin, Charles O. *Atlas of the Historical Geography of the United States.* Washington, D.C.: Carnegie Institute of Washington, 1932.

"Plat of the Colony of Altenburg, August 5, 1840." *Plat Book, Towns, and Villages.* Perry County, Mo., 1855.

Rafferty, Milton D.; Gerlach, Russel L.; and Hrebec, Dennis J. *Atlas of Missouri.* Springfield, Mo.: Aux-Arc Research Associates, 1970.

Soil Conservation Service. Land area resource maps for the following Missouri counties: Gasconade County: Lawrence County: Miller County: Perry County.

Soil Map of Missouri. Columbia: University of Missouri, 1931.

Surveyor's Plats, no. 1. Perry County, Mo., 1840–1863.

Topographic Quadrangles, State of Missouri. Prepared by the Missouri Geological Survey and the U.S. Geological Survey, for all counties in the study area. Scales 1:24,000; 1:62,500; and 1:250,000.

Newspaper Articles and Serials

"Amish in the Ozarks: The Old Days Returneth." *Springfield Leader and Press.* Springfield, Mo., 29 February 1968.
De La Haye, Charles. "Grape Stands Return to Rosati as Vineyards Stage a Comeback." *St. Louis Post Dispatch.* St. Louis, Mo., 19 September 1956.
"Family Reunion at Rosati Recalls Town's Early History." *St. Louis Post Dispatch.* St. Louis, Mo., 27 September 1934.
Farmer, Frank. "The Contrast of Half a Century." *Springfield Leader and Press.* Springfield, Mo., 8 March 1972.
Fink, Oliver F. "Missouri's Old French Pocket." *St. Louis Post Dispatch.* St. Louis, Mo., 20 February 1955.
Freeman, Dale. "Ozark Trappists: The Happy People . . ." *Sunday News and Leader.* Springfield, Mo., 6 September 1959.
"La Guignolee." *Independence Journal.* Potosi, Mo., 18 January 1951.
Missouri Weekly Patriot. Springfield, Mo., 3 October 1867.
Niles' Register. 1832–1837. Baltimore, Md.
"Ozark Vineyards: Fresh From the Hills." *Chicago Tribune.* 20 May 1945.
"Wine Grapes in the Ozarks?" *Springfield Leader and Press.* Springfield, Mo., 17 October 1971.
Wyatt, Judd. "History of the Knobview Fruit Growers Association." *Rolla Herald.* Rolla, Mo., 7 March 1935.

Unpublished Materials

I. Theses, Dissertations, and Oral Reports

Apprill, Arthur William. "The Culture of a German Community in Missouri." M. A. thesis, University of Missouri—Columbia, 1935.
Blume, George T. "Spatial and Social Relationships of Rural Churches in Six Selected Areas of Missouri." Ph.D. diss., University of Missouri—Columbia, 1957.
Clendenen, Harbert L. "Settlement Morphology of the Southern Courtois Hills, Missouri, 1820–1860." Ph.D. diss., Louisiana State University, 1973.
Gerlach, Russel L. "Rural Ethnic and Religious Groups as Cultural Islands in the Ozarks of Missouri: Their Emergence and Persistence." Ph.D. diss., University of Nebraska, 1974.
Henderson, John Russell. "The Cultural Landscape of French Settlement in the American Bottom." M.A. thesis, Illinois State University at Normal, 1966.

Langendoerfer, Martha. "Geography of the Hermann (Missouri) Region." M.A. thesis, University of Missouri—Columbia, 1930.

Lowenberg, Carla. "The Historical Analysis of the Mennonite Cultural Landscape of Franklin Township, Lee County, Iowa." M.A. thesis, University of Nebraska, 1971.

Mann, Clair V. "Frisco First: A Source Materials History of the St. Louis and San Francisco Railroad, 1845–1947." 4 vols. Rolla, Mo., 1946. Manuscript in Frisco offices at St. Louis.

Post, Lauren C. "Acadian Ethnology: Material Culture on the Prairies of Southwest Louisiana." Modified form of a paper read before the human geography section of the Southwestern Social Science Association, Oklahoma City, Okla., 1935, mimeographed.

Rafferty, Milton D. "Persistence Versus Change in Land Use and Landscape in the Springfield, Missouri, Vicinity of the Ozarks." Ph.D. diss., University of Nebraska, 1970.

Spitz, Lewis W. "The Germans in Missouri: A Preliminary Study." M.A. thesis, Washington University, 1930.

Stegen, E. F. "The Settlement of the Saxon Lutherans in Perry County, Missouri." M.A. thesis, Indiana University, 1933.

Velikonja, Joseph. "The Italian Contribution to the Geographic Character of Tontitown, Arkansas, and Rosati, Missouri." Paper presented before the Convegno Sull' Emigrazione E. Sull' Opera Degli Italiani Nagli Stati Uniti L'America, Universita di Ferenze, Italy. Institute di Studi Americani, 27, 29 May 1969. Translated by Don Fischer, Southwest Missouri State College, Springfield, Mo., 1971.

Vogel, Phillip. "The Holland, Nebraska, Locality: A Comparative Study of Dutch and Non-Dutch Occupance." M.A. thesis, University of Nebraska, 1957.

II. Miscellaneous

Absentee ownership file. County collector's office. Gasconade County, Mo.

Abstract of original land entries. Perry County, Mo., 1894.

Agricultural Stabilization and Conservation Service. Individual farm data cards for the following counties: Benton County: Gasconade County: Lawrence County: Miller County: Perry County: Ste. Genevieve County.

Archives of the St. Louis-San Francisco Railroad Company. St. Louis, Mo.

County court records, vols. 1, 2. Perry County, Mo., 1821–1832.

County land assessment and tax books, 1970, for the following counties: Carter County: Douglas County: Gasconade County: Osage County: Ozark County: Perry County: Ste. Genevieve County: Shannon County.

Data on location, membership, and date of establishment of Catholic churches in Springfield-Cape Girardeau, Kansas City, and Jefferson City dioceses of the Catholic church.

Land register for 1867. Gasconade County, Mo.

Manuscript records and church publications contained in the archives of

the East Perry County Lutheran Historical Society. Altenburg, Mo.
Parish records of births, baptisms, marriages, and deaths, dated from 1787
in St. Joachim's Church, Old Mines, Mo.
Parish register, St. Joachim's Catholic Church. Old Mines, Mo., 1972.
Recorders of deeds, real estate transactions, 1968–1971, for the following
counties: Dallas County: Gasconade County: Lawrence County: Oregon
County: Osage County: Perry County: Shannon County: Stone County.
State of Missouri, Department of Liquor Control. Number of retail outlets
for the sale of distilled spirits, beer, and wine by county for 1972,
mimeographed.

Index